A Wider Giving

A Wider Giving

Women Writing after a Long Silence

Edited & with an introduction by
Sondra Zeidenstein

Chicory Blue Press   Goshen, Connecticut

Chicory Blue Press, Goshen, Connecticut 06756
© 1988 by Chicory Blue Press. All rights reserved
Printed in the United States of America

Book designer: Virginia Anstett

Typeface: ITC New Baskerville

This book was edited, designed and typeset using Macintosh
computers. Quark XPress was used for page make-up.

Typesetting was done on a Linotronic 300 by Hoblitzelle
Graphics, North Haven, Connecticut.

Printed by Eastern Press, New Haven, Connecticut.

Cover painting, *Självporträtt* (1914), by Sigrid Hjertén is
reproduced by permission of Malmö Museum in Sweden.

Excerpt from "Wreath of Women" by Muriel Rukeyser is reprinted
by permission of International Creative Management, Inc. Copyright © 1944 by Muriel Rukeyser, COPYRIGHT RENEWED.

Excerpts from *Parrots' Wood* by Erma J. Fisk are reprinted with
permission of W.W. Norton & Company, Inc. Copyright © 1985
by Manomet Bird Observatory.

Additional acknowledgments appear on page x.

Library of Congress Catalog Card Number: 87–72314

ISBN 0–9619111–0–7

For George, Laura & Peter

Women who in my time
Move toward a wider giving
Than warm kitchen offering
And warm steady living

from "Wreath of Women"
by Muriel Rukeyser

Contents

Acknowledgments

The following works are reprinted by permission of the publisher and author.

Cathy Stern, "Poetry Reading in the Downtown Library," *Bayou Review;* "Swimming in the Gulf at Fifty," "Love Poem," "Talking," *The Leaf Raker;* "Thirty-ninth Anniversary," "Old Loves," "Those Places," *Shenandoah.*

Sondra Zeidenstein, "Rough Passage," *Women's Review of Books;* "The One Dream," *Yellow Silk.*

Patricia E. Powers, "The Storyteller," *Ascent.*

Adele Bowers, "The Hunting Season," *Creeping Bent.*

Sadie Wernick Hurwitz, "all the shirley temples," *Riverrun;* "Duet," *A Kind of Attachment;* "Tsivya," *Ohio Review.*

Arlene Swift Jones, "Silences," "Going Home to Iowa," "Symbiosis," *The Insisting Thistle;* "Poussin's 'Martyrdom of St. Erasmus,'" *Tar River Poetry;* "Rheumatoid Arthritis," *Calyx.*

Yvonne Moore Hardenbrook, "Socks," *Poetry in the Park 1985;* "History Lesson," *Whalebone and Royal Blood;* "Pink Thread," *Pudding 7;* "Night Vision," *Pudding 14;* haiku, *Amelia;* "Pushing Off," *What It Can't Save.*

Jeannette S. Guildford, Preface to *Twelve Months at Arethusa* and "October 12, 1892," *Foothills News.*

I would like to thank Virginia Anstett for support far beyond the professional duties of designer and typesetter.

Preface

A Wider Giving: Women Writing after a Long Silence is an anthology of poetry, prose and autobiographical narrative by contemporary women writers who made their major commitment to creative writing *after* the age of forty-five. These twelve writers, ranging in age from their fifties to eighties, are representative of thousands of women who are starting writing careers after child-raising, after widowhood or divorce, after retirement from jobs and careers – later than our culture assumes one can take up creative writing and produce good work.

Born between 1905 and 1932, of races and classes who benefited from time-saving modern technology, birth control, medicine and education, these women were silenced by early marriage and childbearing, by cultural pressure to give themselves to others in the home, in volunteer activities and care-providing jobs, to think of themselves last. Launched on the narrow path of traditional female roles, experiencing the often unexpected consequences of that course, they have lived long enough to emerge into a world that has made the entry of women into the arts more acceptable. (Some of them, in fact, helped prepare that world for their daughters.)

In each the impulse to write survived. Or was kindled. Even so, they had to struggle against the tug of their upbringing. To spend hours drafting a story or polishing a poem does not feel like giving – these tasks require that the door be closed to people who might need them, dinners postponed, a distracted look, letters unanswered. Not only that. The act of creation, in spite of the painful self-doubt every artist experiences, is filled with an intensity and joy which feels very much like self-indulgence. In making deliberate choices to give *themselves* to their art, these writers give voice to the experience of many women who were silenced; they extend the vision of their generations – a wider giving.

.   .   .

The new writers in this anthology are part of a recent phenomenon – in their numbers probably a unique phenomenon in history. They are not a group or a movement; they don't have a common politics; they don't even have a name. Are they "new/old" writers or "promising old" writers – that juxtaposition of adjectives is peculiar to the ears; are they "late bloomers" or simply late-developing writers? Whatever they are called, their culture seems uncomfortable about them. When one of their works gets national recognition – Harriet Doerr's *Stones for Ibarra* or Norman Maclean's *A River Runs Through It* or Erma J. Fisk's *Parrots' Wood* – there is an element of curiosity and surprise in the reviews: how could such fine work emerge from artists *beginning* to write in their fifties, sixties or seventies?

In our culture and century, age is often viewed as primarily a time of loss and decline. The assumption that beginnings are exclusively for the young hangs on in spite of the gathering of empirical and anecdotal evidence to the contrary, in spite of the theoretical support of major adult-development studies. Becoming a creative writer in one's later years certainly addresses the tasks Eric Erikson sees as the primary concerns of maturity and old age: establishing and guiding the next generation and accepting one's own life cycle as something that *had* to be. Although Daniel J. Levinson does not include men much past fifty in his study, *The Seasons of a Man's Life*, a new commitment to creative writing fits his pattern of "structure-building" and "transitional structure-changing" periods throughout life. And the essential nature of creative writing fits his thesis that the later years are a time when "the voices within the self become . . . more audible and more worthy of . . . attention."

But no student of aging or the arts, as far as I know, has looked directly at this phenomenon of undertaking the rigorous discipline of an artist late in life. Certainly the general public does not acknowledge it. Becoming a writer is almost always associated with youth, the precocious teens, the bright and energetic twenties and thirties. Our culture is more comfortable with old people taking up untutored folk art, "homey" writing, art as a hobby. The writing networks are dominated by the young and middle-aged; the increasingly commercial underpinnings of our publishing industry offer little encouragement to the promising old.

And not just the writing world. Our whole society, even as it becomes predominantly old, is devastatingly ageist. Along with the struggles inherent in creation, late-developing women writers face negativities of ageism and sexism. Because these negativities are often internalized and experienced as inadequacy rather than oppression, as Jean Baker Miller explains in *Toward a New Psychology of Women,* they are hard to identify and combat.

. . .

A Wider Giving is based on the premise that women writers who start late are important to us, that we need to welcome them and help them continue. The anthology has several mothers. Tillie Olsen is one of them. In her groundbreaking book *Silences,* she describes the rare combination of talent and circumstances that enable a writer to begin and continue her work:

> Bent (far more common than we assume), circumstances, time, development of craft – but beyond that: how much conviction as to the importance of what one has to say, one's right to say it. And the will, the measureless store of belief in oneself to be able to come to, cleave to, find the form for one's own life comprehensions. Difficult for any male not born into a class that breeds such confidence. Almost impossible for a girl, a woman.

With passion and eloquence that come from personal experience, she examines the various ways in which writers who have begun to produce are silenced: for example, by poverty, by exclusion, by the necessity for political action, by censorship, by lack of time and support, by alcoholism and suicide. In addition, she refers to a kind of silencing that is "almost unnoted." She calls it the "foreground silence," silence *before* the achievement, writers who may have exhibited early the capacity for writing but who did not write or publish until late in life. The writers of *A Wider Giving* are in *this* category. In breaking the silence imposed by their culture, they have had to give themselves time and permission, seek out training, face rejection and self-doubt, fight the negativity sometimes ingested from their own mothers, begin to develop their craft and, hardest of all, summon the strength again and again to continue.

A Wider Giving has two other mothers, both younger than I am – one, my therapist Jean Greggs who helped me discover the springs of creativity clogged since infancy and the other, the poet Honor Moore who tenderly supported my infant steps. Once I became engaged in the unique struggle creation involves, I was filled with self-doubt about beginning at an advanced age. I was not sure it was possible – I only knew that the writing impulse was incredibly strong. I looked for affirmation and encouragement everywhere. Was anyone else doing it? Was it too late? Wherever I went in my local circle of writing groups, workshops and readings, I always found one or two other new/old writers. I was impressed with the quality of their work and moved by its inclusion of experiences familiar to my life that I did not find in other writing. If these late-developing writers exist in my own circle, I thought, they must exist in other places as well.

But they were not attracting much attention. I was aware of publishing efforts in support of older-women writers. The anthology *Women and Aging,* published by Calyx in 1986, featured the work of older-women writers on aspects of aging. Charlotte Mandel set up the yearly Eileen W. Barnes Award for unpublished older-women poets and her Saturday Press has been publishing the winners. *Vintage '45,* a new California-based literary magazine for and by women over forty-five, has extended its distribution nationally. I was also aware of the work being done in nursing homes and senior centers where poets like Kenneth Koch and Gerald Stern were helping old people to express themselves creatively in poems and stories. But I was not aware of any attention to late-developing writers – who face the double problem of being older *and* beginners – beyond references to age in book reviews of late-developing writers and an informative article in the February/March 1985 issue of *Coda* on the problems new or unpublished older writers face getting into mainstream competitions and the literary marketplace. I decided that the first publication of Chicory Blue Press would introduce the work and experiences of new/old writers to the reading public and to each other.

. . .

Through notices in *Coda, Writer's Market, COSMEP* and other magazines and newsletters where writers watch for calls for materials, I solicited manuscripts from late-developing writers. My notices were picked up and reprinted in a number of regional newsletters. I wrote to poets and fiction writers who, as teachers or through other contacts, might know of such writers, to university-based writing programs and unaffiliated writing centers. I solicited work from nationally known writers who fell into my category – Harriet Doerr, Erma J. Fisk, Olive Ann Burns and lesser-known, sometimes unpublished writers whose work I knew from personal contact.

I asked for "fiction and poetry by writers who made their major commitment to writing after the age of forty-five." On the basis of my own experience, I felt that was the age when changes in the body make it undeniably clear that we are not young, that we are mortal, that the future has shrunk. Unlike forty which seems the end of something, forty-five seems a turning point, a beginning like adolescence. Children are usually out of the house, reproductive life is a thing of the past, change seems possible. By "major commitment," I meant a determined effort involving time, attitude and self-identification as a writer to follow where the writing impulse leads.

In response to my solicitation, I got three hundred

manuscripts, about equally divided between prose and poetry, from sixty-seven men and two hundred forty-three women. They came from all the sources I had solicited and, in addition, from senior writing centers I had not known how to reach. They came from rural and urban areas of thirty-three states and several provinces of Canada, although the large majority were from the East Coast and California. The writers' ages ranged from forty-five to more than ninety, the average being sixty. Both men and women were, for the most part, in careers or jobs or in retirement; only a small minority of the women had not worked outside the home. Men were in law, medicine, dentistry, education, politics, the telephone company; women were teachers, librarians, social workers, psychologists, journalists, bookkeepers, farmers, secretaries, nurses, artists. With few exceptions, they were heterosexual, white and middle class. Almost all the women were married, widowed or divorced with two, three, five, eight children.

Most of the writers had had some of their work published in books and magazines, a very few with major commercial publishers, some with small presses, many with literary journals – the most and least known – and a few were published in local newspapers. Some were self-published, a few not at all. They exhibited both the most and the least sophistication about how to submit manuscripts. Their submissions ranged from popular or "homey" verse and true-confessions stories to finely-crafted poems and, to a lesser extent, well-crafted stories. About seventy-five percent of the work was in the mainstream literary tradition.

I do not know why fewer men than women submitted their work – perhaps simply because the editor is a woman. It is likely, however, that men of those generations and backgrounds who wanted to write, may not have had to come to a halt as definitively as women who were raising children and functioning within narrowly defined roles. I cannot explain why most of the men's work did not meet my criteria of craft and emotional honesty, why a significant proportion of their submissions was commercially-oriented adventure stories without character development, sexual wish-fulfilment stories, facile humor. Since the work of just one man made it to the final round, I decided that I would focus the book on the more intense writing of women.

In making selections I let go a few good stories because my taste does not often include the macabre or dark humor; quite a few finely-crafted poems because they lacked the kind of energy I respond to in poetry; many deeply felt stories because they lacked art. I wanted the works to be as representative of place, subject matter, kinds of talent, stages in the writing process as possible. Although I did not solicit children's stories as a genre, I asked for Jeannette S. Guildford's story, "October 12, 1892," because of its unusual way of preserving the past and because I was aware of the strong response it draws from adult audiences.

. . .

Each of the twelve writers has a distinct voice. Their settings are varied, ranging from the Metropolitan Museum in Arlene Swift Jones' poem, "Poussin's 'Martyrdom of St. Erasmus,'" Dhaka, Bangladesh in my poem, "Blue Sari," the land of magic in Geraldine Zetzel's poem, "An Old Story," Broadway in the Great Depression in Francine Julian Clark's "Eligible Impulses – '44." Their themes include the consequences of a munitions economy in Yvonne Moore Hardenbrook's poem, "History Lesson" and of the killing instinct in Adele Bowers' "The Hunting Season." Forms include Erma J. Fisk's journal entries, Cathy Stern's domestic love sonnets, the jump-cut juxtaposition of passages in Naomi Feigelson Chase's story "What Can You Do about Love." Moods range from the self-mocking humor of some of Sadie Wernick Hurwitz' poems to the lyricism of Patricia E. Powers' story, "The Storyteller." At the same time, the included works share elements like mature characters and depth of memory and refer to such subjects as aged parents, widowhood, long marriage, arthritis, pension checks. Love and passion, not only sexual – in fact not often merely sexual – pervade their work.

. . .

Following each writer's work, a long autobiographical narrative traces the thread of her writing history through her life story. I transcribed, edited and condensed these narratives from tapes of three- or four-hour interviews I held with each of the writers. I asked them all the same questions:

> What were the creative influences in your childhood home?
> Did you write as a child or in high school and college?
> What kept you from continuing to write?
> When and why did you make a commitment to writing?
> What trained and supported you?
> What were your obstacles?
> What is your writing process?
> What is your publication experience?

All the writers were open and honest in their answers. In editing their responses, I tried to bring out what was unique in each story and what was common to all of them. I expect that each reader who is a late-developing writer will find a particular set of experiences she can identify with.

In brief, the interviews reveal that these writers were born before 1932, lived through the Great Depression, and, for the most part, were affected by the feminine mystique. As children, all of them loved to read and be read to, some were the family or neighborhood storyteller. At least five of them wrote stories, poems or essays during childhood and adolescence; several of them felt even in college that they were or would become writers. At least three did not write at all. Almost all of them married around twenty and had children soon after marriage. In addition to raising children and caring for their homes, most of them had careers or jobs (five in teaching, two in social work), and the rest were involved in volunteer, community and political work. Most of them experienced short bursts of writing in their thirties and forties, but even if they sent their work out, they did not consider themselves writers, did not know how to revise or improve their work, and most important, did not continue. Many of them, however, did other kinds of writing during these years at home or on the job: letters, case reports, public-relations releases, journalism, advertising copy, investigative reporting. All of them made a serious commitment to creative writing in their late forties, fifties, even seventies. In making that commitment, many of them were supported by a particular teacher, mentor or group. Major steps in the development of each were learning to write in the contemporary vein – i.e., catching up with what is going on thirty years after they left off – and learning how to revise and polish their work after the first outpouring. The obstacles they identify include self-doubt, lack of time and difficulty in getting published. Many of them regret not having found more time to write when they were younger, and all of them are deeply grateful to have the chance now.

.   .   .

If I want to *experience* how much I value the literary voices of women my age and older, all I have to do is imagine the absence in the last few years of works by Grace Paley, Adrienne Rich, Doris Lessing, to mention a few. Without them, important events, troubling emotions, unspoken thoughts would lack the validation that literature so uniquely gives to experience. I treasure the voices of women and men writers much older than me – there are few. My favorites include Robert Penn Warren, May Sarton, Stanley Kunitz, M.F.K. Fisher. What a wasteland would lie ahead of me if they were not humanizing existence up to the edge of incapacity and death, bringing that experience into the fold. How silent the future would be except for tape recorders running urgently in nursing homes and on the broken steps of farm houses as oral histories are gathered before time runs out. How abrupt an abyss for younger women, without linkage, balance, a sense of continuity!

Women over fifty-five make up almost one-fifth of the adult population of this country. What percentage of women writers are over fifty-five? What percentage of *all* writers are women over fifty-five? Young men and women, the brilliant lights and the merely promising, fill our writing schools, competitions, and commercial publications. Darlings of the literary world, they are pushing out their middle-aged teachers and mentors, most of them men. What will happen to the vision of the old? The young can do a lot brilliantly, but few can do well at imagining, not old people, but the vision that comes with age – a vision that sometimes contradicts youth's sense of experience as "unique and my own," that finds pattern, repetition, compulsion in what once felt like free will. It is like the way hills flatten and sea spreads out as you climb toward a village at the top of a mountain, the heightened experience of sounds and smells in steps taken more slowly, the evocation of deeper memories with sharper elements. It is the strange combination of feelings a grandmother experiences as she caresses her grandchild and, at the same time, knows how it all turns out.

How exciting, that in addition to those older writers who, against many odds, got an earlier start and are now well-established, we can welcome *new* older writers whose experience has not found voice before. Only if we continue to fight the kind of exclusivity of subject matter and form that for so many years was fostered by graduate schools and other centers of power, the narrow range of talent they "accredited," will we have more new voices and, equally important, from more *varied* backgrounds. We need them desperately. They should be sought out, nourished, cherished now, but we should also, thinking of the future, support and encourage *first* beginnings in grade school and high school and college. Even if a writing life cannot be sustained during the middle years, whatever groundwork was laid, whatever pleasure taken in books and early efforts to create, will remain a foundation for what emerges later. This lesson is another gift from the writers of *A Wider Giving*.

Sondra Zeidenstein
Goshen, Connecticut
August, 1987

Cathy Stern

Poetry Reading in the Downtown Library

In *this* rain, I wouldn't have come myself

but I'm one of the readers. So I'm here
crossing the lobby, going past the shelf
of bestsellers, down the escalator

to the blue-carpeted room where a few
friends, shaking out raincoats, seem glad to see
me. I'm glad to see them, I'll tell you.
I thought my husband and mother might be

the audience, plus a couple of friends
of Jim's – he's reading after me. But now
I'm up at the mike, there's a strange old man's
bleary, unshaven face in the back row,

empty eyes on me. I open my slim
folder of poems and I read them to him.

for Jim Ulmer

Swimming in the Gulf at Fifty

Going out, I never think about dying.
Or maybe I always do. I concentrate
on sand moving under my feet,
on the rush of rising water,
how it touches my skin – insistent
as a lover's hand.
The deeper waves have their own compulsions.
I give in to the lift and fall
until, out past the breakers,
I lie down in the slow swell
and everything glides away.

But this time, coming back,
the hidden currents found me out.
I swam minute after minute
in the same deep spot,
held in the heavy motion
of the waves. My arms ached
with water, my breath became water,
water drew me down and whispered:
this is when they let go.
Before my foot touched the ground,
I saw my hair turn to seaweed on the foam.

Talking

A painted kitchen table covered with oilcloth –
a criss-cross pattern of yellow and green,
nothing special. Only it is.
It's where they like to sit,
my father and my grandfather,
while a summer evening eases into night,
poking their spoons into glasses
of crackers and milk, pointing
the spoons as they talk, intent
as checker players who've long since
known each other's moves by heart.

They never agree about Roosevelt or God,
but it doesn't seem to matter
because the table joins them,
as it always has. What matters
is the talk, that they love it,
that they hold the words and sentences
like treasures, turn them
into music I keep listening to
when it stops, into small bursts
of fireworks I keep watching
after they fall.

Love Poem

It would be hard to say when I first sensed

the change, noticed myself watching you
again, as you swept the floor, or as you rinsed
the dishes – you knowing how I hate to do
most domestic things;
                              harder still to decide
when the sudden waves of tenderness
returned – you lying there, as always, beside
me, touching my arm before sleep, a caress
so ordinary, so familiar as
to be too dull for books;
                              hardest of all
now, to know how to speak of it – how it has
changed and changed between us, how the small
things have become the largest – how an old promise
turns, becomes new.
                              But you know all this.

Thirty-ninth Anniversary

Another small, blue tile fell from the wall
this morning near the edge of the tub, one more

small thing to fix, the house ungluing after
years of holding on. Outside another squirrel

runs up the leaning pine again, another fall
is here, the wood fence losing out to weather.

We've hardly seen it happening – layer,
and crust, and crack – and I've scarcely questioned all

the years I've slept secure with you. But now
sometimes, afraid, I wake up and lean over

in the middle of the night to listen for your breath,
holding mine like a pain, remembering how

we always thought the future was in the future,
and now it's now, its wingbeats overhead.

Old Loves

Tonight I've drummed up my old loves – a mere

(out-of-style) handful before you, less to
be truthful: at fifteen, that earnest Air
Corps boy kissing me at the USO,

he and his aftershave gone, overseas,
within the week; a playwright's genius son
who read me Nietzsche one summer, wrote pleas
for "*spiritual*-physical union;"

my high school steady, his fifty-dollar
Ford, his gentle hands; the Mozart man, my
philosophy and so forth instructor;
and some moustached ex-soldier, the one I

fell in love with unexpectedly – you
remember – who's still around, old, but new.

Those Places

It's early when I drive to work and thread
the final Main Street slot between the Texas
Historic Building and the XX Video Arcade,
Open 24 Hours, Ladies Free.

Each time I hope that I won't see the young
lost man again, with his dirty, white blanket,
carrying his life across the street.

He's put it down in a corner of my mind.
He's curled up there and he won't move
where I can't see him when I close my eyes.

Now the nights are cold. I've had to put
another blanket over him, or would
if I could find him anywhere
in all those places I tried to move him to.

Keeping

All this keeping, for what, keeping, for when, keeping.
A quirk in the usual urge to divest.
Chaos stacked against Chaos.
Weathered magazines piled on the window seat,
holding back the April air again.
Oh, none of the above, really, odd,
old Gertrude Stein could have told you
your wily words would always only fall apart
in the face of your fears
(and that even that's too pat).
So what's left but outright confession.
I'm the scared keeper in this house,
presiding over a stew of the catalogs
that clogged the mailbox all year,
pages turned down at the corners:
red espadrilles, glass dessert sets,
dehumidifiers, magnifying mirrors, all
never ordered but somehow comforting.
The part about the magazines is almost true
but actually worse because they're everywhere
and every kind, with half-read newsletters
from dozens of organizations mixed in,
along with marked up pamphlets from
book stores and university presses.
I've sixteen frying pans at least,
useless ones nested under good, and
clips full of recipes I plan to try
some summer. Clothes and shoes
in the back of my closet are almost
in style again and of course I'd
like to say that's why they're there,
but of course it isn't so.

The real truth is I never even move
the furniture around or pictures
on the walls because I can't.
I have negatives from every snapshot I ever took,
socks in a sewing basket I'm afraid to mend.
And I can't get rid of letters
because they have a kind of life:
the answered and unanswered ones
here on my desk, the rubber-banded ones
from my father, who died in 1964, that
I keep in the other room in a shoe box,
that I still can't read. And I wait
for it to happen, knowing all along
I couldn't hold on to a thing
if the earth should tilt this morning –
a great seed-pod in the San Andreas Fault
opening in a sudden paroxysm of spring –
everything sliding sideways down and down
through all the pink azaleas massed to protect us.

The Ordinary Strange

That morning we drove north in heavy rain,
the dark blossoms of a spring night storm
hanging over a hundred miles of day.

It began then, small strobe-light flickers
on the edge of perception, slivers
behind thought, just out of reach.

We turned into the freeway's early grey,
the no-color realm of trucks and paving crews,
and one-to-a-car commuters checking

their own reflections in rearview mirrors,
their faces as unfamiliar
as the road's known landmarks

suddenly seemed to us, as you
seemed to me, a moment's vertigo,
the underside of the world rising.

Within its sameness the rainlight changed
and changed, the highway rolling slowly
into the East Texas woods,

redbuds breaking out like brushfires
here and there among bare-limbed
or feather-budded trees. And farther north

white explosions of dogwood
back in the pine forest, massed
petals luminous under a low sky,

glowing from nowhere, flashes of dark
light back of the brain, outside in.
My hand was on your arm to hold us still

as we kept moving, as I kept slipping
away, or you did, nothing the same
although everything was, and changing.

Cathy Stern

Nobody was practicing an art in our family unless it was the art of writing and speaking well, which my father, I think, got from his father. Their entertainment was sitting around with crackers and milk in the kitchen, talking. I was fascinated with all their conversations about religion and politics. It was clear that they didn't agree at all, but they were very devoted to each other. The argumentation was full of love and, at the same time, full of caring about those words. My father, who was a private-school principal for most of his life, was very much in love with language. He was very well-spoken, he made beautiful speeches, he became an amateur Chaucer scholar.

My mother, who had studied Liberal Arts at Boston University, was interested in the theater and had had some bit parts in the early silent movies of the East. She was a teacher before we were born but when we were growing up, she did volunteer work with the disadvantaged. We moved around a great deal. I was born in Kansas City, then we moved to Syracuse, to Wilmington, to Staten Island, to Cincinnati where I lived for six years. Then my parents were divorced and I started going here and going there to be with them. I think I had a reasonably happy childhood except when my parents got divorced – I thought that was very difficult.

I started writing early. My mother told me I wrote a single-line poem when I was about six: "Listen to the music of the night." She thought it was very poetic and wrote it down. I was always interested in poems, I guess because they rhymed. And I would write little plays when I was very small. I had my whole family dress up in costumes and made the neighbor kids come in. I had very dramatic performances, like one about fishermen who drowned that involved a garbage can full of water which I poured down the driveway.

I went to progressive private schools where they often published the things that students did. The first place I had something published, a first-grade poem or something like that, was at the Staten Island Academy. I used to do little newspapers when I was in elementary school and junior high, but my first real memories of writing are as a teenager. One extraordinary memory is connected to Pearl Harbor. I was living in Sarasota with my father and on that Sunday afternoon, I was sitting out on the dock writing a poem about how the stillness had been broken by the flight of a plane. After I got through writing my poem in my notebook, I went in the house and my father said, "The Japanese have just bombed Pearl Harbor. We are going to be in the war."

At that time I wrote a lot on my own but all I can bring to mind is some line like "the ironic tears of God." It was typical fourteen; the rain was God crying, the world was a rotten place – the whole weltschmerz of the fourteen year old. I wrote a lot of letters during those years. It was the time of purple ink and brown ink and designed exclamation marks. We all printed; that is the result of private school. We were keeping diaries that were almost like illuminated manuscripts. They weren't just about boys; they were about the big questions, What are we doing here? What is the purpose of all this? Is there a God?

In high school I had some things published in school publications. One was a sonnet that my father helped me finish. Later I was an editor of the school paper. During my senior year I was in a special class of three students who were set to work writing literary criticism about modern poetry, about Archibald MacLeish, Dylan Thomas, Stephen Spender and Auden. I don't remember doing much writing outside of school during those later years, although I do know I wanted to be a writer – in the sense of having *already* written all of it. My college applications asked how you pictured yourself at the age of thirty-five. I remember my answer was, I would be married and have three children and I would be a writer.

I went to Antioch College in the last year of the war. It offered a five-year work-study program, the general idea of which was to introduce you to the work world while you were in college. It was right down my alley, the whole place. It was very politically oriented; I joined the Civil Liberties Union and other organizations which expanded my horizons tremendously. I loved my jobs. The first was as nurse's aide at Mt. Sinai Hospital in New York City. I lived in the employees' dormitory there and worked in the pediatric semiprivate wing. In a writing course the following year, I wrote a series of vignettes based on that job. One was about the death of a little boy. When I loaded up the toys of this little boy and took them down to give them back to the parents, the father wanted to give me a two-dollar tip. I said, "Oh, I couldn't take that"; I felt as if this child had been almost like my own. I wrote about eating in the employees' dining room with the scrubwomen, listening to them talk, the contrast between being on the social bottom of the world and where I was in my real life. For my second job I went to Washington because my father worked for the government during the war. I worked as a file clerk in the Foreign Broadcast Intelligence Service, in the Far East Division where they intercepted Japanese radio broadcasts. That is where I was when we dropped the atom bomb on Hiroshima.

That summer I met Herb again. He had just come out of the army. We looked at each other a little bit differently than we had when he was a senior and I was in the fourth grade, or before he went overseas when I was fourteen and he was twenty-two. And we just sort of fell in love at first sight. I was nineteen and a half when we got married. At first we lived in Cincinnati where Herb had a job. I stayed out of school for about half a year and then went to the University of Cincinnati. Since I did not want, any more than my sister did, to be a teacher – because we were the children of teachers – I majored in psychology.

I was about to graduate when Herb got transferred to Houston. I actually considered staying behind and finishing the degree, which would have been radical at that time, but he seemed so distressed by the idea, I thought, "Well, it is a big move and probably we should go together and I can just finish school somewhere in Texas." When we came down here, I audited some courses at Rice and then completed my degree at the University of Houston. I took a writing course there and though the teacher was a novelist, what I seemed to be interested in doing was writing poetry. I can't tell you what the antecedents of that are, but suddenly that is what I wanted to do.

Nancy was born a year later in 1951, Peter in 1954, then Charlie in 1960. I figured my job was to be a parent. Most of the time I was very busy with children, but still a friend and I managed to take Great Books together for two or three years when the babies were small. We would sit and talk afterwards in one driveway or another, until the husbands would come out and see if we were even there. And I belonged to the League of Women Voters for many, many years. When Nancy was a baby, I was doing research on constitutional revision. With one foot I was pushing her back and forth in her stroller and with my hand I was writing a chapter for a book on methods of constitutional revision and the history of the Texas constitution. Much later when the Girl Scouts wanted someone to teach their "My Government" badge to Nancy's troop, I decided I would do it and found I really liked to teach. I was also very active in politics and was a precinct organizer for the Liberal Democrats one election.

I think I was home with kids for twenty-seven years before I was alone again. These particular three children took up a tremendous amount of my time. They were extremely active and I was the chauffeur. They were all in different schools for the longest time. In the same year one of them started kindergarten, one, junior high and one, high school – that was the most crazy first day of school. They were here, there and everywhere, they were like whirling dervishes. Nancy had dance class, Peter was taking private trumpet lessons and was in the marching band in high school, Charlie was in Spanish tournaments. Herb had the kind of job in which he was gone early in the morning and got home at 6:30 at night. If I had vanished from the earth, the whole thing probably would have fallen down because I was the one who held it together. I don't think I have been sorry; their careers and leadership abilities came out of all this.

That is probably why I did not do any writing. But I did write limericks. If somebody had a birthday, I would dash one off. Once I wrote limericks about everyone of fifteen or sixteen people coming to a party, trying to capture the character of each one. That's very tricky because you only have so much space and only those two rhymes and you have to get it all in there. And I once wrote a fund-raising skit for The League of Women Voters, rewriting all the lyrics of *My Fair Lady*. We took it to the state convention of the League.

I always assumed that I would go out and do something later on. So in 1969 when Nancy was eighteen, I went back to school. At first I thought I'd follow the psychology route and become a high-school counselor, but I found you had to be a teacher first. To get a master's degree in psychology you had to go full time, so that door was closed. And to study social work was full time or nothing. So I decided to go back to school part time and become an English teacher. It was 1969 and I was 42.

It took three years to go through all that mess. Education courses were so bad that at the end of one of them, I wrote, "No wonder you have trouble finding teachers. What you ask us to do is insulting to the mind and the intelligence." I did my student teaching at a blue-collar high school where I asked to be placed and later was hired to teach there. Peter and Nancy were away at college, Charlie was in the seventh grade. That first year of high-school teaching was one of the really difficult years of my life, but the next year was a pleasure. I taught there for three years and won a teaching award, one of the ten "most-wanted" teachers. I loved teenagers and found out I related to them very, very well. I thought, This is what I am going to do.

But in the spring of 1975, while I was recuperating from a hysterectomy, I started thinking that I really didn't know enough about English and would like to go to graduate school for a year and then go back to being a teacher. I said to Herb, "I am going to take the GRE and if I get the proper score I'll go." I did really well, told the school I wanted a leave of absence for a year and started studying English in the master's program at the University of Houston. Almost everything I was studying had to do with poetry. I felt a great reluctance to stop going to school and was no longer certain I wanted to be a high-school teacher. At the end of that year I resigned from the Spring Branch School District and the next year I entered a graduate writing workshop at the university. That's where I started writing poetry again. That's so long ago mentally, but it is not even ten years. I was almost fifty.

I had to put up with some pretty tough criticism. I remember I had written a poem with the eye of a hurricane as the metaphor. It was about searching for some kind of identity – with this whole family business going on – in solitude, in "the eye of the hurricane." I am sure the young people didn't read it that way, but how could they? One guy said, "Aw, we have heard all this stuff before, about the storm." I was taken with that metaphysical sort of thing since that is where I had left off, with the New Critics, paradox, irony, conceits. The first thing I had to learn was that all of that was *out.* Don't use conceits. Forget about irony. Forget about paradox. Metaphysical poets were out. Romantic poets were in. Later I found out everyone was writing about their childhood. It had never occurred to me that that could be subject matter. I was still the fourteen-year-old girl who thought you were supposed to write about love and death, the great questions of the world, all these terribly heavy things. I didn't even think of writing any funny things outside the limericks until later.

Partly because I was given some encouragement by the workshop teacher and partly because I was petrified of writing an academic thesis, I decided that for my master's thesis, I would choose the creative writing option and write a book of poetry. I just jumped into it. I don't know where the poems came from. I tried everything – I have poems about political issues, poems making fun of graduate seminars, poems about sexist billboards and nursing homes, all kinds of things, abstract and concrete, angry and not angry. I was still dealing mostly with moods; I thought that was a major subject matter of poetry – you were feeling depressed or whatever. I tried all kinds of different forms. But I think most of the poems were rather glibly written; I just didn't know how hard you have to work. Later on I came to know an entirely different experience when I was writing, much intenser, much deeper, much more isolated. But that fifty-page book of poems was the twenty-six years I stopped writing; that is how I look at it. It wasn't all that good, but I can see the seeds of the poet I was to become.

It was a wonderful experience for me. From my thesis advisor, Jim Cleghorn, I learned that not everything I gave birth to was perfect on the page. I learned from him how to reconsider the order of things. Once, in a conference, he said to me about a poem, "Maybe you ought to take the last stanza and move it up to be the first." I came home and said to my husband, "Can you imagine what this man said to me? Take my last stanza and use it first! Oh, what a terrible thing! He is tampering with my work!" I also learned what to veto. And I learned to read when I couldn't write. Even now when I am stuck on something, I may just pick up someone's work, not necessarily close to my own – I am not sure what I expect to find, maybe just a way of getting out of a corner. He was very patient, very encouraging, not as hard on me as other people in the full-fledged creative writing program that began in 1979 would be, but for what I was doing, which was trying to catch up twenty-six years all at once, he was good.

I didn't write for a whole year after I did that thesis. This was, in part, because – having missed teaching – I had recently become a teaching assistant at the university. (I've been teaching ever since.) But it was mainly because I had to "recover," in a sense, from *doing* the thesis; I had to get some perspective on what I had done. Then, in the spring of 1980, I decided to apply to the new Ph.D. program in creative writing at the University of Houston. Since I was already in the Ph.D. program in literature, it would have been a sideways move. But I was not accepted. That really was a bit of a blow. I kept saying to myself, "I don't care," but I really did care. I got a form letter that said, "We think you need to take some undergraduate poetry workshops." I wasn't pleased at all, because I had a master's degree in English/Creative Writing from this same school. But I wasn't going to give up, so I signed up for the undergraduate courses.

I studied poetry with Thomas Lux; what I learned from

him was: clarity, clarity, clarity. And I learned from him to resist writing that final line in the poem. After we get all through with a poem, we want to say to the reader, "Hey reader, just in case you didn't get it, I am going to put on this final line that tells you exactly what this poem means." Usually it is better to leave it open. I also took "The Personal Essay" from Phillip Lopate which I would recommend as a wonderful exercise for poets.

But my transition in writing came in Stanley Plumly's graduate class in poetic theory which I took, at his invitation, in the fall of 1981. He is a lyric poet, which is what I aspired to be, and the kind of work he produces is the kind I wanted to produce: very clear, translucent, perhaps deceptively simple, with depth. The things he asked us to do were very helpful to me. He said, "Play the diction against the form," so I tried to write a sonnet in conversational language – it was "Love Poem." Or, "Write a poem of fifty lines, at least four stresses to the line." I had never written anything long and I thought I would never be able to do it. I wrote a poem called "August: On the Texas Coast," the first time I had ever touched upon childhood. He had us try to write something that was totally against our own style: I wrote a poem about someone who made me angry. We did exercises on other poets, for example, tracing how the poem moved down the page. I learned from Stanley that I had not stretched my mind whatsoever in what I had written in the past. He let me go on to study with him in his graduate poetry workshops, though I was not officially in the writing program. He opened up a whole new world for me of things to think about and ways to go about things, some of which didn't sink in till much later. That is what I needed.

I do very well with assignments. Try that or try this. Like the forms course I took in 1985 with David Wojahn: write a villanelle, write another sestina. I want to see if I can do it. It may not be a successful poem but I will have learned something. Here I had the opportunity to hear a different opinion about my work. David Wojahn said, "I like your quirky stuff, like 'Keeping' and 'August: On the Texas Coast,'" instead of picking out my sonnets and lyrics. All this time I thought I was supposed to be making a better sonnet, a better lyric, and that these assignments were stretchers but not, perhaps, the real thing. And then suddenly I perceived them as another form of the real thing. I studied with Ed Hirsch a year ago last fall. His work is rougher, more pedestrian sounding, more prosy than Stanley's. Now I want to move somewhat in that direction with my own work.

In the course of these years, working with a number of poets and studying with great enthusiasm many aspects and periods of poetry, I somehow slipped over into the creative writing Ph.D. program in 1983. But by that time I was more interested in writing poetry than in getting the degree. Then last spring, when I felt I was through with graduate school, I heard that Richard Howard was coming, and then Howard Moss, and I decided not to drop out because it is the only way I could study with them. They are my own contemporaries and for almost the first time I would be studying with someone my own age.

Richard Howard said to me, just the other day, that he wants me to put "Those Places" into iambic pentameter. He said, "Your perceptions are very formed, the way you deal with your experiences. I would like to see that poem not so rough." Here is someone who is telling me the opposite story, that he likes the formalism of my work and wants me to stay that way. I know I don't have to agree with him. I may go back and tell him, "No, I can't do it," or "It will throw it off." I may do it on another poem because I am not a reviser. But I will *try*, because I consider that he, like other distinguished writers, has wisdom I haven't earned yet. They have been at it so much longer.

There is something about going to school, about having spent eleven years now as a graduate student, half time or full time, that has done something for my poetry. I can't underplay the academic side of my development because having studied the writers of the past, having re-fallen in love with Chaucer, for example, has done a tremendous amount for my writing.

School has tended to be the superstructure but I don't want it to be that way anymore. I want to get off into some superstructure of my own invention. I am going to try to put together a book, to broaden what I do in some way that I don't understand yet. I have succeeded to a certain point with the lyric. Now what? I never thought I would get to the place where I would say, "Okay, I have learned how to do this, now I am going somewhere else." When you succeed at a certain level in the creative world, you are faced with a whole other set of problems that come from success rather than failure.

In addition to the workshops at the university, I have belonged for the past six or seven years to a poetry-writing group. There are twelve or thirteen of us, all women, our average age around fifty-five. What I have gotten out of this group is the great joy of sharing work with people my own age who understand my life experience in a way that many young people cannot. For example, "Old Loves," which is a very tongue-in-cheek poem about the "old loves" of a now middle-aged woman who married for life at nineteen, has been continually misread. Anyone our age knows that the moustached ex-soldier from forty years ago, one of my old loves, is also the "you" the poem addresses. But this perception is completely lost on the young students. And one young woman said, "This poem is grotesque, just grotesque. She has given these people such short shrift." And another said, "She's really a snob looking down on these old loves, giving such thumbnail sketches of these people." They cannot, for the life of them, understand what that can possibly be about. And they probably never will, because their lives are not going to be like that. They are going to have forty-five old loves, five of them live-ins for two or three years apiece; it is going to be a whole new world from the one we know about. And then I took it to the workshop of middle-aged women I belong to and of course they loved it, because they all came from the same background. I often take a poem to the workshop at school and then to the middle-aged women's workshop to see what different reactions I get. The women will giggle at the right places; the young people won't. They won't know what I am making fun of. I haven't felt any standoffishness with people in their twenties and thirties, nor have they with me; they have been very nice, very supportive. But there is this strange myopia.

.   .   .

When I sent out some of the things from my thesis and everything came back, I thought maybe my stuff wasn't good enough. It wasn't. Now I know it is, but I am still going to have a lot of trouble getting it published because there are hundreds of people out there whose work is also good enough. I contributed seven of my poems to a book called *The Leaf Raker,* a collection of work by my women's writing group. Each of us put in $150; it came out in 1983 and was in bookstores around here. One bookstore gave us a party.

I am very proud to be in this book, but I am sorry on one count, because it prevented me from having my very first piece of published work in the *New Yorker.* It is a rather bizarre story. When Howard Moss visited the writing program in 1983 and I set up a conference with him, I knew he was poetry editor of the *New Yorker,* but I never thought he would be interested in publishing any of my work. I gave him what I thought were the best of my poems, including some that were published in *The Leaf Raker.* The conference was canceled because of his health but later at the party given for him, he said to me, "I enjoyed reading your poems. Would you mind if I took them back to New York and sent you some comments. I particularly like 'Love Poem,' and 'Poetry Reading.'" I should have known, but I was too naive. Right before New Year's I got a letter that said, "I am happy to say that we have accepted your 'Love Poem' but we would like to call it 'Hard to Say.'" Well, the hardest thing I ever had to say was, "I am sorry, it has already been published." The one thing it gained for me is to bypass the slush pile. I never get form rejection slips from the *New Yorker;* I get letters from Howard Moss.

The thing that gave me the greatest confidence was winning the Houston Discovery Prize for Poetry, a competition sponsored by PEN Southwest, the Houston Art Museum, the Cultural Arts Council of Houston and the Creative Writing Program at the University of Houston. I entered the Discovery Prize contest for four years and won second place in 1984 and first prize in 1985. To be chosen as the winner by Robert Hass, a Yale Younger Poet, and given second place by Richard Howard, a man more my age, made me feel that it wasn't a fluke.

The reading I gave as part of the Discovery Prize was quite

an experience. I spent quite a bit of time deciding what to read and in what order. I practiced because I used to read too fast and drop my voice. I went to listen to David Wojahn give a reading and we talked about it later. He said it is a really good idea to stop after each poem and let it sink in and give a little introduction to the next poem. When you read them glued together, you lose everything. So I took two swigs of whiskey in the ladies room to take the edge off and read ten poems, with a little chitchat in between and before I began. The many years of teaching stood me in good stead. I was very nervous the first or second poem. The art museum auditorium is a bad place to read because you are way down at the bottom of an amphitheatre and they lower the lights and you can't see anyone. But then between poems, when I said something amusing, they laughed and I knew I had them. From then on I loved doing that reading.

I have also entered the Houston Festival and read in it a couple of times. It is a citywide festival, mostly in the downtown area, with poetry readings, dance performances, ethnic food, puppets, bands and theater. I read once on a corner while people were eating cotton candy and then later in the downtown library during a terrible rain.

I know that my work is good enough to be published. I just haven't had it published. These days, I send to the *New Yorker, Georgia Review, Southern Poetry Review,* and *Poetry.* I don't have time to start down with some piddling little magazine; I know my work is better than that. I want to start at the top and just drop down as far as I have to before I go up again. I wanted to get something published before I was sixty, which will be this summer. Clearly that is now going to happen. The *New Republic* will publish a new poem, "Once Removed," this spring. And "Those Places," "Old Loves," and "Thirty-ninth Anniversary" will appear in *Shenandoah.* And my poems are in this anthology. But if I didn't make that, I would have moved it up to sixty-five.

. . .

I am disciplined while I am writing but I don't write every day. I can spend two or three days writing a poem and then I might not write another for six weeks. I am going to be more like Elizabeth Bishop, I am not going to produce scads of finished work. I am a very painstaking writer – I will write the first line and scratch it out, I will write two lines and then scratch them out. Until I get the beginning right, I don't do the rest. I spend a lot of time, so much so that I lose track. I mean I would give up eating, I would give up anything as long as I am doing it. I don't live in this world when I am doing it.

I show almost everything I write to Herb. I will listen to him before I listen to anyone else because he is not a poet, he doesn't have a literary background. After all we are not writing, I hope, just for other poets but for an educated adult person. If Herb can't understand it, I figure I am in big trouble.

In regard to process, I very rarely start with the language – much as I love language which is a thing I can almost touch, like pearls in your hand. I figure that will come. I don't start with the line, I start with the idea, an experience usually, and I have to live with that experience for a very long time to discover what it was really about. For me the writing process goes way down deep and that is where I stay till it's done. For example, "Poetry Reading in the Downtown Library" was an experience I had. There was a derelict who had come in out of the rain at a poetry reading I gave during the Houston Festival. I thought, I would like to deal with this, but how? The real problem is how to put yourself on both sides of the issue. Ten years before, I would have looked down my nose at the derelict in the poem and never known the difference. I had a lot of trouble with the last two lines because there was a little shadow of condescension in there and I had to get it out. I changed "I open the slim/folder of my poems and I read to him" to "I open my slim/folder of poems and I read them to him," just a fine line of difference. I spent a long time on that change, maybe two hours trying to figure out what to do.

The same thing happened with the young man crossing the downtown street with the blanket, that became "Those Places." I had been thinking about him day after day. The truth was, I didn't want to see that man again. I drove that way early every morning and I kept thinking, Please God, don't let me see that man again, I cannot handle this. And I wondered, Why can't you handle this, what is making you so upset? It took me a very long time to face the content of the poem. I sat on it for maybe two months and finally I had to deal with all those feelings: you really don't want to have anything to do with those street people even though you know you should, and then the next day you want to have everything to do with those people, but you can't. It was that ambivalence that finally came to be the message of the poem. But I didn't know that at first.

.   .   .

I think the advantage of starting writing so late is having been around a long time, having been all these different ages and all these different people. The great advantage is experience, a whole slew of things to draw on. Sometimes I think, Suppose I had written all those twenty-six years, maybe I would be somebody. But I would not trade the children and the life that I had. I might do it slightly differently but not the big parts. I would have married the same person and I would have had the same children – I am very happy with the way they are. But I would have gotten out of the house more and felt less guilty about it. And I might have started writing sooner.

But this is a gift, what has happened to me. This is a second life and most people don't have a second life. I don't really want to be famous. It is the doing of it. That is something I wouldn't have wanted to miss. You create something, make something that is new in the world and that is what is so wonderful. Though I can't write about everything, I make something out of my life into art. It is a way of keeping your life.

Francine Julian Clark

. . .

Eligible Impulses – '44

And so I had passed my childhood disguised to myself as an observer, not a participator. As one who rummages around on the outside of my life – a stubborn family tradition apparently among the women. But now all I need in order to have a future, is to design a future I can manage to get inside of. One that is not clumsy. One that is not filled with forlorn fury. One with clean sheets, a four-poster bed with a canopy. This whole picture of domesticity has got the upper hand of me, entirely. To accomplish my goal I learn to dance the rumba, the conga, the Lambeth Walk, the samba, the boogie. Java, java, java, java, uhhh. I develop a fiery temper; men like it when they're courting, not after. I need to create a climate. My life needs a thermostat.

I have had a fever of one hundred and three for the month of June and half of July. Mornings it is down to ninety-nine and evenings it starts its climb. When my head hits my pillow at about two in the morning, I'm raging, drenched, crying, telling myself I must be happy.

But the matter is not totally one of aesthetics, not now. It's one of what man to place between the thighs, so that I can at last begin life. I confess frankly to many hours of quiet sadness mingled with absurd musings about the only future I can envision at the moment. What color geraniums will I have in my window boxes? What color towels will I have in my bath? I wait for better days. And one final thing, just to make sure it's understood: I do not consider for one moment the use of my ability, my talent as a means to my future. A view that might have seemed absurd in any other society.

I have a summer job in a public-relations agency that is based on Broadway near Times Square. I keep the purchase-ledger in the accounting department: accounts receivable. Mother is ecstatic, a little more money coming in. She's happy I'll be associating with a "better class of people" rather than those "ineligible, rapacious boys you go dancing with." Adultery has made its brand on my thoughts. In my imagination I see that festering "A" on the foreheads of women. The common opinion is that adulterous women should be killed, branded. Or kill themselves to rid the world of their stench. Most important, I have to go to my Prince untouched. No used-goods for him. But that's not all. Here's the irony of irony: I must be a molten, quivering lotus when the hallowed moment arrives. I must fulfill without question all his fantasies. He must be left totally calm and satisfied. The job must not be bungled. I have been officially informed: "No ineligible impulses until the right moment."

My boss Davis seems to like me.

"Good morning, Bub," he says as I hang my bag in the locker that stands outside of his office.

"Hi," I say. He is sizing me up to a fare-thee-well.

I'm tall and excruciatingly thin, yet round and fleshy too. I have a mane of blond hair that, for office propriety, I have tied in a Gibson Girl roll around my head, allowing the fringes to fall. Norma has made me an "office dress," a draped crepe dress with long sleeves and a high collar reminiscent of clothes worn at the turn of the century. "This will help you get ahead," she tells me.

Outside my office window, a male model's face on a billboard puffs cigarette smoke out onto Broadway, advertising Camel cigarettes. The ticker-tape that travels around the Times building reads off the number of war casualties each day, all day: the battle news. On the triangle below our office windows there is the shouting and activity of a constant War Bond drive. Hollywood movie stars sing, holding megaphones to their mouths. At lunch time some of the girls and I go to Toffenetti's restaurant or to Schrafft's. On payday the girls and I go to the Piccadilly restaurant and if they order a cocktail, I drink Carstair's rye and ginger ale. In the evenings after work we go to the Astor bar or the New Yorker hotel and sometimes, to be very daring and if someone has a car, we drive out to the Glen Island Casino. A block away from the office is Walgreens, the famous theatrical drug store: where actors buy their grease paint and cosmetics and lounge at the soda fountain talking about their auditions. One day I see Danny Kaye buying cigarettes. The starlet Geraldine Brooks is with him. There is a famous theatrical agent on our floor near our office: Aaron Stern. Beautiful women, actresses, go in and out of his office; stand waiting by the elevators holding their hips, smoking, impatient. Sometimes limousines wait outside the building for them. When I have extra time at lunch, I stroll by the stage-doors in the theatrical district.

Davis is tall and broad-shouldered and often wears a gray tropical suit with pleated trousers, a blue shirt and a maroon knit tie in the current fashion of Zoot. A watch chain to which he has attached a heavy load of keys hangs low on his pleated trousers. Keys to his office door, the building doors, the wash-rooms, the filing cabinets, the office safe and keys to his fami-ly's house in Pelham Manor where he lives with his parents and two sisters. His mother grows cabbages in their yard and kohlrabi and huge tomatoes. He brings these in to work and passes them out to the staff. Also, he has a key to the armory where he is a lieutenant in the National Guard. Davis is 4F because of high blood pressure and sticks out like a sore thumb in nineteen forty-four. There are few men of service age around wearing civilian clothes. But it is nice getting attention from a man rather than the boys I know at church.

After work, after I have bathed and changed my clothes, I time my exit from the tiny flat Mother and I have, to her exhausted arrival home from her job in the department store. I scheme to avoid her, her quizzical looks, her strangely angry interest in my comings and goings. She keeps her back to me when she asks me questions about my life. When I hear her dry footsteps on the stairs, I pop three aspirin and start down. I see the banality of that crossing, the old and the young.

"Going to church," I say, slithering by her on the landing.

"Oh," she says, already lonely. "I thought you'd stay home tonight."

"No," I say, "Stan Kenton is playing at the Mall in Central Park. We're all going over." I am the flickering candle, she the powdery moth, a tight pressure growing in her head. That crossing is to me like trying to envision mortality, visiting your own funeral, putting flowers on your own grave. Eager and relieved, I take the Madison Avenue bus uptown.

Most of the boys in our crowd at church are waiting to be called up, ready for officer-candidate school: the air corps, the navy, the marines. Some of the older boys have already washed out and are in the Seabees and infantry. We meet at church and walk into Central Park together heading for the Mall. People stroll arm in arm. The park is fragrant and cool. That lever that springs New Yorkers into high gear hasn't made its inroad yet.

Hammerhead waits for me by a drinking fountain near the bandstand. He is a famous seducer in our crowd, romantic and without reticence. No cramped innuendo in Hammerhead. He grabs me and we walk together. Fervent Hammerhead, wearing a suit.

"What do you want from me?" he asks.

"Nothing," I reply. "You don't have to be sarcastic."

"Are you going to let me tonight?" he asks, circling his arm about my waist. He claims to understand the female heart. "You know you want to." And jealous. "Don't dance with Donald even if he asks you."

"Why not?"

"He rubs against girls."

"Oh he does? Gee, he must like crowds," I laugh. "What a precisely described scene."

"Don't give me any of that lofty talk. Have you been to the doc yet about your fever? How am I going to kiss a girl every night who's burning up?"

"Who says I'm going to kiss you every night?"

"Come on, you know you will. My parents are in the country. The house is empty. Come on sweetheart, let me."

The Mall is given over to cliques of kids who come together, dance together and leave together, taking a meeting place at the edge of the dance floor to join up after the sets. There is no traffic sound, birds and crickets chirp, people sit on benches and the grass and smoke. Everyone smokes.

When Hammerhead pulls me out onto the dance floor, he's greeted jovially, a celebrity. "Hey Hammer," they shout. Then they look at me trying to decide about me. If I do. When Hammerhead dances, it is as though he has come down from some celestial castle just to make everyone happy. A happiness God. You have to wear two pairs of panties when you dance with him, or even tights. He is first of all gigantic in size, a figure I can imagine standing stoking coal before a blast furnace, the fire silhouetting his arms and legs, his massive body, his rather small head thrown back, laughing. He has large, flat German lips and white teeth like a shark's but even. I decide that is how he gets his nickname, the shark. His real name is Vic. But the boys laugh when the girls call him Hammerhead. An inside joke. And he has just broken up with Deenie, the only girl in our group who does it.

The *Daily News* sends out a photographer to shoot pictures of him. He is usually shown on the center page. The caption once read: "The Lindy Hop, a Tribal Fertility Rite." He comes in to you low on his legs, the flashbulbs click, his pelvis thrusts forward, the flashbulbs click. All but a public copulation, shaking his knees in the boogie, his mouth pursed. He grabs me by my hips and raises me in the air over his head. Then he swings me between his knees, turns around and catches me midair. I throw my legs around his waist. He buries his face in my flouncy clothes. "Oh cookie," he whispers. "Let me."

"No."

"Why for Christsake? Oh, I know, you're saving it."

"We have to be equal in our destiny, you know."

"Virgin Sturgeon." He looks at me and laughs. "You are one funny girl, but I tell you, you're going to regret not being with me. You're really going to regret it. This is how girls go wrong," he cries sagely. "Oh *marrone*, this is how girls go wrong." He claps his hands to his forehead.

After the dance, we walk deep into the park and sit on a

bench and neck for hours. "I can't stand much more of this," he whispers breaking away from me. "It's wrong." He emphasizes wrong with a religious indignation. "Nature should not be denied." Then, "Hey, you don't think I'm going to hurt you, do you?"

"You're being called up in a month."

"So what?"

"You'll leave."

"I'll write you. You'll be my girl."

"I've come a long tired trip to get here, Vic. I recognize all the signs of long distance in others."

"I won't leave you."

"I need someone steady."

"Love chooses us. We can't fight it."

"I'm not sure that I believe that. Anyway, it's different for girls."

"I won't get you caught, if that's what you're scared of."

"I know you won't and . . . it's not that I don't want to," I say quietly. "Because I do."

"Oh my Christ, then why not?"

He walks a few yards away. "Hell, blast and damn."

"Besides, I'm only seventeen."

"And I'm only nineteen. So what?"

"You have everything you need in life."

"So this is how it ends."

"If you say so."

"I'll tell you one thing. And this I know for sure. You'd better leave your mother."

I creep into bed without waking Norma who sleeps on the other side of the room. I dream of Hammerhead and the dream and my fever take me almost to delirium. The next day Hammerhead sends me a telegram: "Dear Tangerine. I have for you Perdido. Take the A Train with me. Your Hammerhead."

"Who is this Hammerhead?" Norma asks.

"A boy I dance with."

"That's a funny name. Is he dumb?"

"He smiles like a shark," I say and watch her face for recognition. A female recognition of the quality in Hammerhead every woman knows, feels to the marrow, avoids, sailing for saner waters. To think back on later. To remember with breathless wonder.

"It doesn't sound good," Norma says.

The next day, Davis asks me out to lunch. We find an Italian place on Thirty-ninth Street. We drink two glasses of chianti one right after the other. It is as though we need a quick release. I notice that Davis has knotty, powerful hands and that they are nearly constantly clenched. His face stretches before a strong emotion, crumbles and ages like an ancient papyrus. And when he is calm, he hums. He talks about a car he would like to have, a house he would like to have. I am suddenly quite bored, but my feelings for him deepen; that's the funny thing. He seems to read something of what I'm feeling and he lights a cigarette as if waiting for a storm to pass, as though he is only comfortable when the feelings have passed. His forehead wrinkles with the effort, his eyes widen. I know for absolutely sure that he is thinking he might like to marry me. This realization moves in on me like a fog moves in at the beach. I think that I like to be square and open with people, especially men; with girls I can say daring things but there's a lot of hiding. But I feel myself going underground with Davis, to a more protected place. I smile. He yawns widely. We walk slowly back to the office.

"I like the sound of your bracelets," he says.

When we part and I hang up my bag in my locker, I have the feeling of getting rid of an enormous responsibility. But something in the tone of things with Davis says that he will offer me the freedom of his sheltering protection. That he needs in return a respectable household, an ordered life and, above all, complete commitment. When he says good-night at five o'clock, his wrinkled brow tells me he is already sure that I will marry him, but if I don't, I will be depriving him of his needs and that will be most ungracious of me.

I've got all the time in the world, I say to myself. The whole of my life. And then suddenly, as if remembering something: People always think that. People always think they have lots of time and then life catches them up in a trap. I feel his frown lines reassert themselves on my face. And suddenly I have a great pain in my chest.

The next time I see Hammerhead, Tommy Dorsey is playing at the Mall. Hammerhead is dressed in navy whites and
paired off with Audrey who is new to our crowd and whose
family have taken an apartment in the city but maintain a
house in Old Lyme, Connecticut. Her talk is colored dreamily
with events at Old Lyme, the hay rides, the little coffee shop
called "the Dumps" they all go to after basketball games and
parties. Everyone drives a car in Old Lyme and everyone rides
out to High Point, the lovers' lane. And of course, in Old Lyme
all the girls do it. They have booze at parties.

Hammerhead dances with me once, a fast Lindy. "Come up
to the midshipman dance this Saturday," he whispers into my
neck. "I'll be there at Columbia until they send me to Pensacola. We can go to the Lions' Den afterward. Bet you can't do the
Lindy to 'Hayfoot Strawfoot.'"

"What will Audrey think?"

"Come on, they've got Nellie Lutcher's 'Hurry on Down'
on the juke-box."

"I like your haircut. You look . . . good."

"Dance, will you. Stop dragging. Have you seen the doc
yet?"

"No."

"Little suicidal bitch. I can feel you burning."

He dances the fox trot with Audrey all evening, holding
her hand in the small of her back. She keeps flickering looks at
me over his arm. An almost audible groan comes from inside
me.

Next morning I call in and tell Davis I'm ill. Actually I'm
exhausted from dreaming about Hammerhead. We were being
married in a chapel in New Orleans, making love on a throne
to the tune of "Perdido," a chorus in the background dressed
in waiter's clothes sang "Hayfoot Strawfoot" while shaking
maracas.

I can literally hear Davis straightening his tie on the other
end of the phone. "I've been meaning to ask you," he clears his
throat. "Would you go out with me Saturday night? I'll be in
town all day at the armory. We could meet afterward and do
whatever you like."

I am almost too fevered to understand anything but I hear myself say: "I'd like that."

"Who are you going out with," Norma asks as she watches me dress: a little violet-colored skirt, a white linen blouse and high-heeled shoes.

"My boss, Davis. Let's see: he's twenty-six, unmarried of course, sort of nice looking, lives in Westchester with his family. What else?"

"You're in good form," she says, turning her back. "What time is he coming?"

"I'm meeting him out."

"Oh, I know you." She's hurt.

I hug her. "I understand Mother, you want to be busy. But not with him."

"Do something about your cheeks, they're so pale."

She pinches my cheeks. "This Davis sounds substantial. Not like that Hammerhead with his Perdido. Thank goodness you broke with him."

"How do you know I broke with him?"

She knows by the looks of me, the sick look of one past emotion. She sees the little tight line in the corner of my mouth, the expediency line, the line of the good marriage, life plan, wife plan. I'm linked up with an ancestral tribe of good women who embraced the cool sheets of fortuitous matrimony. They nod approval and join hands to dance a ring-around-the-rosy about my fevered body. Let's not deceive ourselves, Norma married my Italian, panther-eyed father, but always felt she'd missed the boat.

"Let's make one thing absolutely clear," she says. "Make a good marriage or you'll rue the day. You'll rue the day."

Davis and I meet in Howard Johnson's. I tell him I'm meeting him there because it's more convenient, but he knows I don't want to bring him home. He gives me a little assuring pat on the hand, as if to say: Eventually I'll have to meet her. I have a chocolate soda and he has a vanilla soda. We stroll up Fifth to Central Park and sit near the Bethesda Fountain waiting for the crowds to gather. Cab Calloway is at the Mall. The place is wild: kids down from Harlem, from all the boroughs, the dance floor is jammed. But out in the middle, with a crowd standing around watching them, Hammerhead is dancing with . . . Deenie. He is dancing with do-it-all-Deenie, not Audrey. Small, stocky Deenie moves into him with her hips gyrating in the boogie, she pauses, throws her head back and thrusts into him. He watches her like a man watching his baby girl take her first step. His face glows with appreciation. Deenie hits him, he grabs her, swings her into the air. The cameras flash.

Davis and I dance the Westchester: a fox trot with little or no movement. We hold our hands twisted around behind me, self-consciously. When we do move we set out determinedly in a straight line from corner to corner, pause briefly, rear up on our toes, then surge ahead with little bursts of frenzied movement. Then we swing into reverse and retrace our steps, making a box in the other direction. At each set break Davis leaves me and goes to the men's room.

Hammerhead drifts over to stand by me. "How's my little furnace?"

"Back with Deenie, I see."

"Man cannot live on bread alone."

"If that's what you have to do. If that's what eases your mind."

"More than my mind, honey."

"Have you ever thought about sexual counseling?"

"Don't you know I'm with her so I can have you?"

"Then why should I object."

"I think you're jealous. Who's the bimbo you're with?"

"My boss, Davis Todd."

"She's out with her boss . . . *caramba.*"

I see a strange light, a crossroad, an openspace. I have seen this openspace many times through the years, but instead of moving toward the light, saying the things I'd like to say to Hammerhead, I close up and say: "Davis is a very nice man."

"I'll be overseas in six months. You won't feast your eyes on me for a while."

"You'll be okay."

"But will you, Iceberg Lady?"

"I love you, Vic. I do. But I don't want to sleep with anyone. Anyone do you hear." I stamp my foot.

"With me, honey, it has to be that way. Anything else would

be a lie." And then he adds, almost as an aside: "With the equipment I've got." Davis is approaching us. "I told you you'd regret not giving it to me. But honey, sweet baby, oh, my sainted aunt, I didn't know how much."

I introduce them. Hammerhead shakes hands with Davis with an air of affable deviousness and saunters back to Deenie. Davis asks: "That guy hang around you a lot?"

"Yeah," I say. "I like him."

"He looks like a specialist in sex information."

He holds his arm around my shoulders as we drive out of the park, presses his lips to my hair. Home in a taxicab. He helps me out of the cab, walks me to my door, takes his cigarette from his mouth and kisses me lightly on the cheek. "Sweet dreams. Sorry I can't do the Lindy. My blood pressure. I gotta be careful."

"That's okay."

As the cab drives away, I see Davis smooth his pompadour with his cigarette hand. Something very appealing, yet stony, about that gesture, upsetting in a way, that private gesture.

A terribly hot spell in August. The smell of manure everywhere. The city swelters. The rusty iron railings on the fronts of buildings and stoops give off the smell of dirty underwear. I take a cool bath and I'm immediately soaking wet. I have within me a significant feeling of foreboding. A doom feeling. That sad knowledge that must be behind the drawn faces of very old people when there is no longer the prospect of much future time. After they have bought the plot. I think I'm dying on my feet, my little bobby-soxed jitterbugging feet. A spirit in my body yearning for its freedom is now no longer a doodler. It's going to get out if it has to shuck me off like a corn husk. A little demon digging in my guts is now turning its malevolence outward, wants to be rid of self-absorbed me, needs to find fresh fields.

I go out to a public phone booth and call the outpatient department of New York Hospital and am told to come during clinic hours. After an examination, I'm bid to return after lunch to be admitted. They will have a bed then for me.

With a dollar left from payday, I treat myself to lunch at Lamston's counter on Lexington Avenue. A plate of chicken croquettes and potatoes with gravy set in little craters on top of the cones and smeared all over the croquettes. Rich tan gravy. Two white rolls. I have thirty cents left. I call Norma at work and tell her that I'm going into the hospital. She sobs such wracking sobs she has to hang up.

I'm in a ward with twenty women. To my right a Jewish lady who speaks only Yiddish. Across from us there is a woman who is reading Henry James' *The Turn of the Screw*. Each night she cries out: "Haunts. I see haunts." Her husband is a used-car dealer. She tells the ward about his girl friends. How she pursues her husband and his girls with a flashlight in and out of abandoned buildings, on roof tops, in back alleys, in the A&P warehouse in the Bronx, through the Botanical Gardens in Brooklyn. She makes us laugh. She laughs. She has a smile quick as a lizard's tongue. She is sick with an enlarged liver. Her liver is so big she has to have help turning over in bed. She looks like her skin has been dyed a rich, squash color. At intervals during the night she screams "Haunts."

Hammerhead is now on a naval aircraft carrier in Pensacola. I receive a postcard every few days mailed to the apartment. Davis has sent me yellow roses.

On the other side of the central corridor of our ward there is a girl my age named Ilsa who has been in the ward much longer than I. On Sundays her entire family comes to visit her dressed in black, like a steerage going-away party on shipboard, with baskets of fruit, looking overwrought and funereal, premature mourners. Ilsa stays in bed. I'm allowed to walk a little, so I go to see her once in a while, sit by her bed and we talk. I've never seen anyone so contented as Ilsa. She seems totally pleased with everything: her bedpan, her pills, her chart, her doctor's visits, her radio, her books, her letters to write. We compare our symptoms: a high fever, a high white count, nodules on our legs and joints. I feel she doesn't want me to come too often. She's responding to a celestial tide too deep for her even to sense. I know this. We are both riding the deep stream.

The Yiddish lady rings for the nurses and then can't tell them what she wants. She lies in bed wiping the frown lines from her forehead, agitated and forlorn. Somehow I'm able to tell them what she needs. How, I don't know. When her family comes to visit, she tells them I help her and they nod their thanks to me. When they speak to me in Yiddish, I shake my head: no, I can't understand. They keep nodding, thanks.

I find my breath is coming shorter, my head is swimming. I am lost in daydreams, puzzling over things, brooding. Sometimes I wake up in the dark laughing flamboyantly, but I'm blurred, confused. Can't remember what's funny. Waking in the night to small stabs of searing heat. The fever doesn't go down even in the daytime. This is what it's like, a voice says. Poor me, poor, luckless Patchin.

A wan, tearful Norma visits me each night after she gets out of work. I feel that she is pleased to find me in the same place. Put in my place, so to speak. I am, however, the recipient of her boundless love. She brings me snapshots of her ancestors, a shoe box of my baby clothes, things she made, excellently faggotted, tucked, smocked baby oddments she has saved commemorating the most exalted time in her life; a worn high-topped shoe, a name bracelet from Brooklyn Hospital where I was born. She brings, smuggles, dried prunes, yeast, lifesavers in many flavors and slips them under my blanket. Smith's cough drops, Kotex. It is as though she is stocking a tomb. Things she thinks I'll need in the afterlife. She is muddled and exhausted, but there is a new translucent beauty in her, a light. A frightening light.

I notice that a young intern visits my bed late at night, stands by my side when I cry out, holds my wrist. I keep a bottle of Tweed perfume on my night stand. He picks it up and sniffs it, puts some behind his neck. He is short and stocky and has red hair and freckles.

"What's wrong?" I ask him.

He shrugs.

"What's the matter with Ilsa?"

He shrugs again.

"Do you like to dance?" he asks. "I put myself through med school by dancing coast-to-coast with a Big Apple troupe."

"I love to."

He takes my bottle of Tweed, sprinkles it lavishly on us, dances the Big Apple grinning, holding a dancing dress up to him, pretending it's me.

The ward sleeps.

"Listen," he says finally. "Don't accept it. Fight. Okay?" He pulls the curtain around my bed.

We have a whole lifetime conversation in whispers. He half lies next to me, one leg on the floor, one leg next to me on the bed, and whispers to me softly in my ear. His stethoscope explores me under my nightgown. I tell him things that a chaste young woman might not know. We laugh in whispers. He kisses me, long, hard kisses. We touch. All in whispers. There is a steady snoring in the room with an occasional cry of "Haunts."

I waken one night to see Hammerhead leaning over me.

"What you doing in bed when old Hammer is on leave?" he asks.

"Dying, I think," I say.

"Hey, you can't do that."

I see he thinks so too. "How'd you get here?"

"Night nurse let me in. I bribed her with a promise of untold glory in the closet later."

"You have a heavy inventory of girl friends," I say with difficulty.

"You got to be ready for Hammer when he gets stateside again. I'm shipping out tomorrow."

"Where you going?"

"Don't know but I think the Pacific. Oh, those hula girls."

"I'll miss you."

I was in pain then.

The nurse tells him to leave. "Bye, baby. Think of me."

I'm released from the hospital the second week in September. I trudge home in my summer clothes, walk into our apartment pale and shaky. Norma sits on the sofa with her hat on, her bag next to her, smoking a cigarette. I see she is grim and determined. I am heartened to see her though. Then she hands me a box of stationery and tells me to write to everyone I know, to all my friends and tell them that I can't see them for a while, that I must stay in bed and rest, that I'm an invalid.

"I won't," I scream at her.

I walk to my closet and pull out a red print dress that has a big, black velvet bow in the front.

"What are you doing?" She rises to come toward me.

"My God, stop," I say. "Don't touch me."

"You can't go out. I won't let you," she screams.

"Watch me."

"You're defying nature." She is appalled by her loss of control. She glares at me, puffing her cheeks out, searching for the right words.

"Do you want to hear something sad," she shouts. "Ilsa's aunt is a nurse at the department store where I work. The poor girl died at home in bed."

"Best place for her."

"I have tried and I am beaten," she gasps, breathless with anger.

I take an hour to make up while Norma wrings her hands outside of the bathroom. I roll my hair into two large pompadours in front. I make up my mouth wide, wide, wide. Like Joan Crawford does. I put on silky-black stockings and a pair of black patent-leather shoes with a stiletto heel that kill my feet. When I leave, she is in a dancing rage. I run down the stairs. Norma screams a terrible scream.

The boys at church are all gone.

There is a notice on the bulletin board in the lobby of the church house. Hammerhead's ship went down in the Pacific. No survivors.

The girls are wrapped up in talk about Hammerhead and the others who are lost. I leave, stop at the corner drug store and buy a carton of Pall Mall cigarettes. Then I walk into the park and stand by the bandstand in the Mall and smoke a dozen cigarettes.

In the morning I call Davis and ask for my job.

After this there is nothing to do but get down to realities.

At Christmas time when I tell Norma that Davis has asked me to marry him the following summer, she is so pleased. Totally pleased. "Well you're grown-up enough," she says. "Such a nice boy, dependable, a good provider, reliable, steady." And I must agree. He is all of those things and more.

A man who, if you are ill, waits patiently until you return home, but doesn't visit. Sends bouquets, little notes, get-well cards, telephones often, but doesn't visit. Who can't handle the less than perfect. A man in a tiny, sealed-off country of his own.

Not a man who dances the Big Apple by your bed with a bottle of Tweed in his hand. Who kisses you hard, who says: "Fight." Not a man in navy dress-whites who persuades a stern charge-nurse to let him in to a hospital ward in the middle of the night, to see his sweetheart.

But I have learned things. I have to believe there must be something, some design to this.

"I have to ask you a difficult question." (Davis, on the night he plans to present me with my solitaire engagement ring.) We are standing under the big clock in the lobby of the Biltmore hotel waiting for colleagues of his to join us for a cocktail. We will sit in a bar and they will talk about the war.

Life bustles by us.

I'm wearing a camel's hair polo coat: my Christmas present. My hair is piled high on my head in curls. I feel frail and bright. Davis has a great white muffler around his neck. His collar is turned up. He wears a soft, large-brimmed hat. We are on our way to his parents' house for an engagement party. Norma has gone out on an earlier train loaded with presents for everyone.

"Please, I beg you darling, don't be upset. I have a delicate question to ask you. It's essential I know."

"Oh, be pleasantly surprised," I say.

Francine Julian Clark

I wasn't raised by parents who listened to classical music or read books or went to concerts, museums or art galleries. Yet they had an almost absolute adoration for anyone who lived or tried to live the life of an artist, and they gave anyone in the performing arts their highest respect. Art was their currency, art was what they believed in. My father's grandfather had been a cellist and conducted a well-known orchestra in Europe. My maternal grandmother wrote poetry, painted landscapes and played violin and piano. She was thought to be half-crazed by the men in her family because she was not at all interested in keeping house.

My mother and father were really so oddball, yet the kind of life they lived jazzed up the imagination, especially mine. Before she married my father, my mother was in the Ziegfield Follies. That came about because Mother's sister, who was in the Follies, was caught in a bad marriage and wrote my mother, who was in art school in San Francisco, begging her for help. Mother, who for some reason always deferred to her sister's wishes, left art school and came East. Her sister introduced Mother to Ziegfield and he offered Mother a job; it was as simple as that. Mother never had any ambition to be in show business. All she really wanted to do was paint, but the lure of being on Broadway proved to be too much. And that is how my mother met my father, at the stage door of the Ziegfield Follies.

My father had run away from home when he was still just a kid in Brooklyn. Somehow he made a three-horse parlay at Belmont race track and took the money and went to Chicago. He played the piano well enough to get a job playing in honky-tonk bars. Later, during Prohibition, he had a speakeasy in Chicago called Dago Franks. I heard Alberta Hunter, an old-time blues singer, say on a television program that that's where she had gotten her start. My father also wrote songs. He and his cousin, Jimmy Monaco, who went on to become a well-known song writer, started a business publishing music while they were both still living in Chicago. Later, when I was a little kid, my father had his own music publishing business in New York.

I don't think my parents ever tried to live a normal life. They couldn't stand everydayness. Anything that happened in their lives, even the most ordinary events, always became very dramatic. They thought of themselves as different, and because my father had run a speakeasy and known gangsters and my mother had danced in the Follies, I was different too. It was a burden I carried all through the time I was growing up. I remember one of my girl friends had a purse and a clean handkerchief that was just for Sundays. I looked with absolute hunger at families like that, that had an ordered life.

The Great Depression came when I was very young. Up until then my father's various business ventures had prospered and we lived in Queens, New York. But with the depression we had to move. We were tossed into the maelstrom, into the struggle to survive. We moved into Manhattan, into a walk-up flat on the East Side. I remember times I was outside playing on the sidewalk near Second Avenue, when I used to run and hide in doorways as the elevated trains went by. Life became not only disjointed but marginal, as I suppose it did for most people who lived through those times. We lived from day to day, hand to mouth. Listening to my parents talk, I was constantly trying to decide just how drastic the situation of the moment really was, whether my life was threatened or whether I had time to be happy. But even when times were hardest, my parents talked constantly about the artistic life. To my ears it was a life of constant struggle and sacrifice but filled with incredible romance and consummate reward.

In answer to my pleas, my parents, as poor as they were, let me start dancing lessons at the age of five. We had an old victrola and my father always managed to bring home records of the latest in popular music. Often after dinner, my parents would play their favorite songs and I would dance for them. It was the only time they ever really paid any attention to me. Performing seemed the only way I could get them to recognize that I was there. After I danced for them, my parents would discuss my future. They said the same thing every time. My mother would say I had great talent and that if I didn't become a professional dancer, I should become an actress and go on stage. I would become famous. My father would say, no, I should become a writer, that I had great talent as a writer, and that I would write great novels and stories and become famous. What gave him that idea I don't know, especially since I never saw him read a book or even a story in a magazine. Perhaps it was because my parents had begun to argue over everything and the topic of my talent was no exception.

My parents sent me to summer camp to get me out of the city. Though I was terribly shy and I constantly plotted how to escape almost all camp activities, especially sports, I became the camp storyteller. During the day, kids would beg the counselors to allow me to tell them a story at bedtime. As a reward for good behavior, after taps had sounded, the counselor would sit in the middle of our dormitory room and shine her flashlight, making a pool of light on the floor. In that safe, darkened space, I would weave Agatha Christie-type stories, using the campers as characters. I'd hear gasps and excited moans from the campers, and I would always stop at the most exciting place . . . to be continued.

I began to write when I was eleven or twelve. It started when I wrote a composition for school in which I compared what I remembered of life in Queens with life on Second Avenue. It was a grief-stricken outpouring. I contrasted my past life in a semi-rural surrounding with little gazebos out in the back, vine-covered, and a great grassy lawn, to the tense, fearful city life I hated. I used the noisy, hideous Second Avenue El as a kind of metaphor for my journey into the world of dirt and terror. After class my teacher, Miss Gorman, took me aside. She seemed quite moved by what I'd written and said I had talent, that I wrote well for my age and that I shouldn't stop. I could never really believe anything my parents said about me, but I believed Miss Gorman.

I began to buy copy books whenever I could and fill them up, one after the other, with stories and poems and plays. I even started a novel. It was all kid stuff of course, stories about kings and queens, heroes rescuing ravishing young women from great peril, rich and beautiful people traveling to far, exotic places, tragic love affairs. The closest I ever came to writing about my own experiences was a poem I wrote about the Grand Concourse in the Bronx. My father had driven us there one Sunday, in the days he still owned a car. It was a windy spring day after a heavy downpour. My parents let me stay by the car while they conducted some business of theirs. To me, the wide avenue of the Grand Concourse seemed like pictures I had seen of foreign cities, like the avenues of Paris. I wrote a rhyming poem called "Walk after Rain" with many, I say *many* verses describing my planned escape from the terrible state of childhood with its hidden fears and dependence on the whimsy of unstable adults.

During those years I showed my writing to just two people. One was Bernie Glick, a sailor who married my mother's best friend. He was my confidante. When he was home from the Navy, I'd go over in the afternoons and read him what I had. He was very good about it. He gave me criticism and told me he thought I was good. I remember him asking me questions about myself, what I did during the day. That may have been his way of trying to lead me into writing something that had some real meaning. But he always said that I should keep doing it, that I could learn how to do it well, that I would be talented. And the other person was a Broadway theatrical agent by the name of Max Hart. I used to go to his office and cook for him on his hotplate and run errands for him because he was very sick with cancer. He used to read my poems and tell my father that someone should do something about me, that I had some sort of ability. I kept on writing until I was sixteen and in high school. Then I remember looking over the stories and poems and saying to myself, This is junk, I can't do this, I don't have anything to say. Even after Miss Gorman's encouragement, it never occurred to me that I should write about the people and places and events in my own life.

The girl friends I had at school seemed to have only one ambition in life and that was to meet the right young man, fall in love, get married, have a home and raise a family. All those Betty Grable movies! By the time I finished high school, we were in World War II and all the boys I knew were in the service. I got a job working in an office and more or less waited for the war to end. My parents had long since separated and I lived with my mother in a small apartment for the duration. I gave up all ideas of anything that I wanted to do personally for the dream of getting married and having a family. That was the one most important thing that I was going to do.

I was married at the end of the war when I was nineteen. Within a year I found myself living in a small house in a Long Island suburb, spending my days taking care of an infant daughter and waiting for my husband to come home quite late each evening from the job he had in the city. That was the way things were supposed to be. For me it was grim existence, to say the least. My mother used to come out every Tuesday with a coconut layer cake she bought at Cushman's bakery. It never occurred to me that she realized how desperate I felt. It was after one of those Tuesday visits that she called me on the phone and said, quite matter-of-factly, that if I wanted to take lessons or classes anywhere, she would pay for them. It was as if some magical event had suddenly occurred in my life. I said I wanted to become an actress. Mother said, again quite matter-of-factly, that I should get whatever brochures were available on acting schools and the next time she came out we would sit down and figure out what she could afford. When I told my husband what I was going to do, it didn't register with him at all. Not at all. I remember he looked at me over the top of the evening paper and said, "Shouldn't you be in the kitchen?"

The acting school Mother and I selected was called the Harrison Lewis School of Acting for Screen, Stage, Television and Radio. The first day of class I was almost too frightened to go in. I remember standing on the sidewalk leaning against the building, trying to screw up enough courage just to walk into the lobby. At the end of the first day, we were all told to find a scene in a play, learn it, rehearse it with another member of the class, if possible, and bring in the scene ready to go. I spent the week terrified at the thought of performing before a group of strangers and dreading the moment my name would be called. But once on that platform, all fear vanished. I was suddenly in another world. I loved it. I said to myself, This is for me.

After eight months at the Lewis School, I became part of Brooklyn Playhouse, a winter stock company in Brooklyn Heights and for the next three years, I was in a different play every two weeks, at first playing supporting roles and then leads. I remember the camaraderie and the feeling that I belonged, but mostly I remember the audiences. They were marvelous. When I began to work, commuting to the suburbs, especially late at night, became next to impossible. I told my husband that I was going to move to New York, that marriage was not what I wanted and that I wanted a divorce. I hardly expected him to beg me to stay or to swear his undying love, but somehow my decision would have been easier to make if he had at least raised his voice in anger at what I was doing. Instead, he sat in his chair and looked at me as if I were an appliance that was no longer serviceable. He nodded his head and told me that as soon as I found a place, he would help me move. For a long time afterward I wondered why or how I could have married a man who seemed so devoid of feeling.

When the Brooklyn Playhouse closed, I was doing summer theater with good Equity companies and managed, in the winter, to get bit parts here and there on television dramas, some work on popular variety shows, some commercial movie work. I was on the Donald O'Connor show, the Jimmy Durante show – just dancing, or I'd jump out of a cupboard or closet and do a little boop-oop-a-doop type of dance. Occasionally I had a few lines.

It was after I came back from a summer with a stock company in New Jersey that I met my second husband, terribly handsome, fun to be with and very much into show business. I wanted a career, but I also wanted a home and family. After we were married, I had a second child, a boy. In addition to his job as TV producer, my husband was trying to raise money to put a play called "The Lawyers" on Broadway. Ralph Bellamy had expressed some interest in playing the lead role. We held backers' auditions in our apartment to raise money; I was essentially hostess, passing canapés and smiling a lot. Unfortunately the play didn't make it, and the marriage didn't either.

I moved into a small apartment overlooking the East River and for the next two years devoted myself exclusively to taking care of my two children. It was during this time that I decided to try writing again. I wrote short stories based on my life as a divorced mother of two small children. They were about dating strangers, about coming back to the apartment with an amorous date and two kids sleeping in the bedroom, about getting mauled in a taxicab, about nice men who turned out to be married. I wrote stories about nursemaids I overheard talking about their employers as we sat with our children in the park, about trying to raise kids, earn money and have some kind of a life. I used to write at the kitchen table, early in the morning or late at night. Nothing ever got finished though. I never had time to polish anything or solve any of the ideas in the work that I was dealing with. But I knew that writing would become a safe harbor for me someday, where I could channel my creative drive, where I would be able to have control over the material and also of my life.

It was also during this time, in the early 1960's, that I met Ted, a salesman in the city who was trying to write on the side. As he put it, he was having great success collecting rejection slips from the best magazines in the country. He was fascinated by the fact I was an actress. We talked for hours about the theater and about writing. I would show him the stories I wrote and he would offer criticism and encouragement. But in spite of this, I was doubtful and restless about writing. I knew in my bones something was missing in me and the way I approached the craft, something I couldn't define or put a handle on.

I decided to go back to acting. Both my children were in school and required less and less of my time and attention. I went down to the Village and enrolled at HB studios in a class given by Aaron Frankel and then studied for four years with

Uta Hagen, a marvelous actress and wonderful teacher. And I started to work again in off-off-Broadway theaters and doing commercials. Things started to perk up a bit and it looked like I was going to go more solidly in theater. But I didn't go on the road, I didn't take parts that would take me away from home, so I was kind of limited. I kept trying to write during the day, but whenever I sat in front of a typewriter nothing would come that really meant anything to me. Since acting classes helped my development as an actress, I thought a class in writing might help. So I submitted several of the things I had written to a well-known writer who had a class in New York and was accepted.

The format of the class was that one of this teacher's "regulars" would read a long piece, often taking up nearly the entire class time and then there would be a discussion period that seemed not to be dealing with the story we had just listened to, but some kind of one-upmanship as to who could find the most challenging and witty language to offer their thoughts on a variety of ideas. It was a new experience for me and I felt completely out of place. I could barely drag myself to class. For me, it became a lesson in cruelty. I hated the teacher and soon came to hate most of the students, but I stuck it out to the end, thanking God all the while for the more selfless and collaborative way theater people critique each other.

After that disaster I turned all my attention to the theater. I continued to take acting classes, this time with Myra Rostova. By then I had taken the step up to off-Broadway and occasionally I would land a bit part in one of the soaps. When my son was old enough to go to camp, I felt free enough to try stock again. Ted and I married and when he was offered an excellent opportunity to move his business to the Hartford area, I suggested we buy a house in Northwest Connecticut so that he could easily go to work in Hartford every day and I could come up from New York on weekends. For the first year the arrangement worked rather well despite the fact we saw less and less of each other. I worked at an ad agency during the day, off-Broadway at night and on the Cape in summer stock. We managed to stay together that way for four years when it finally became clear to us both that we really had separated. As crazy and hectic as it was, I loved the life I was living. There seemed no way to reconcile my husband's needs and mine, so we agreed to a divorce.

I kept the house and went there as many weekends as I could. One weekend, in 1976, I stopped in a charming country inn in a nearby town for a sandwich and cup of coffee, looked at the almost empty dining room and found myself thinking how it could be arranged as a dinner theater. It was then the idea came to me, Why not form an acting company of my own and start with a small dinner theater? I called actor friends whose work I knew and soon had a company. The first show ran for six weeks. Producing, directing and acting all at the same time was exhausting, but it was profitable enough to be encouraging. I made another decision: I would stay in the country, put on more shows in the summer and, in the winter, devote myself completely to writing. As a serious student of acting, I recognized how impatient and sporadic my efforts had been in trying to master the craft of writing. I moved out of the city completely and settled down to write.

I soon found out it wasn't going to be easy. At first the hardest part was the adjustment to living in a small town and the business of keeping house. I have never been one who found pleasure or satisfaction in the accomplishment of small tasks. Making breakfast, cleaning house, preparing supper, washing dishes is not my style. When it's time to dust the furniture, I'm ready to go out. Disciplining myself to write every day was also difficult at first, but I forced myself into a routine. Get up early, have coffee, sit down at the typewriter and write for four hours at least. If the well begins to run dry on a story, put it in a manila folder, label the folder, put the folder in the file drawer, start another story. If an idea for a story came to me when I was doing something else, I would write it down before it got away and put the paper in a box I kept next to my typewriter. By early spring I had a box full of ideas and a drawer full of stories, some just begun, others almost finished. None, I felt, were ready to send out. They were about love relationships, the wild, sad business of falling in love, how it affects various people, why people abandon each other, why they stay together.

That May, I formed another acting company and produced

another show for dinner theater. That winter, in addition to writing new stories drawn from my inventory of ideas, I began to rewrite what I had done the year before and I began to send stories out. When they came back, sometimes with a brief encouragement on the rejection slip, I wasn't really that surprised. I still felt something was wrong in the way the stories were written, but I couldn't put my finger on it. It was late that spring that I saw a small notice in the local paper announcing that a writer named Honor Moore was going to hold a summer workshop for women called "Women Writing/Women Telling." I had never heard of Honor Moore, but I submitted part of one of my manuscripts along with a covering letter saying I wanted to join. A week or so later, I received a letter welcoming me to the workshop.

Looking back, I realize what a turning point that workshop was for me. The first thing that struck me were the other women in the group, twenty-two of us, all from different backgrounds, but all feeling the same need to write. The second thing that struck me was how at ease I felt. I had never before felt entirely comfortable being with a group of women. I think that many women of my generation were raised to compete for men and in that arena it doesn't take much for another woman to become a mortal enemy. But most important was Honor Moore herself, the relaxed and easy way she conducted the workshop, the way she approached writing, the way she respected our work and what it meant to each of us as individuals, the way she cared. Of course in any group there is competition, but the competition in the workshop was not over who produced the best work or who was going to succeed. The competition was, for the most part, for everyone to succeed, everyone across the river, nobody left behind. In the meetings that followed, no story or poem was ever brought in, no matter how meagre, that was not addressed and understood and appreciated as meaningful to the person who wrote it. I don't mean there wasn't plenty of criticism, because there certainly was plenty of that within the group. But the objective was always to find the truth, the emotional truth as well as the literary truth behind what had been written.

I have always thought there are a great many similarities

between acting and writing. I know from my growth as an actress that there comes a time in the development of an artist when he or she has to start taking extreme risks. In the case of acting, I refer to those times when an actor or actress, through some almost magical power, carries an audience beyond the words written on the page and the words spoken on the stage to an almost apocryphal understanding of life. I think of it as getting out on the high wire. What Honor Moore gave to me, and I do think of it as a gift, was a trust in my own feelings, in my own thoughts, in my own truth. What the other women gave me was the knowledge that there are chords common to the individual songs we sing. I discovered that the ghost that I felt haunting my writing was me. Afraid to come out. I was trying to hide behind what I wrote. I think that ghost has been exorcised.

From 1979 on, as many summers as Honor Moore gave workshops, I attended them. The writing group of six or seven women that developed from the workshops and lasted until 1986 has been everything to me. If I were to sum up what I found in that group, it is the understanding of trust, its various aspects. I felt I could bring anything there without offending and know that the work would be evaluated, that my right to deal with the subject matter would never be challenged. The group immediately knew if something wasn't organically truthful and resisted it. And when I read something to the group, my *own* ear resisted when I heard something that clanged, what I call the "clinkers" or the "clams."

The group gave a number of readings at libraries and colleges, each of us reading for ten or fifteen minutes. I think we're very vulnerable when we go out to read our material to strangers. There's always this feeling that what has become so full and rich and understood might shatter a little bit when we get it out in public, that it might be illusive, it might be mirage. There's part of that wonderful area of risk. But people have responded well, we've all had nice things said.

. . .

In regard to process, I always have to settle the idea at first – what I'm writing about and what I feel about it. I may circle around an idea, live with it for a long time, sometimes months. If it continues to show me new ideas, I know it's alive. And then there are those incredible times when the story lands in a nearly complete form and I rush to the machine. It can be very, very fast. Sometimes I've gotten on my hands and knees on the bed with a pencil in the dark and just scrawled – the rush, you know, where you're sort of falling on top of your material, slightly sobbing and you get it out that way. And then I go back and put more in. It's very satisfying when it works that way for me. But more frequently it's a daily layering on of words and feelings.

For a long time, I thought I could only write in the morning. If anything jarred me, even a phone call I didn't like or if I was worried about something, I felt the edge was off. Lately I find that I can pick it up at various times of the day, even the afternoon, but I can never write in the evening. I compose in longhand and then put it on the word processor. I have struggled with a basic hatred of machines but now find the PC invaluable.

I'd like very, very much to be published but the driving ambition has been to develop my craft. I am totally taken up with what I think are my responsibilities to the craft. I have wanted to have a body of work before I start sending things out. I'm coming to it. I spent the better part of last year rewriting some stories, putting aside others and generally getting my house in order. I now have fifteen short stories almost ready to go, plus ten more in various stages of growth. I've also completed a novel – its working title is *Sonata Street* – that has to do with a theatrical family that lived through the depression. "Eligible Impulses – '44" is a section of that novel.

If I were to try to understand why it's taken me so long to get to my writing, I would say that I was socialized without much direction. I didn't have a workable set of priorities when I was beginning. I spent too much time worrying about how I looked and whether I was being attractive to men. You could say my adventures into romance are like the number of bicycles in China: set end to end, there would be enough to go around the whole earth. In other words, I've put in a lot of mileage on love. But I don't think I have any problems related to starting late. Nothing has been wasted. I'm not concerned about the years passing. I am absolutely delighted that I have this now and don't feel that I have blown it or that I've wasted all that other time, I suppose because I was doing theater. I see myself much more clearly now; I feel much more kindly toward myself and others. It's a lot easier just to exist at this age and that makes room for writing.

Sondra Zeidenstein

Achille Lauro

I refused to read about it
but this morning in the tub
helpless to turn off television
I heard how they shot
one old man in a wheelchair
and dumped him in the sea
I saw the wife
platinum like my mother

Which of you are Jews, they asked

I don't want to leave my house
my russet dog
the red fox I saw dash
across the highway
into the golden field
the flaming maple

but when they hold the gun
at my forehead
the turquoise sky
promising Jerusalem

(they made them sit without hats
platinum heads in the sun)

may I remember how
the red fox slides into gold
how the geese in Dragor
where Danes shipped
their Jews to safety
chew the grass with a constant
chip chip chip

may I still despair
that I cannot mourn
the Palestinian child
dark with wild curls in the rubble

only the Jew, only the old Jew
at the ship rail

Grandson at the Pond

My sagging body
is an armchair
for the leggy boy
who shivers

in his fish
silver trunks – only
one nick so far
on his shin

where he snagged
ragged metal.
I wrap him
in a brown towel

hold him deep
in the clutch
of my thighs
until he stops

shivering
and the hot sun
drains purple
from his thin jaw

and he wriggles up
to leap stones, pause
at the forest curve
and is gone.

Rough Passage

Mother the sissy, stomach all flab,
feeds me but I read while I eat
and stay bony. Trim boybody,
I walk the street shirtless
loving the wingbone I raise
bending my arm behind my back,

loving the knobs of my spine
my countable ribs. Clam-clenched
twelve-year-old whose areolas
soften perfidiously. *They hurt,*
I tell her. Twelve-year old
still running faster than boys,

I catch one of the plagues
we number at Seder (dipping
a finger in wine, sprinkling
pink on the napkin), boils
almost as big as breasts.
Even the doctor is shocked.

It's in the blood, he tells Mother.
She spreads salve black as
eggplant, snowy gauze, prim
adhesive. (The blue-rinsed
Latin teacher inquires politely.)
My arms gets hotter, throbs,

finally I whine. Persistent
not wincing, she draws them
with steaming pads, until one prick
with a flame-blackened needle
releases: teardrop, pearl, worm
trickle – the hole still too small.

Deftly she presses. I grip myself,
the membrane slits. Gusher.
We breathe in unison. Out flows
lava, river. I tear out gauze
after gauze, she turns them
ooze to ooze until it comes

watery. Stern she forces
one thick white clot through
the torn place which can heal
now. But I will not stop
winning. My calves pump,
I wear undershirts, resist.

And when the last bandage is peeled,
scars gone pale, I wear
a white cotton bra
under itchy sweater, clean white
gauze between my legs,
the first blood black, refusing.

Last Rites, Miami

1

He lies in an unlined box.
They have taken his glasses, tinted
his skin, shaved stubble from ruts

in his slack flesh, his yellow
knit shirt is open at the neck.
We ride behind him a long way

out of the city, huddle under
a canopy – it is not raining.
The slot, sharp-cornered, lines up

in the rectangle of grass the way
he placed a stamp, edges cleanly
separated, on an envelope. The dapper

rabbi slices our black ribbons,
chants the magnitude of God, a cup
of sand is passed. We sprinkle it.

Two Haitian men unwind the box.
It sways a little in the onshore
breeze, enters without nicking.

2

Back from the burial,
Mother leaves the door ajar.

They come on walkers,
canes, in wheelchairs,

they tell their stories:

My husband. Ten days
in intensive. The children
slept on cots outside.

My son at thirty-nine. WHY,
I begged the rabbi.

Yours was a blessing,
not like mine.

Slowly Mother begins:
Oatmeal for breakfast,
the way he liked it.
I heard a thump. He was
still warm, curled
like a baby sleeping.

She makes a cradle
of her stubby fingers, cups
word-pulsing air.

3

White sun. Endless flat. Growling
flight path overhead. We stand
bewildered on the grass,
zoysia daggery and coarse,
not like a lawn up north.
                        Xeroxed map
provided by the cemetarian, we track
Mt. Sinai section, subdivision Mt. Tabor,
then sixteen paces from the path:
his plot, the temporary nameplate
overgrown.

   I should have brought
scissors, Mother says.
     Sweat pearls
her forehead. *I wanted aboveground,*
my brother has one, what do you call it . . .
a crypt?
    Mother, come out of the sun.
He didn't say 'I'm dying' or anything.
Skull-rattling rumble. Another
jumbo levels out, then surges north.
He won't like the racket.
     Mother!
She comes away with a shrug,
her wordless what's-the-use-anyway,
turns back to flap her fingers down
at grass – hello-and-goodbye –
the way she dismisses
a daughter's ritual two-day visit.

 4

Our mothers,

all of them blond and curly
sit by the pool in flowering

. latex, sandals stretched
to the spread of their bones:

Milly broke her hip
falling in the lobby.

Sadie couldn't climb
out of her tub all day.

A sun-stained woman,
at ninety-one the queen,

starts out of her drowse.
Selma's days are numbered,

she pronounces. Gold heads
turn. She dozes.

Dinner I put a book
in my hand, put the food

in somehow,
I don't even know.

The queen wriggles forward
on her aluminum throne,

tries once, twice –
give me time – rises,

creeps toward the elevator
holding the wall,

stops a moment leaning,
all eyes on her.

Blue Sari
(Dhaka, 1973)

How shall I speak of a nameless woman
in a blue sari, coarse village weave?
Gardener's wife we called her
or *Sunil's ma.* No one remembered
her birth name. What can I tell
of a moon face I startled once
before she slid from me
wrapped to the eyes:

I stay in a white-washed house,
concrete surrounded by concrete.
The gate creaks.
Through its fretwork thin wrists
stretch, palms cupped: *Ma! O Ma!*
Launderer, gardener, nightguard, cook
guard me. There are grates
on my windows.

You can sleep above the garage,
we tell the gardener,
*but don't bring your wife
and babies from the village.*
(If you let them bring one,
we are warned, they bring them all.)
Bony ankles, soles pale as wheat,
she scuttles, blue head
at the window above the garage.

.   .   .

I stay in cool at my desk, its faint
grain sealed in shellac, and write
about women in villages:

how they marry at twelve, bear
at fourteen, the farm work
they manage unseen – the air
conditioner rattles, sucks damp
from my pages, muffles the song
of the mango seller, scent
of gardenia – *how they are wasted.*

I come into the glare head down
and a blue slimness glides
through gardenias, past tatters
of banana tree, five blue yards,
smooth flanked, sharp at the elbow,
practiced at camouflage
through the delta's daggered plantings.

                .   .   .

I get away for a week to a nonchalant
city – walk among women, bargain
for silk, dark-veined teak, carnelian
to make up in brooches. She persuades
the gardener to let her go alone
to New Market, filled with nylon
chiffons, brassieres, satin burkas
a woman can walk in like her own tent.

Blue clasped in her fingers, tight
over her mouth, hooding her eyes,
she threads tangles of rickshaws,
betelnut hawkers – glare
without shadow. It comes from nowhere,
two giant eyes high above her, driver
wheeling, horn blasting through
the scattering poor. She freezes.

The gardener explained how he found
her, her thigh ripped open. *Mangsho*
he said, for meat, *har* for bone.

    . . .

If I had said, *Come in, unwrap
your smooth arms,
show me your eyes,* it would have been:
memsahib, memsahib.
If I insisted she call me
older sister, still she would mean
memsahib, memsahib.
Launderer, gardener, cook and nightguard
the beggars, the heat:
I was afraid they would all come
like a tide rising.

But if I had said, *Come in,*
we could have fingered discs of mirror
stitched into pillowslips with thread
the color of hibiscus, we could have
traced tendrils vining the carpet,
sprouting preposterous blossoms.

The One Dream
(A Spell)

for George

Over this longmarried pair sprinkle nepenthe
Let them forget for an hour on Sunday
    Afghanistan   Palestinian camps   child's face
    crumpling under a threat
Clear the airwaves honeycombed with sorrow

Let the sun flash through maple flowers tasseled
    like earrings   through smallpaned windows
touch their peach duvet   peach flannel sheets
Let karmas of cramped children   stunting parents
    give room
Shut the sad brain   let it be skin only
Draw a circle around their cherrywood bed for this hour

Let the peach cave in a cave burnish away their imperfections
Let their eyes be slits   discriminating
Let hands soften   hips unknot   backs let go
    old compressions
Let failures spice their soft bellies   their tinder
    take fire

Let them not be young betraying each other   oh not young

Let them touch each other's eyes smiling
Let words move sweetly in their saliva
Let her breasts be richly complicated
Let his penis rise wise and humble
Let him seek her in his fingertips
Let her moisten a sweet nectar
Let them be careless   slippery   forgiving
Let their cries enter brooks rushing the gorge
ring in the calls of Canada geese   red-eyed vireo   raccoon
Let that saferoom spread its held heat into the world
and let them naked entwined sleep
dreaming like Vishnu
the one dream

Sondra Zeidenstein

My father was the child of very poor Jewish immigrants from Rumania. He lost his father when he was fourteen and from then on had to support his mother and sisters. After he married my mother, he became a furniture salesman and eventually owned his own store. He moved a wife and four daughters from depression poverty, evictions and all, to comfortable middle-class life. He was a serious, inward-looking man who seemed to get his emotional sustenance from long walks in the park. He read a lot: business magazines, history books, nature and philosophy. As far as I know he never read novels or poems. Still, I think of him as someone who, though always very much under control, responded deeply, even passionately to life.

My mother was a dedicated housekeeper and children-raiser, who struggled to get us to eat, kept us bathed and scrubbed and safely and comfortably tucked in at night. She subscribed to all the women's magazines, belonged to one or two book clubs. She always had the latest popular novel and would curl up with it on the sofa after the long day of meals and baths and cleaning. Neither my mother nor father paid much attention to the arts beyond what was offered on the radio – they had no opportunity to. Still, we all got piano lessons and some of us got dancing lessons, though I had no talent in either.

But something was very wrong in my growing up. My parents say I turned suddenly from a quiet, content infant to an all-night crier who became a terribly shy child. I wouldn't talk, I wouldn't look up into anyone's face. When I was school age and not much improved, my parents thought I would be helped by elocution lessons. Miss Reardon, my first elocution teacher, would come to our house once a week and bring "pieces" for me to memorize. They were comic or maudlin, usually in dialect, and I think uncomplimentary to Irish, Jews, Blacks. She also gave me exercises to round my vowels and taught me to project and to curtsy. I performed her pieces in school, at ladies' luncheons, once at the local movie house which had a monthly amateur hour. I liked the applause.

Maybe because they were embarrassed at what I was "reciting," my parents eventually found me another teacher, Mrs. Jacobson, a refugee from England who was making a living for herself and her daughter giving literary talks on the women's-club circuit. She taught not elocution, but dramatics. No more dialect humor. Nothing I could recite for school events. The pieces now were from the works of Shakespeare, Keats, Shelley or the Bible. I learned whole scenes from *Macbeth, Othello, Romeo and Juliet* and, with my best friend who took lessons too, would perform them on the luncheon circuit. I came to love the taste of words, their music, the intensity of emotion they sustained.

From the beginning I was in love with reading. I am told I learned to read at three and a half from our maid Mary, a Polish farmgirl, who sat me on her lap and read me poems until I "read" them back. I remember the first book that was my "personal property" as if I still had it in my hands – it was about the adventures of a red-cheeked fireman. It was given to me by my father's secretary when I had my tonsils out and always carried the smell of medicine the doctor painted my throat with. I can remember my first poetry book, coverless, the pages thick and swollen from all the thumbing. I read all the time. I read at every meal except Sunday dinner when my father was at the table. I read myself to sleep every night; I read poetry on the toilet; I traded stacks and stacks of comic books. On summer vacations I would read six thick novels a week.

But I never ever felt the itch to write anything myself.

Through all of grade school and high school, I remember only one personal writing assignment: to write a page about something we did during the summer. I must have been thirteen or fourteen. I described a trip we'd taken that summer to visit some caves and how, when the guide suddenly turned his flashlight upward, we'd seen giant bats swirling. I used the Latin name for bats as the title and kept the horror as a surprise ending. The writing got applause from the teacher and from my father; I think I was pleased with the trickiness of it, the fact that I could control the reader's response. But I didn't try again. I couldn't understand how my friends could make up lyrics for shows or write for the school paper. Making words seemed a feat beyond my imagination.

I loved school. My career ambitions after the cowgirl stage wavered for awhile between English teacher and librarian, and then, irrevocably, settled on English teacher. When I graduated from high school in 1949, I went to the University of Michigan. In freshman English the assignments were on abstract themes like "justice" and "equality." I felt terribly inadequate and didn't know what to write. But mostly I was in an excited frame of mind. I especially loved music lit, art appreciation, Great Books. I became an atheist. I stayed up late at night over coffee and sardines, talking and talking. Otherwise, college was mostly about sex and terrible tangles with my family. I upset my parents by falling in love with a "bohemian" – they made me come back home to Pittsburgh for the last two years of college.

I majored in English, according to life plan. I enjoyed all my literature classes as more chances to read and think about books, but the course I really felt I belonged in was literary criticism taught by the only spokesman for New Criticism in the university. We were taught, implicitly, that writing was a highly exclusive act. Explicitly we learned there were strict tests for what was good: stories and poems were ranked for qualities like "sincerity" and "irony." Much of the critical jargon was unintelligible. But I loved figuring out how stories and poems "worked." And of course the mystique of it all supported my own assumption that writing was for the inspired few.

. . .

The summer before my senior year, I met my husband, George, on a blind date. By the end of a week we decided to marry, though we had to wait for six months until I graduated and could join him in Cambridge where he was in law school. I worked in a boring job for six months to help support us and then we sold our wedding gifts so that I could go to graduate school at Radcliffe. There I loved the passionate teaching, the research papers, the reading periods and even the essay exams which gave me the chance to integrate masses of knowledge. But since I wanted us to have our children early, I was several months pregnant with Laura when I got my master's degree in June. She was born in 1954 and Peter in 1956.

We moved to New York and I stayed home with the children for five years. When I couldn't stand it another day, I got a job at a community college. I enrolled at Columbia for my Ph.D. and for the next five years was teaching and studying literature and raising my children. Then, in 1965, George decided to leave Wall Street law and work for the Peace Corps. I gave up tenure at the college, took a leave of absence from Columbia and went to live in Kathmandu, Nepal for three years.

During those three years I taught Shakespeare and Renaissance drama at the university, lectured on American literature, wrote local color articles for the *San Francisco Chronicle*, wrote an essay about Beat literature that was translated into Nepali and translated a Nepali novel into English. I was amazed at how much time was available to me for work as a result of having a cook, a laundryman, a maid/*ayah*.

When I got back to New York in 1968, the scene had changed radically. It was a time of upheaval – long hair, miniskirts, the Beatles, student protest, sexual revolution, political action. I took up teaching again and started writing my dissertation about the prose of William Carlos Williams. I was very restless with graduate school. So much was changing around me and I wanted to be part of it, to catch up. We had open admissions where I taught, and I became involved in new ideas about education. I was marching and petitioning about Vietnam and civil rights and I was becoming a feminist. Somehow, on the side, I got my Ph.D. in 1970, but it was so peripheral to my real interests that for years and years I had a recurrent dream that the dissertation wasn't finished. As soon as I finished the Ph.D., I wrote an article about changes in my teaching – trying to keep the student at the center of the learning experience rather than following a fixed curriculum in a passive classroom. It was my first piece of writing – since the bats – that was centered in my own experience. The changing culture and the feminist emphasis on the validity of the personal made possible a connection between me and language that I had never felt before.

Three years after we got back from Nepal, my husband was offered a job opening the first Ford Foundation office in Bangladesh. I resigned from teaching again and this time went to live in Dhaka for four and a half years. As I was about to leave, a colleague and dear friend gave me a purple folder full of crisp white paper. On the inside of the cover she warned intruders that this was "my booke." At thirty-nine, I started to keep a journal for the first time. I arrived in Dhaka a high energy feminist and found the streets empty of women, the heat overwhelming by ten in the morning. I decided that the only way I could last without my own work, my own friends, with a diminishing sense of the relevance of my own experience, was to distance myself and become an observer. I picked up a wet green pen and began writing in my journal, an addiction that continues to this day, sixteen years later. In the beginning, except for the too frequent refrains, "I am depressed today," "I slept all afternoon," "I had a big argument with George," I wrote impersonally, reporting everything I saw or heard about women.

In Dhaka, I spent all my time working. Again, a household of servants freed me from hours of chores. I taught literature and lectured and wrote about women. Eventually, as a result of my writing, I went to work for the Bangladesh Government as advisor to a national effort to direct economic resources to rural women. My "boss" was Taherunnessa Abdullah with whom I wrote articles and, with financial support from the International Labour Organization and the J.D.R. 3rd Fund, researched and wrote a book, *Village Women of Bangladesh: Prospects For Change.* Later, under her tutelage, I wrote a textbook to train field staff of the national program she had developed.

When I returned to the States in 1976, I moved to the summer house in Connecticut we had bought shortly before we went away and worked as free-lance consultant for UNICEF, Ford Foundation, Population Council and other international development agencies, traveling to Barbados, St. Vincent, Thailand and, frequently, to Bangladesh to write about the economic life of rural women.

I loved the writing life, but more and more I had trouble translating what I'd seen and heard into the gray language of the institutions I was working for. I thought of going back to teaching, but there was a glut of Ph.D.s in English and besides, I wasn't willing to leave my house in the woods for concrete, crowds, traffic. I was becoming a rural woman myself. When I wasn't at my desk, I was working in the too-large garden my son had fenced in. Though I had edited a gardening book in Bangladesh, I literally did not understand even that seeds need water to germinate and sun to grow, but I threw myself into learning by doing. I started thousands of seeds under grow lights in February, on my knees weeded every inch of soil, with George made gallons of harvest soup in November. I think the garden was my first strong connection with the world outside my head. It was free of words, full of images. I germinated.

At the same time, I was in long-term therapy which I had sought because, though I was surrounded by family, students, friends and colleagues, I felt lonely. I had always considered myself an appreciator not a creator, but as I emerged through the process of therapy, I began to understand how shut down I had been, how isolated, how frightened under the guise of capability and competence. At forty-five, I began to let go, to experience a range of new feelings and finally a terrible grief that would have been overwhelming if I hadn't learned how to be comforted.

None of that taught me to write. But a thirst for words was wakening. I began to think about publishing my journals. As I was typing out pages of journal entries to submit to small presses, a friend pointed out a notice in the local paper advertising a women's writing workshop in our area. The workshop was called "Women Writing, Women Telling" and was being given by Honor Moore. I immediately applied.

In 1979, when I was 47, I met with twenty or so women on six summer evenings in the community center of Kent, Connecticut where Honor read to us, talked to us about women and writing, gave us assignments, listened to our work. What I responded to was her belief in women, in the power of writing, her strong sense that a source of that power is our willingness to reveal our vulnerability. When you are writing and begin to feel scared, she would say, when all you want to do is get up, get a glass of water, make a phone call, anything but write, then you know you are on the track. Keep going, keep going. If you feel like gagging, like crying, keep going, keep turning the pages. Stay with the image, "walk through the senses," keep going. What reaches us in a poem or a story comes out of that depth of opening.

That is what I heard. Those six weeks were full of risk and adventure. Listening to Honor, I wanted to try what was most difficult, what I'd never done, never said. Yet, at the same time, I didn't expect to be asked to write on demand. I was a journal writer. Period. Of course my defiance was self-protection. If anyone had laughed at me or criticized me, I would have pulled in even further. I could so easily have been nipped off. But instead I was welcomed as if I were as much a writer as anyone else. No one judged how I said things. I began to open. I am so grateful for Honor's commitment to working with writers like me, which came, perhaps, from the fact that her own mother had started writing in her forties, a few years before she died.

I was hooked immediately. My therapist encouraged me. Okay, I said, I will sit down and write for a year and see where I am. When Honor seemed amused at the idea that one year could reveal much of anything, I said, "Okay, five years. And then I will start a small press." So in April, 1980, the day after I finished the report for a difficult consultation, full of "institutional" words like "administrative machinery" and "infrastructure," I sat down in my study and wrote a story about a dinner party which launched me abruptly and totally into this world of creative writing.

I kept my same writing hours, the same routine of writing and gardening, but the source of my words was new. From the beginning I wanted to write about large themes, political issues, what I know having lived in other cultures. But what came out seemed out of my control completely – it had to do with parents and sisters, children, husband, friends. I tried to write stories but for the most part they came out sketchy autobiographical fragments without artistic distancing. I tried to make stories out of my journals. For two years I wrote from nine to two, five days a week, with time off for small consultancies. By the end of 1982, I began to write some shorter things, or reduce longer ones radically. Timidly I called them "pre-poems," not daring to believe I might be able to make poems. But that was what I wanted to do more than anything. For the last four years, I have been moving on from there.

.   .   .

All the artists I know say it takes ten years to get your own voice, to begin to get control. And they all say writing is a process, that you only move forward by *doing* it and by reading others. That advice has helped me very much during these apprentice years. I do read voraciously, especially women poets who I feel are opening new territory. Their work encourages me in my struggle to explore as honestly as I can the tensions a woman experiences when she tries to fulfill all her potential within a "traditional" lifestyle. In my New Criticism or my Columbia days, I didn't read *anything* that was about the central issues of my life. I return to the greats – Yeats, Shakespeare, Keats, Donne, Dickinson – for pleasure, but also for a better understanding of how poets achieve their effects. Once in a while I go to a poetry reading, not easy to find around here. I have a few tapes, Audre Lorde and Muriel Rukeyser and Langston Hughes, that I listen to on my long drives to visit friends, all of them spread out among small rural towns. I read biographies of poets and artists, all the interviews I can find about how writers write. I take hope when what they do resembles what I do. I love when writers say you can't tell at the beginning what a writer might become. I lose hope when they are the least bit exclusive. And for good luck, I wear gauzy scarves and put lovely, glass paperweights and crystals around my room.

I find I learn my poetry lessons in their time, not mine. By that I mean, that only when I get to a certain place in my writing, can I understand the significance of something that didn't register before: how the poem looks on the page, the function of titles, trusting the image, finding strong verbs, getting immediacy, knowing when to end, learning to play with sound, being concrete and very specific. And over and over – to *show* not *tell*.

During these apprentice years, I have felt supported and encouraged in a variety of ways. For a year or two, Honor gave several daylong workshops. Each one opened up new material and increased my sense of control over it. She gave me several private lessons, reviewing a sheaf of six months' or a year's work I brought her and offering me invaluable advice. For six years I belonged to a writing support group that grew out of Honor's workshop and had the same underlying commitment to emotional depth and honesty. I counted on that group as the place where I was accepted and my work was understood, where I could bring anything and never feel embarrassed. Sometimes in the early stages of floundering toward poetry, I even asked that they give me *no* criticism at all – I just wanted to read out loud in front of trusted friends, to sense if people felt *anything*. Later, I craved detailed discussion and criticism.

Gradually, when Honor was no longer free to give workshops, I began cautiously to look for other resources. I felt fragile, a beginner, but with strongly held feelings about why I was writing, what poetry meant to me as reader and writer. I watched the spring listings in *Coda* and *The Writer,* but when I saw the "big" names, I drew back like a turtle. I couldn't think of showing my tentative work to strangers.

I did go to two weeklong workshops that were important for me, but even in retrospect they seem like mostly negative experiences. The first was advertised as for beginners and so I felt comfortable in the group. It was the right context for me in that respect, but at that early stage when I was unsure about whether tradtional forms suited me, I felt they were being stressed, that that's what I had to do to be a poet. (Whether that *really* went on, I don't know.) For a year after that, I worked trying to put extremely potent material into traditional forms and merely managed to weaken it by distancing it.

Two years later, feeling in need of training again, I found a workshop that was being given by a feminist in the right place at the right time. That week, I learned about titles and got good examples of the wide variety of forms in which poets can operate. I was better able to make use of them because of where I was in my own development. Unfortunately, I had the experience of having a poem cruelly ridiculed and laughed at by the teacher. I don't think I had ever before had that experience, even in all my years of school. I had to pinch myself to keep from crying in class, to keep from telling her to stop it. For the whole five-hour drive home I raged and raged to exorcise the deep sense of inadequacy she had provoked.

Enough of that, I decided. That is not how I learn. Receiving criticism in a less than warm atmosphere is antithetical to what I am about. Yes, I can survive and learn even in the most negative setting, but why bother? And then unexpectedly, when I was deeply engaged in editing this book, I saw a notice for a "competitive" workshop in New York given by Joan Larkin whom I had once met and whose poetry I deeply admire for its courage and craft. I applied. In my application I said I didn't have much support in my environment for taking risks in my work. In Joan's workshop, I got exactly the support I needed. In the first moments of the first class, she said that poetry writing involves taking risks, going to the place of danger and hanging on past the point of fear. I felt I'd come home. Joan created an egalitarian, nurturing atmosphere, as if in respect of the pain and struggle we underwent in writing our poems. At the same time she offered and supported tough criticism as what poems require. Her assignments were exciting: write about the truth of the body, write portraits, write using repetition as a form, write about "something I was never able to say," about "a lie I told," break a taboo. I spewed up material that will require a year or more to work through.

In addition to workshops and support groups, I look for criticism in other ways. I regularly exchange poems, usually by mail, with three or four women whose criticism I value, who are well ahead of me in many ways and are willing to comment. I show my poems to my family and non-writing friends and they are very encouraging. George loves to read my poems – in fact he reads them over and over, and recites lines back to me. Laura, a midwife, painter and martial artist, responds both to my work and the *fact* that I write with great enthusiasm and absolute support. Peter is cooler, but he has been writing since he was thirteen and earns his living that way. As I open to my artistic nature, I understand his better.

In regard to seeking publication, I have moved slowly. Having studied and read and taught poetry all my life, I am painfully aware of how my work compares with "great" poetry. But at the same time, I want to share what I have written. In 1984, after I'd been writing poetry for a year, I "collected" my work – twelve or thirteen poems – in a folder and covered it with a drawing I made of an amaryllis. (I started sketching at about the same time I started writing poetry, but I do not take it as seriously.) I gave sets to twenty-five friends and relatives and each one responded with comments, what they liked and why. I was thrilled. The next year, I began sending out poems. After the obligatory ones to *MS* and the *New Yorker,* I sent to small magazines mentioned in *Coda, COSMEP, Poets' Marketplace* and other places where there are calls for manuscripts. I try to buy and read magazines carefully to see if what I write will fit. I have had ten poems accepted in small magazines including *Creeping Bent, Connecticut River Review, Letter from a Friend, Anemone, Yellow Silk,* and, most recently and gratifying for me, *Women's Review of Books.* I've had two stories accepted, one of them in *Vintage '45.*

I've found readings more rewarding than publication. Four or five times, our group, Women Writing, Women Telling, read at libraries and colleges to audiences as large as sixty. Twice Honor introduced us, setting us in the context of women ending silence. She talked about the courage it took, the loneliness and negativity we battled – she dedicated our reading to women who were still silent. People who came up to us afterwards included silenced writers who were inspired to try again. Years later, people still tell me how special those readings were. For us it was inspiring to hear the laughs and gasps and intent silences and know the audience was with us. Recently, after several years without seeking opportunities to read, I participated in two readings, one at a Women's Fair. Maybe because I am writing out of a deeper place than before, I felt more scared. I kept hoping I could find a way to get out of the obligation, woke in cold sweats for a few nights, but they turned out to be the best of them all. I still can call up an image of the audience – thirty or so women in a warm, wide grin – that makes me feel deeply rewarded and affirmed.

.   .   .

I feel nothing will stop me from continuing to write, but at the same time I struggle with fierce problems. Often I feel humiliated about being a beginner in my fifties. At this age, I feel I should be passing on my experience to younger people, working at a job where I already know how to solve the problems. My self-esteem has suffered a lot. For four years I have had to say to people my age, educated like me to consider writing poetry a mysterious process, that I am learning to write poetry. Depending on my level of confidence at the time, I either quickly change the subject or boldly discuss my new venture. When I do the latter, someone's eyes inevitably light up. On one of my consultancies in Barbados a few years ago, for example, an energetic, effective admininstrator opened her eyes wide with pleasure and said, "That's what I really want to be doing. Writing is my secret dream."

Another obstacle is the feeling that I don't fit anywhere. As the child of first generation Americans with watered-down rituals and an exaggerated gentility, I feel I have no depth of tradition. My poem "Last Rites, Miami" is about that nakedness in the face of painful life experiences.

I fight demons of self-doubt, swing from the joy of writing to terrible negativity about my work with such violence that I sometimes think I can't continue, but I also can't stop. After lunch on almost every writing day I feel depressed; in the middle of the night I wake in a cold sweat: What do I think I'm doing, this is ridiculous, give it up. I am always eager, indeed desperate for criticism, but sometimes I feel whipped, defeated by it even when it is offered in the most caring and loving way. When I have taken a poem as far as I can and it is found seriously wanting, when it is not praised, I sometimes wonder how I will ever be able to finish a good poem on my own. But when I sit at the computer or with my notebook and feelings and images flow out my fingertips, or when I work at reshaping and refining as if I'm smoothing clay, there is no other life I would choose. I have never felt such despair or such joy.

.   .   .

Being a publisher satisfies my love of literature, my desire to serve it in some way, the need I feel to challenge my competency, but not my need to be a better writer. And it robs me of time. I was never able to write on command, or quickly, but I am learning to write faster. When Joan Larkin gave weekly assignments or suggestions for writing poems, I wanted to take advantage of a special opportunity I may not have soon again. I have always taken the first hour of the day for my poetry, no matter what else I have to do, but in addition I reserved – really commandeered – Wednesday as my poetry-writing day, from the time I get up until I collapse at midnight. (Since George works in New York City and lives there half the week, I have several days without "domestic" interruption.) I taped the poem I was working on, played it in the car, edited in my head. I would carry the draft poem and a pencil in my hand on the long walk to the poetry workshop and stop and lean against lampposts to scribble changes. I learned I could speed up the process considerably, but my idea of heaven is still to have five or six days, uninterrupted except for an occasional phone call or dinner with a friend, during which I can enter that open, soft place where there is no time, only my own rhythm. I try to schedule retreats, blocking out days in my agenda where I have no engagements but it doesn't always work. I can never really get enough time. I want to be with George, be available to children and friends *and* have the poetry. I feel I am always wading upstream to get to it. Someday I may apply to a writer's colony, but I can't imagine a more inspiring place to write than this quiet house in the woods.

I write everything that comes to me. George is in the next room and I write about our quarrel or some negativity or secret – he comes in, and I turn the screen dim. But I have to write about everything or I will not write about anything. What I would keep secret is where the energy is. I must open to that. What I decide to do with the revelations comes later. Showing George or my children or my mother poems that may contain negative feelings or things we don't like to remember or talk about is a problem I haven't resolved. But I cannot keep silent. I can't wait for people to die. I want to be whole. Sharon Olds' courageous honesty makes her a heroine to me.

.   .   .

Poems can come to me like an itch, a few words and an agitated feeling which I must get down. Otherwise I lose the poem. Then I have to have time – while I am in the same mood – to let it out, expose the rest of it. That's an hour or two or three of unstoppered writing, trying to keep it sensory, the images in focus. The next step is a process of discerning the core, the pattern, the language, the rhythm in the mass of material, carving out the poem like the face a sculptor sees in a tree stump. I revise endlessly, play with words, line breaks, the whole form, study how other writers do it and am still very easily influenced by what I read. I don't know what my form is, though more and more I think it will be open. I want to become simpler and clearer, to enter images more deeply, to make the poem more self-contained.

I *need* to write every day, often churning up new material into my journal which I always have with me and in which I note evocative words or apt phrases. When the right time comes, that material will re-emerge in a poem. Keeping at it every day and in Joan's workshop, making sometimes two or three poems in a week, prepares the way for the real poems when they come. "Blue Sari" and "The One Dream," both of which I wrote in response to assignments that had to do with form, are in that category. From time to time I had written in my journal about the incident that "Blue Sari" narrates, but it was Joan's reading of a poem by Muriel Rukeyser that got me started. I had thought a lot about the experience of "The One Dream" but felt frustrated I couldn't find a satisfactory way to get into it. When Joan suggested the class try to write "a spell," I then and there jotted the word or two that started the poem.

It was one of the easiest and most enjoyable poems I've written.

.   .   .

I like being a new writer in my fifties. There is an advantage in having reached this plateau, this freedom from being driven by reproductive energy. So much material is available from the past, the present is heightened by the sense of mortality, a constant awareness of time slipping away. I have so much to learn, so much I want to write. Writing poetry uses all of me. At this age, I feel it is one of the few experiences that matches the intensity of life. Almost everything else seems partial, or not able to *contain* the feelings aroused, as Stanley Kunitz wrote, by living and dying at the same time. I like that it is never ending, never accomplished, like my too-big, too-weedy garden. I couldn't have done it sooner – that is simply my history – but I am totally grateful that I have it now.

Patricia E. Powers

. . .

The Storyteller

Today her father is in one of his deep sleeps when Lily arrives. Rigid under the sheet, his head and shoulders raised by three pillows, he is a stranger. His nose, like a mountain ridge, is sharp, big and crooked. His cheek bones, mouth and chin mere bony outlines. Gaunt, chiseled, he is imperial and cruel. In these long journeys his face takes on masks as if he were rehearsing the possibilities of the lives he might have inhabited in past years. His aging is like peeling down to the first matrix.

"How is he?" she asks her mother, tracing with her eye the spare shape of the body on the bed between them. She lifts his hand, an intricate architecture poised on his chest. He has had Parkinson's Disease for so long that Lily finds it hard to remember when it began.

Her mother reaches across to smooth an invisible wrinkle. "I take good care of him," she says as if she were the curator of a great treasure and Lily the visiting inspector.

Lily feels she has slipped into a role without proper preparation. What precisely are her duties? She remembers going to Mass with her mother last New Year's Day.

"It's a new priest," Mother whispered. The young man had glossy black hair to the tips of his ears, and smooth skin the color of smoke. "I've never seen a priest like that," she said.

"He's from India," Lily said. A modern wise man, she thought, from a far off country bearing precious gifts.

His sermon was different too. It opened with a Chinese legend about how in olden times when parents grew feeble, their child would take them to a distant valley called "The Valley of the Dead" where they would lie down and die. The way there was long and arduous, through forests and over streams, so that the old people could not return. One young man, seeing his mother break twigs from the trees and scatter them along the way, asked her why she did this. For you, my son, she replied, so that when you return you will not lose your way.

A difficult lesson, she thinks, releasing her father's hand.

"Lily is here," Mother says bending over him. It is one of her stratagems. If she treats him as if he were the same man she has always known, she might trick the stranger out of him. But she gives up the effort to reach him. "Sometimes I'm afraid." She touches his hair with her long delicate fingers. "I'm afraid he wanders."

It's not wandering, Lily thinks, it's arrangement and rearrangement. It's her students confusing myth and history, fiction and life.

"How is the teaching?" Lily's mother pours tea into china cups. Every week when Lily visits they stir their tea with silver spoons and ask each other questions.

"How is the teaching?" she says. The teaching. Not your job or your classes or your students. The teaching – as if it were a commodity like cloth that Lily cuts from bolts and delivers in neat packages to her students.

She teaches Introduction to Literature in a community college. The students don't care for essays or poetry, but they like stories that don't have hidden meanings or at least meanings that are not too deeply hidden. They say stories should be true to life.

When her students leave school at the end of the year, she pictures them going off like pilgrims or explorers looking for stories to live in.

This year it is her turn to teach an elective, and she has chosen Irish Literature because she was born in Ireland and has always wanted to be truly familiar with its literature. She finds that teaching involves a subtle shift of roles in which she learns more than the students, although this class is enthusiastic. Most of them have Irish forebears, and they want to know about the Celts and the Druids, and the heroes of old and new times.

Her father was her first teacher about Ireland, telling stories from her earliest days so that history and fairy tales, politics and magic, John Bull and earth shaking dragons blended into gorgeous, mystifying shapes as real to her as the mossy earth of the back garden or the worn cobbles of the streets they walked. She could see the evidence of his stories in the ruins of King John's Castle when they went to market on Saturday, and on Sunday at Saint Peter's on Chapel Street she could see in the stones of the center aisle the footsteps of the ghost who came to say Mass there.

Only last week he was waiting for her in his wheelchair, dressed in fresh shirt, pressed slacks, brown polished shoes, white hair neatly combed, looking as though prepared to have his portrait painted. He beckoned her to him.

"That day in Dublin," he began, but his voice was so low (the Parkinson thrust for that day) that she had to pull up a chair next to his and lean so close that she could feel his breath on her ear, a sort of Morse code tapping his story into her brain. "It was a beautiful day. The sky so blue!" He paused to collect the details. "We were on holiday and up to Dublin for the races." She knew the story well.

He had gone to the Fairyhouse Race Meeting on Easter Monday, April 1916 – just a kid up from school for the holidays and had strayed into O'Connell Street in time for the charge of the Lancers on the Post Office. Bewildered and excited, and finally afraid, he ran with the crowds. Images leaped out of his memory – dead horses, one with its feet in the air, wild-eyed looters, finery hanging from their shoulders, food, boots, and silver in their arms, a big red-bearded man admonishing them, a drunken woman with her blouse undone, a boy as young as himself dead in the street. He hid in a cellar, in gardens, in doorways, slipping from one to another after every burst of fire.

From that time on, he had become absorbed in the history of Ireland, reading and rereading the accounts, reliving its wars, fighting the battles again and again. Over the years the casual collision with The Uprising had become transmuted into heroic participation, and that, leading him back into history, made him a participant of other battles. No wonder his stories had always been so real. He had had a role in all of them.

She knew from photos that he had been a slim youth with large dark eyes and dark hair. Handsome and delicate with a look of wonder in his eyes. Her eyes. And the same wonder she felt as a child as each day brought its surprise. A castle bombarded, a wall scaled in a story. A rabbit skinned for dinner in the back garden, a chicken plucked and singed, old wallpaper torn off the dining room walls revealing damp stains like continents, the sounds of a party downstairs after she was in bed at night.

"But we were betrayed. The forces in the countryside never came in. What could we do? Pearse, Plunkett, Connolly – just the handful of us." His voice was no more than a bit of dust from O'Connell Street of 1916. He grasped her face so he could see into her eyes.

"They are only stories!" Mother turned away impatiently. She had heard only shreds, but she knew by his rapt eyes that he had strayed from the path, had wandered.

"They are history!" He slapped the arm of his chair, but no sound came from his outraged mouth.

"His story. Your story. It's all nonsense. They're dead and gone." She leaned forward from her chair near the window to turn the small pot of geranium on the sill. It had one brilliant red bloom. This is the here and now, she seemed to be saying.

. . .

When Lily's students learn about the Hunger Striker in the Maze Prison in Belfast, they become very excited. They cut pictures of Bobby Sands from the newspaper. They repeat anecdotes about him in class, finding significance in every detail. They are awed by his youth, his courage, his suffering. At last they have found a story that is life itself. It is so fresh and new its ending is not yet known. It is as if they are writing it themselves.

She tells them about the Hunger Striker of ancient times, inventing descriptions because they wanted them, couldn't get enough to feed both their hope and fear he would succeed.

She told them that it used to be the man who was put upon, the grieved one, came at sunset to the house of the man who had injured him. In sackcloth, maybe, and barefoot, with only a stick to lean on, and his hair bound in a special way, marks painted on his cheeks, his chest slashed. And this plaintiff would stand outside the rath or the ditch or even right in the doorway under the crown of skulls that gaped on the lintel, black holes for eyes. He would be fasting. The moon would come up and lengthen his shadow, disturbing the sleep of the defendant and of all his neighbors, making his suffering their suffering, transferring his grief from his body to theirs, the whole community becoming one, and finally the defendant would emerge, fasting himself, in a fresh linen tunic and would give a sign . . .

She was sure they were picturing Margaret Thatcher in something like a bathrobe, holding out her hand to the emaciated Bobby Sands. They would be elated that he had succeeded but also secretly disappointed that they had been cheated of the other ending, his death.

.   .   .

Her father is also excited. His eyes shine deep in their sockets under the thick white brows which seem to have grown longer and more tangled. He follows the television news avidly, turning the sound high and moving from channel to channel as though he were hurrying events on.

"It's a powerful weapon," he says. "Remember Gandhi. Bring down the empire!" He flies through the channels again filling the room with confusion. "Of course, he got it from the Mayor of Galway. Fine IRA man, though I never knew him myself."

What has Gandhi got to do with the Mayor of Galway? East and West, the twain have met. She watches his hand on the dial remembering how she used to marvel at his knowledge and power. She looks for the Fourth of July scar on his right hand. What a wondering little immigrant she was. Father with the big bag of firecrackers containing packets of red tubes that danced across the yard as they exploded, punk to hold like a cigarette, sparklers to hiss into galaxies, fiery wheels to spin though the dark. And the Roman candles. He lifting the long tubes, she holding the edge of his pocket for safety, and waiting for the low sucking thunk from inside the candle and the flowering high in the dark, crimson petals slowly falling back to earth. Until one exploded in his hand leaving it like torn crepe paper.

"He has no right! It's a sin against God and man." Mother says.

"The suffering is fierce. They turn black. And the nerve endings on fire. At the end they go blind." He rests at a channel occupied with an ad about telephones. "We have to get word out to the others," he says.

"What on earth for?" Mother is annoyed.

"To be ready!"

"They will not let him die." She touches her soft creamy cheek with her finger. She seems to have suddenly lost interest in the matter.

"He will die!" He starts from the chair, quivering, balanced on his toes, like an arrow leaving its bow. Lily eases him back into his chair.

"It's unnatural," Mother says. The days are warmer, and she leans forward to feel the breeze that gently moves the curtains.

.   .   .

Her students write on the blackboard each time they meet: 50 days, 52 days. She begins to think he will die for the world is watching and he is trapped in the mechanism of his own story. She is surprised for she had assumed it would end short of death. She begins to study television news reports too, reading the rough painted signs on the walls of Belfast, watching Bobby Sands' mother enter and leave the prison between shots of masked youths hurling flaming bottles. She finds herself picturing her father, the young man with large wondering eyes, lying on a pad on the floor of the cell, skin turning black, going blind.

Her students go to rallies, and one evening, feeling that she should participate, no matter how remotely, she goes too.

BUTT-CHA, THAT-CHA
MUSS-COW

BUTT-CHA, THAT-CHA
MUSS-COW

The voice of the crowd bowls down the side street as she approaches Lexington Avenue where the British embassy is.

A dialect, she thinks. Muss-Cow. Medieval spring festival. A ceremonial outing, the men in short pants beating the ground with staves and stamping their hobnails. Perspiration coursing through the hair on their legs into the wool knee socks.

It is indeed warm. The back of her neck is damp. If she had a ribbon she'd tie up her hair. She wishes she hadn't worn a coat.

At the corner a policeman leans against the pillar to which a wire basket is chained. She steps around him to see the crowd, and their words become distinct.

BUTCHER THATCHER!
MUST GO!

A picture of Bobby Sands floats toward her on a stick, bouncing up and down, nodding to her.

BOBBY SANDS!
MUST NOT DIE!
BUTCHER THATCHER!
MUST GO!

"Come on, come on!" Two of her students, looking triumphant, wave to her as they pass.

Oh, I should, I should, she thinks, for the O'Briens, the O'Neils, Robert Emmet, Kevin Barry, McSwinney, Parnell. For my father. But she is rooted to the sidewalk. The persistence of the faithful rebuke her as they pass. Old men and young. Even a woman with infant in carriage.

The bodiless young Bobby Sands smiles at her again from the top of a stick. He is multiplying, popping up from the crowd in instant reincarnation.

THE BRITISH ARMY!
MUST GO!

Her father would leap from his wheelchair and careen down the line of march. "UP THE REPUBLIC! UP THE IRA!"

Four young men carrying a rough-hewn black coffin call to her. "March for the Hunger Striker!" and "March to prevent his funeral!"

"Communist murderers!" A thin woman in a black coat grasps the wooden barrier next to her. "Heathen killers!"

ACT NOW! A banner snaps as it passes.

Lily backs away, knocking into a box marked, "Pennies for Northern Ireland Aid."

MUST NOT DIE! the crowd roars.

Her belt buckle catches in the wire basket, pulling her coat down from her shoulders, pinning her arms.

MUST GO! The crowd insists.

She struggles to free herself.

MUST NOT DIE!

"What are you doing?" The policeman grasps the wire mesh basket.

"I'm not responsible," she says, and pulls free from her crippling coat.

She dashes away. The crowd roars.

MUST GO!

.   .   .

The news shows an emmisary from the Pope leaving the Maze Prison. Everyone knows now that the last chance is gone. The Hunger Striker will die.

.   .   .

Mother calls in the night. "Come at once. I can't rouse him at all."

.   .   .

Father is in his chair, head bent far back as if the neck bones had broken. His eyes are open but vacant, fixed on the ceiling. His breakfast tray is untouched.

"Dad!" Lily leans over him. "What's the matter?" She touches his face, dry and flaky with a harsh white stubble.

He gives up his study of the ceiling and fixes on her, tries to speak but fails. With one finger he indicates the space before him. Lily holds out her hands and he grasps them. She pulls him forward, and he slowly gains an upright position. Walking backwards, she leads him to his bed where he lets his shoulders fall back on the pillows, and she lifts his rigid legs into the bed.

Mother takes off his slippers and pulls up the sheets. Lily straightens his arms. They feel as though they might crack.

.   .   .

The doctor bends over him, looks deep into his eyes, takes his pulse. "Has he been taking his medicine?"

"Of course." Lily and Mother look up at the tall dark haired doctor as though to challenge him.

"He is in shock." The doctor is pitiless. "From lack of Synomet."

Lily goes to the table where Father takes his meals and the pills are administered. She finds two under the table, four in the bowl of dried flowers. In the pocket of his bathrobe she finds more. "Bring down an empire," he said. She looks at the slight body hardly interrupting the sheet. "It's those who can suffer most."

"From now on you must watch him. He can't be trusted to take his medicine," the doctor says.

Can't be trusted with his life, Lily thinks, feeling that she has touched on something important, but she is busy with the Synomet, slipping the pill into his mouth, tipping his chin to make him swallow. His tongue is dry.

"When the balance is restored, he will lose the rigidity." The doctor snaps his bag shut.

How powerful it must feel to promise the future, Lily thinks, putting the kettle on for tea.

.   .   .

"Where do you think he goes?" Mother asks as they stand next to his bed, the revolving lamp changing their nightgowns from red to blue as if a miraculous sea was rising and falling.

She says she doesn't know, but she remembers reading about going into the unconscious, free-floating without gravity or bearings, an extraordinary trip from which some never return.

"I think he must go back to when we were young. Life was never again as lovely." She touches Lily's arm as though she would pass the scenes through her fingers. "We used to sail in the Regatta on the Shannon. Everyone came out for miles around, waving from the shore and leaning over the bridge to see us pass. At night there was a big dance, and I wore a green silk dress with black straps. It was very fashionable." She takes Lily's arm again. "And do you remember picnics at the lake? You had a polka dot bathing cap."

The clear water gently lapped the shore, wetting the smooth stones into color. Father sat on a rock and rubbed her dry with a towel. The sun was quite warm.

"And that rogue, Pat Donoghue. He had his harness shop on the other side of our garden wall." Lily remembers the tall wall. Do not go out of the garden gate. There's danger over there. Big troughs of water for the horses. A child could drown. Pat's hammer on the horseshoes or the wagon wheels clanged through the day, a big timekeeper counting out the hours.

"We went to Bouremouth one warm summer. It was a fine resort, known for its waters . . ." She turns to her bed.

Lily gives the midnight dose of medicine and goes to her cot near the window. She hears Mother at her prayers and turns away. In a space between the sill and the blind she sees a strip of sky. She pictures all the prayers of the world pulsing up like a quasar from the earth, assaulting the gates of heaven where the Hunger Striker stands, staff in hand, grievance on his lips.

In the morning Lily scalds the teapot and Mother butters toast. Pale nightgowns, soft robes – morning apparitions that reach around each other, take down cups, pour milk. The toast wilts, their cotton slippers whisper on the floor. There would be silence, but they have turned on the television in the living room filling the small apartment with a stranger's voice.

Bobby Sands is dead. Authorities fear violence in this northern city.

They stand in the doorway and study the smiling face of the young man. "I wonder . . ." Mother begins but a cry from the bedroom stills her.

"Hold your fire! Don't waste ammunition! Keep alert! We can hold them off!" They hear the bedroom door slam with a tremendous clap.

As they turn there is a thud. He has locked and barricaded

the door. What furniture could that frail little body move?

"That's glass I hear," Mother says.

"Wait," Lily says, meaning, don't let yourself think he's at the windows.

She knocks at the door. "Dad!"

More breaking glass.

Mother calls him.

"Tom's at Jacobs Factory," he answers.

"Would you like tea?" Mother asks.

"And Michael at Saint Stephen's Green."

"Come out of there." Mother says, and in a softer voice, "Oh God, Lily, what's happening?"

"Check on Four Courts!" he calls.

"I will if you open the door!" Lily calls back.

"De Valera's at the bakery."

In Dublin the weekend of Easter, 1916 had been a glorious one: throughout Saturday and Sunday, there had been a continual trek to the silver beaches which stretch for miles on either side of the city . . . The words from one of the books Liam used to read to her pace out, single file. Pictures form. The Republican flag on the roof of the General Post Office. Pearse, poet turned soldier, standing between the mighty pillars: *Irish men and Irish women: in the name of God and of the dead generations from which she received her old tradition of nationhood, Ireland, through us, summons her children to her flag and strikes for her freedom . . .*

Yes, then the breaking of the windows, the crouching behind barricades, the Lancers' plumes bright, moving up Sackville Street, pennants flying.

Crash! A volley of rifle fire from the GPO. Four Lancers lay dead on the cobblestones.

"Oh Lord, he's back in 1916, in the Post Office," Lily says.

The fighting will last five days, culminate in fire burning them out of the GPO, and surrender on Friday afternoon, followed by executions.

Was Father to act it out to its end? Behind the door she can hear him moving about, speaking the parts of Pearse and Connolly.

"Oh, Lily, is there any hope at all?" Mother asks, but doesn't wait for an answer. She sits in her chair near the window, absently turning the geranium to face the sun. Lily turns to the closed door and pounds upon it, insisting that he not leave them.

He calls someone's name; gives an order.

"They're all dead and gone," she says.

"You'll see," he says, "you'll see the meaning of what we're trying to do."

"You'll be shot and killed," she says, giving in.

"Let them," he replies.

. . .

The doctor says that if they can't get him out he'll send orderlies to break down the door, for he must have the medication. Then, he says, he will have to go to a nursing home where he can be cared for.

Mother seems to shrink. Her eyes seem smaller and more pale. "That's where they go to die," she says. "I will never do that."

. . .

Lily wakes frequently. She goes to Father's door and calls, but he doesn't answer.

She dreams of students. Sometimes they call to her; sometimes they are locked away from her. Parades of black coffins piled with books pass in long lines. "You are responsible," a tall man with blue glass eyes says in a deep voice. Father tries to speak to her but no sound comes from the open wound of his mouth.

. . .

In the first light she goes to Father's door. Still he doesn't answer. Asleep, she hopes, and will awaken clear and strong.

If not, what will I do? Let strangers burst in on the old man at the barricades? Send him to the home, leave him in the valley to wait for death?

They bring tea and toast and gently call. "Dad, it's your breakfast."

"It's changed, utterly changed." His voice is hoarse. He won't open the door. Lily can feel the cold from the broken windows. Did he cover himself with blankets or sit at the window all night?

"Poor, poor man," Mother says.

"He has to have medicine, Mother."

"I promised him I'd never let them take him away."

"It might only be for a little while – till he's himself again."

"Do you think so?"

"Yes, oh yes. I think they will help him."

I am lying to my mother and sending my father to a place to die, Lily thinks. The earth should quake and swallow me up; bullets and cannon shells tear me apart.

"But not to drag him out like a madman, a bad man."

"No. No. We'll find a way."

Time is something you walk around in. She had often thought when she was teaching books of long ago. Now Father is wandering in time. The trick will be to bring him to a time when he is not doomed to die.

Help me now, Father, with your old stories.

.   .   .

The message, she tells him, is from Patrick Sarsfield.

After the smallest hesitation, he leaps to Limerick, 1690.

She tells him that the French fleet has come, too late to save the Irish forces, but in time to allow any *man of the Irish forces to leave the Kingdom of Ireland and go to any country beyond the seas, that the garrison of Limerick might march out with arms, baggage, drums beating, match lighted, colors flying, . . . They will march by the thousands to the French ships . . .*

She remembers Saint Patrick's Day and the banners of the counties whipping in the wind and underneath the old men wearing satin bands printed with their honorary titles.

.   .   .

He wears his blue blazer with the gold buttons. "I'm ready now," he says, and suddenly looks at Lily, a knowing, terrified stare, as if he saw it all entirely, and would say, "No I shall not go to die," but Mother smooths his hair, the banners snap in the cold wind, the men pass with medals and ribbons on their chests.

"Hand me my sword," he says, "it's only ceremonial, but it makes a good impression."

In the elevator he touches Mother's cheek. "You are beautiful today," he says. "Don't weep when the ships pull out. I will return."

.　.　.

Another prisoner takes the place of Bobby Sands on hunger strike, but her students are not deeply concerned. We did that already, they seem to say. Besides it is the end of the semester and they are distracted, rushing to finish old assignments. They yearn to be free for they think there are new stories, their stories, still to be written.

Patricia E. Powers

I was born in Ireland, the oldest of five children and therefore always the surrogate mother, taking charge, bossing sisters and brothers, feeling responsible. My father had a waterworks business which produced bottled soda and seltzer water. His biggest customer, ironically, was the British army, since they could afford to buy the fancy siphons, the carbonated water and tonics. After the Irish Free State, which my father was very much in favor of, and the withdrawal of the British, business went downhill. We came to this country when I was about nine, in the pit of the depression. My father worked first as manager of a grocery store and then stayed on in that kind of work. Mother never worked outside the house.

In Ireland I was surrounded, without knowing it, by the most wonderful language and storytelling. I thought everyone talked that way. When I came to this country, I was confused by the difference between my own use of English and the way it was spoken here. In grade school the nuns used to send me around from room to room to give messages. I didn't know it was because of the brogue. When it dawned on me that this was the little school joke, I vowed that I would get rid of it. No one was going to make fun of me.

My father was – this is an Irish phrase – a "great reader." My mother was a great storyteller. When we were very young, she would make up stories to amuse us. As we got older, she would tell us stories about relatives or people she had heard about. I loved to hear them then and still hear them and enjoy them. It was a very enriching childhood in terms of language, but I was totally unaware of it. It formed me as a writer; when you scratch the surface of my skills, what comes up is the flow of the language I originally learned by ear.

From the time I was three years old, I was in parochial schools. I went to a Catholic high school and, for the first two years, to a Catholic college. I had a truly classical education including four years of Latin in high school. I didn't care to translate any more than anyone else did, but I was fascinated by the words.

Even before I was in high school, I knew I wanted to write. Certainly by the time I was in high school it was a conscious desire, but it just didn't seem to be anything that anyone considered of importance. I remember giving one little poem that I had written to a friend to read. She returned it and pointed out that I had misspelled a word. That was all she said about it and of course that crushed me. My papers would always be picked out by the teachers for being well-written. I remember one time in college when I gave a story I had written to a professor, he said it was very nice but advised me that I really shouldn't pursue writing. There was nowhere for me to go with it, especially as a girl. My work was always praised and yet I think people were saying to me that I shouldn't put a lot into this, because it wasn't going to go anywhere. Looking back, I think they could see that the kind of thing I was writing wasn't going to end up in *Good Housekeeping* or some place else that paid a lot of money for a nice "ladies'" story. And I really didn't know the difference between that kind of story and my own work until, early on in college, I discovered Virginia Woolf and thought, There are other people who write things that don't have involved plots. But still it was a puzzlement to me and took me a long time to see the difference between the commercial short story and what I was writing.

By the time I was eighteen years old, I broke away from parochial education and went to the University of Connecticut. It was very exciting, but that was at the beginning of World War II and the whole world was upside down. I was married at nineteen, in my third year of college, and left school. Overnight I went from a young woman with a background that was like a medieval world to a married woman in the Bronx.

Still, writing was on my mind constantly even though I was the one who had kicked over the traces. I went to Columbia and took writing courses at night. We had no money but I used to keep a mayonnaise jar on the window sill of the kitchen in the Bronx and put change in it to save for the story-writing courses at Columbia. I used to have a little neighborhood girl come in and mind the children while I would run off to school on the subway. I had great encouragement from my teachers there. One of my teachers was Professor William Owens who had just got out of the army where, I think, he had worked in decoding. He used to say to me, "Send your things to *Sewanee Review.*" Perhaps I did send something in those days, I don't even remember. But I have since, and I now have become friendly through the mails with the editor of *Sewanee Review.* If ever I catch up with Professor Owens, I'd like to tell him that.

In the next ten years I had four children and there wasn't much time to write, although I tried. I remember one particular page in the notebooks I kept where I wrote, "This is unfair to my husband and children." Anyone picking that up would have wondered what on earth is this wicked young woman doing that is so unfair. What I was talking about was my writing, the fact that I was taking whatever hour I could steal from my household duties and my children to write. A few years ago when we moved, I found a suitcase full of those notebooks. There were beginnings of stories, descriptive essays, sketches, and me talking to myself about my own life, how much I believed in *other* people, how important it was that I help *other* people fulfill their goals. It never occurred to me that I had not fulfilled some part of myself. I keep repeating, "Of course I'm doing the right thing, of course," almost frantically insisting that it was the right thing for me *not* be writing.

Perhaps I wasn't ready. Perhaps I couldn't give a big enough slice of my life to it. People think you can just sit down and write. You can't. It's a tremendous commitment, and I had no kind of support system that would enable me to devote big chunks of time to it. I had four children – boy, girl, boy, girl, all

fine and healthy – two and a half years apart, the last one perhaps a little more than that.

But the desire to write must have been tremendously
strong. When we moved with the first two children from the
Bronx to a garden apartment in Bayside, I remember trying to
write there. I would get up early in the morning and write. I
don't know what I thought I could possibly do. I didn't have
that kind of gift that I could sit down and write a story in terms
of "here's what happened." I was working almost in a different
medium and didn't know it. I think I probably got very discouraged. And then I gradually stopped.

When I was thirty-three or so, after we had moved with
four children to Long Island and were there a few years, I went
back to college and got my degree and started teaching. I had
no problem. I ran a household, took care of four children,
went full-time to Hofstra and loved every minute of it. I graduated in June, went to work in September in a high school in
Massapequa. And then in the next several years I got my master's degree at New York University and did all my course work
for a doctorate. I left high school teaching and went to Suffolk
Community College where I daresay I spent the happiest years
of my life. I was absolutely at home, able to use all I had
learned, all I had studied. I loved teaching.

And yet all the time I wanted to write. Again I started writing in the early morning, practically the middle of the night. I
began to realize that I was so happy teaching and put so much
into it, there was nothing left over; all my energies, my spirits,
my joys were going into the classroom. A man, of course, can
go home and the rest of the day is his own. I would go home
and start in another day's work. I came to a point when I realized that if I was ever going to write, I would have to stop teaching.

When I was forty-eight and our youngest child went off to
college, we moved here to New York City so that my husband
would no longer have to commute such a long distance to
work. The move coincided with my own thinking about writing.
I knew that if I was ever going to write, it had to be then or
never. It wasn't as if I was tired of teaching or didn't like the
kids or the classroom. By then I was a professor, I had good

courses, I had good hours, I had good friends at the college, everything I could want but that one thing I had wanted for a lifetime and had given up time and again for somebody else. True, I had to give something up now too, but it was for me at last. That was quite a big step. I thought to myself, Maybe I couldn't do it at twenty or thirty or forty, but if I don't do it now then I'm a phony. It was a very conscious decision.

When I came to New York to live, as a teacher and student for almost a lifetime, the first thing I did was look around for a place to learn. Anatole Broyard was giving a writing course at the New School which was just down the street. I sent two stories and he accepted me. That was the turnaround for me. His acceptance was confirmation, it was saying: Yes, it's all right, you *can* write. The seminar was small, between ten and fifteen people, all very good. In that situation it's assumed that everyone can write well, so the little skill you've had since you were born, that makes it easy for you to write, is no longer very important. Now the question is, What are you *doing* with it?

The seminar was very demanding and very professional. At each meeting two people would read their work; it would be discussed by the group and then Broyard would comment on it. Anatole insisted that you have to be a good critic in order to be a good writer. If everyone liked your story, you were floating on air until you read again. I had some very positive critiques and then there were others that were not as well received. That's where it hurts of course, but that's where you learn. For example I wrote a story about a middle-aged man and woman on a vacation in Ireland. The background was lovely, the description of the woman's unhappiness was absolutely wonderful. But a woman in the back of the classroom said, "Yes, but *why* is she unhappy, what is the *matter* with her?" I didn't defend the story out loud, but I was thinking, Oh that's just the way my character *feels,* haven't you ever felt that way? I didn't want to come to grips with why this woman was unhappy. Was it about her marriage? About her life? Did she want to do something else? Did she have a lover? I didn't want to say *anything,* I just wanted to create this feeling. That story still has to be rewritten, but I learned that if I am not willing to say what the problem is, then I shouldn't write it. If I was afraid of that woman's dilemma, her unhappiness, her hazy, misty, free-floating angst, then there was something I was avoiding. It was true, I didn't want to face it. But you can't have a good story unless you are honest.

The class met for three or four years, regular meetings with professional criticism of a very high level. That was my professional training. Then when Anatole gave up the class, a number of us continued to meet on our own. We still only read two stories a night, because we find that's about all you can truly concentrate on. Usually at one meeting we'll say who's going to have something for the next, and if more than two people are ready, it will be the two who haven't read most recently who get the chance. If we have a pileup, we schedule a meeting right away – people don't want to wait when something's going.

The only people I can share my writing with is other writers. I think families can be dynamite. They don't understand what writing a story involves, what went into it, what it took to write it. To have something treated in a cavalier fashion or lightly put aside with a, "Gee, why don't you write a bestseller" – that can be damaging. I find it's safer just to talk to other writers.

.   .   .

I took Anatole's suggestion that perhaps I should be writing novels. I wrote two novels; each one took me three years. It's as hard to get an agent as it is to get published, but I was very lucky. One of the friends in my writing group showed my first novel, which dealt with the Irish IRA in New York City, to an agent she knew who was connected with some well-known Irish writers. The agent sent it out for a good long time, but it was not accepted. Then I wrote another one. It is currently being shown around. About a year ago I began writing short stories again, and it just seems that everything has changed. I've had four stories accepted in the space of a year and all at very good places. I couldn't be happier. In the past six months I've written seven new stories. I've only sent out three of them – I've been too busy writing to send the others out – two of which have been accepted. They all deal with the same characters, they are related – it's a different way of writing a novel – and it utilizes my talents to my best. And obviously with the amount of work I'm doing, I must be at home in it. We'll see if the others go as well as the ones so far.

The stories that began to click came out of the deepest experiences of my life, honestly, without holding back. And that is what made the difference. Wouldn't you think you'd learn that a lot earlier? I think pain made it happen. When you see someone else suffering or you share in their suffering, and the only way you deal with anything is to write, you cannot deal with that suffering in any way less than the very best that you can give it and the most honest. You have to be willing to strip away an awful lot. That's when you hit your stride. That's when you finally discover what's inside.

The source of my writing is deeply held emotion. I have moved toward that. Now when I look at the stories that I first wrote, they seem so artificial. They never went to the heart of things, they were all on the surface. I was very much in control. I knew pretty well how to do things, but I didn't know how to pull up the best of the raw material. Any deep emotional or psychological experience was cloaked, so changed and removed as to be unrecognizable. Not that you don't have to distance yourself from your material – otherwise it will just come out like a soap opera – but you have to manipulate it so you're holding it off and at the same time putting everything in. When you're doing it, you know it. Sometimes I can feel the blood rushing up into my face with excitement, and I know that this is it. At that point I know I have done something. And it happens that those pieces are the ones that get taken. To go back to that woman who said to me ten years ago, "Yes, but what was the *matter* with her?" I didn't give that answer for ten years. It was a matter of stumbling on it. I was writing one day and I just kept on going and there it was and I recognized it, Yes, this is what I have never written. And my stories started being published.

.   .   .

All through the years, every so often I would finish something and send it out. At first when the rejections start coming back, especially when they are just the little printed things, it is very discouraging and you are hurt as if someone did something to you personally. Years ago there would come a point after several rejections – half a dozen, let's say – when I would say "That's it, I just don't have the talent, I can't write" and I would stop for long periods. But I have found in the last ten years that, although at first the rejections were hard to take, it became easier and easier. The best way to get over rejections is to have a big stack of envelopes and stamps, and the minute you take your work out of one envelope you put it into another and send it right back out. The greatest cure is to sit down and write. When you are working you don't think about anything else. By the time you finish your work for the day, you can hardly remember what it was that had you so upset. I know writers who, after a very serious rejection such as a novel being sent back, are plunged into despair and won't write for perhaps days or weeks. I'm afraid if I did that, who knows, I might never write again. I just couldn't take that chance.

I have long since discovered that I don't send to *Esquire* or *Good Housekeeping*. I send to the small magazines. This is my market, it's a world I'm happy in and I wouldn't want to be anywhere else. At first the editors would put a little note on the bottom of the printed thing, "Try us again" or "This one was interesting" or "Well-written" or something like that. I was thrilled. In the writer's world, this is the first step, your wings, or whatever you want to call it. Then I began to get longer ones and longer and longer. The story might still be turned down, but they would take the time to say why. You learn from this and when you send something to that editor again, you refer to his or her comment and you have the basis of a dialogue. You begin to learn what kinds of stories they like. There are certain things I would not send to such and such a magazine, because I know from comments that editor made that they are simply not interested in anything with an historical background, for instance. I try to be considerate of that. In the past ten years I have gradually become at least familiar to a few editors who reply in personal notes. Sometimes one editor will send me to another: "I really like this, but it's not for us" or "I can't use it" or "My fellow editor doesn't like it, but try so and so." That happened two or three times and in two of the cases, the stories were taken by the next publication.

The first story of mine that was published went out, I think, fifteen times until it was accepted by *Kenyon Review* (Spring '85). I have every rejection from that story, everything from printed forms without any notes, to quite nice notes, to a very terse note from a well-known editor who said "This is not a story." I was ecstatic when *Kenyon* accepted my story. The editor sent me a wonderful letter. It was the most astounding, most wonderful experience of my life – I had waited so long. Then shortly after that came the next one and that was "The Story-teller," accepted by *Ascent*. And the reason it went to *Ascent* was that an editor at *Massachusetts Review* said "I like this very much, but I can't use it. Try Dan Curley at *Ascent*." And immediately, he accepted it. And that one had been rejected ten or fifteen times.

Ascent decided to give an award for the best story of the year, something they don't often do because, as Dan says, they rarely have the money. But that particular year they had money and so they asked Carolyn Osborne, author of *A Horse of Another Color* and *The Fields of Memory*, to be the judge. Out of forty or fifty stories, she picked mine as the best in every respect. And then it was nominated for the annual Pushcart Prize. It didn't get taken but I was delighted just to be nominated. By then I had learned a lot about the question of taste, the question of balance in a magazine; so many things go into these choices. So I don't feel as if I was being rejected in any way.

Two others of the recent batch have also been accepted, the first at *Kenyon* and another at *Massachusetts Review* which was sending me to other places a year ago. Probably to someone who publishes in commercial places it's unimportant, but it's the world I belong in and I am really very, very pleased. And feeling that way helps in writing, allows me to be free and to respect the importance of being as honest as I possibly can. My most recent recognition has been the award of a fellowship from the Artists' Fellowship Program of the New York Foundation for the Arts based on a story "In the Yucatan" that has been taken by *Kenyon Review*. And I have been accepted at the Tyrone Guthrie Center for Writers in Ireland. I am going to spend a month there and hope I'll be able to write in all that solitude, when I'm used to Broadway.

As far as my process is concerned, very often I start from an image, a group of words, a phrase. I don't always know why at the start, but by the time I've worked it through I find out. Sometimes I'll write in my notebook things that occur to me and find, days and pages later, that they were really all connected, that they have an internal harmony and architecture of their own. You have to trust this process. The more you do it, the more will come.

When I get blocked, I go walk busy streets. That jazzes me up, gets the electricity going. Something might occur to me or I might see something that will start me off again. Or I'll think it through. I've learned to do a little question-and-answer routine, "Where would he *go*, what would he *say*, what would he *do*?" But more often than not, I just sit down and start writing again. Very often a block comes when there is something wrong, and so I will start again, not necessarily at the beginning, just another scene. Frequently I will find out that I was going in the wrong direction or something was not right and so the material just stopped. Sometimes if you start in another place, even if you don't know why and don't know where it's going to go, but only that this little fragment seems to want to be written, before you know it, there's another little piece and another little piece and it begins to take on its life and move forward.

I don't do a great deal of revision. I am not good at it. I have a friend who is a very good editor and she'll look at something and say, "You should start here, you started in the wrong place." That I can change. But if someone says, "I think you need more detail in the middle," every new line that I write will stick out. Generally speaking, my words have a rhythm, a pace of their own that's internal and essential to the piece. If I come back a few months later and insert something that isn't of that rhythm, it will stick right out as if you put notes into a piece of music where they didn't belong. And sure enough, every time I'll go back and take them out.

"The Storyteller" took about a month. Sometimes a story will take less than that, sometimes a little more, from the point when I sit down and begin in the notebook. That includes the notebook, putting it on the computer, the editing and polishing, but it doesn't include those times when I'm walking around thinking and thinking or just daydreaming, with material tumbling about. God knows how long that goes on, night and day.

I've been a reader all my life but I don't read today the way I used to. When I'm reading, I'm only paying half attention – the other part of my mind is thinking about my own work. I don't often read literary essays. I become too analytical and that is not good for my writing. All the literary criticism in the world will not lead you to one page of a short story, whereas the little things you might recall of your childhood or an old friend or something that you saw some place could be the richest thing in the world. The more you get used to paying attention to your interior life, the richer it is, the more you hear and the more time you spend listening to it.

I'm now interested in doing a piece about the World War II period, something I've never written about. It was a man's world, the war, with no room in it for women or women's cares. We were *just* supporting the fighting men. But now when I look back on it, I think, What a wonderfully rich period of time it was. And so I'm searching for that material. But not in books. I'll be walking down the street and I'll hear a fragment of a song that reminds me of the music of those days. Details are building up now, like a storeroom, and then it will begin to take shape and language. Meanwhile I will be working on other things.

I write everything in a regular school notebook. I write on the right-hand side of the page and leave the left-hand side empty, so that when an idea or question comes, I have the space to put it. As often as not, the things on the left-hand side turn out to be the best ones. Then when I see that a shape is beginning, I put it on the computer. I started using a computer two years ago and had a little trouble at first, but it was such a relief from the typewriter. Now I find it very easy.

Ordinarily I write not only every day, but all day. I really only get in two to three hours of creative work, but by the time I count in all the extra things, the productive part of the day really goes from around ten to three or four. By then I am exhausted. When I'm in the apartment, I have to be alone to write; the emotional awareness of another presence just stops the work. But as long as I'm anonymous, I can write anywhere: bus terminals, buses, airports, airplanes, railroads. Sometimes I get my best things on a bench.

When I started writing full-time ten years ago, I would say to myself, My writing comes first, and I'm not going to let a single thing interfere. But then someone would say, "Meet me for lunch" and I would say, "Sure." I was seeing every art show in town, going here, going there, meeting people. Now I'm ruthless. I don't meet anyone for lunch – oh once in a while, of course – I really don't go on shopping trips, I don't do *anything* except my work. And when I can't work because of physical or mental exhaustion, I walk around the streets of the city, and that jazzes me up so much I come back and am ready to start again.

My telephone hour begins after four. I call my mother at five every evening, and that's when I talk to my friends. You lose friends, in the sense that you don't see them anymore, but you can't be a writer, if you're very serious about it, and be all over town. As a daily matter you have to be very strict, you have to mean it. People get used to it. They say, "Oh well, don't call Pat, not till later" or "She won't go for lunch." And so that's fine. As for entertaining, every woman knows that if you invite company, you don't begin an hour before, you begin a day or two before, planning the menu, shopping, checking that you have everything, then the cooking and serving and then being exhausted the next day. I don't do that anymore. We have friends occasionally. Bert is a great cook; I do half the dinner and he does the other half. That helps. But if I had my way, I'd reduce it even more. I would get it down to utter simplicity, no distractions.

My children are all married and I have eight grandchildren. I am very happy to be a grandmother though I don't at all feel like one. My family is more than willing to support me. I struggled for this and I now have it. But you have to be very strong. You have to be determined and know that this is your last chance, this is now and you can't kid yourself. I'm not great at dealing with things, but when it comes to my writing I am as

I was with my children – I will fight down to the last thing for my work. If I lose that, as far as I'm concerned, I have nothing. I have a beautiful family, I have everything I want in the world, but this is the only thing of importance to me. I'm not exaggerating.

I think I was my own obstacle. Whether or not that is related to growing up in a world in which the ordinary woman's personal and emotional life was considered unimportant, or whether it was my peculiarity, I don't know. I think a lot of women, more so than men, have to discover not just their own identity but their own importance. For me, it was a long time that other people's needs and other people's values were more important. You can't help but say to yourself occasionally, What if I had started twenty years ago, thirty years ago, what might I have done? But I think that is futile thinking, a waste of energy and a waste of time.

Geraldine Zetzel

Difficult Balance

Pigeon dragging a scabby wing,
gull with one leg out of kilter
(mad yellow eye defying help)

creatures needing repair
as dearly as a rose
whose stem wavers under its load,

the blazing crown – our longing is
to mend, prevent. To touch
the tender stalk of this child's neck,

Adam, bumbling across my lawn
his too-big head brimful
of ticking nerves and messages

the whole odd pudding alive
with instant news: each minute's
smell, the taste of every name –

Airplane . . . Red flower . . . Grass . . .
Bug . . . and the power to tell
his thumb, Go squash that bug.

Just as at any moment
that brittle house of bone itself
poised on its stalk, could crash.
Unless held whole with every breath.

Off Season

Redwings hustle over wet fields,
grackles croak and dive
on the March wind: it's time
to plant peas in cold soil, time
to pull up the first witchgrass
poking up through the seaweed mulch . . .

I see him stoop to do these chores
in his blue work-shirt. Dirt
gets under his nails, his skin
smells of loam when he comes in
to warm up, lies reading,
drifting to sleep on the window-seat.
Pale sun warms his lap, his long hands
folded over baggy chinos.

> Later, he lay there dying.
> Then we pretended together
> that that Spring was not our last
> invented the savor
> of every day . . .

Time now to varnish spars,
time to think about shingles
that winter blew down,
to begin making screens,
clean the mouse-droppings
out of the kitchen drawers.

> Time now to rage: that his eyes
> can't see the redwings' play,
> hands can't hold those tools

he loved, that all the intricate
music of that mind had to spin off
into senseless static –
and even that noise has gone
into the patient breathing
of waves against the beach

In the cold rooms
dust films. The light
falls whiter as I take down
the curtains. Somebody
left a cigarette butt
in the clamshell, somebody
made the bed but the blue spread
lies crooked halfway across the pillows.

For A.K. (1924-1970)

Fur

Out of its shoebox coffin
and tissue-paper shroud
this legacy: strip of beige fur
backed with dark-brown satin.
The pelt is soft, thick
as the bodies of old ladies
    (oh gentle flesh encased in whale-bone, feet bound
      in alligator-skin,
      sweet brows winged, crowned with feathers
        of jungle birds . . .)

Lifting to my cheek the piece of mink
saved from some last good winter coat
instead of animal, I inhale
a smell familiar as a chime:
woman. This creamy under-down,
the brown guard-hairs fragrant
with all the years
those little bodies lay
tame around some powdered neck.
                Only the longing

remains, like the acrid thread
of musk that coils in at the window,
summer nights. And you waken
to stare down at the garden, asleep
under its quilt of street-light.
The air is rank with the smell
of raccoon. They grunt and dig
for grubs in the lawn, scuffle
high in the trees. The cries
of their love-making slice
through the city's distant rumble.
The tide of their bodies' heat
rises, pressing against
your shivering skin.

An Old Story

When the King my father got tired of waiting
for us to choose brides, got bored
with stout ambassadors offering
portraits of wellborn girls
he roared: *Enough! let each of my sons*
shoot his best arrow into the blue.
Where it alights, there in that courtyard
he must find him a wife.
And be done!
                    Crown Prince Sergei went first.
His arrow flew like a hawk
over two counties to fall
smack at the feet of a princess –
long yellow braids, sixteen,
fat as butter.
                    Then Kostya the Clever
took aim. Winged his shaft straight up –
so high it must fall back nearby
onto familiar ground
where the Duke's tall daughter
was just then mounting her mare.
Lucky old Kostya . . .
                    My turn.
The bow felt heavy as stone.
A swan flapped past as I drew.
My shot went wobbling into the swamp.
From which hopped forth
a frog, arrow clamped fast
in her jaws. She dropped it
right at my feet, sat back on her rump
waiting for praise.

O how they laughed, the brothers, courtiers,
grooms – the very kitchen-maids
could barely hide their sniggers.
Father, enraged, stuck to his edict.

At the wedding, I put on a brave face,
concealed my disgust until the farce
was over.
        That night, in the marriage bed
I found at my side a girl
with silken limbs, hair the color
of heron's wing. The frogskin
hung on a peg behind the door.
I used to waken at dawn
to watch her mending my cloak,
to smell the fresh bread baking . . .

Still, they would joke over ale-pots
how I was so foul I'd sleep with a
frog, how my clothing stank
of damp, how my get would be born
with pop-eyes and web-feet. My love
saw the hurt, offered at last
to show her human form
just once to the world.
        You've heard
the rest: at Michaelmas Ball
the whole kingdom amazed
at her grace, the shimmering darts
of her speech, her wise unusual face.
At midnight, as she danced
in a circle of tranced admirers,
I ran to the house, grabbed frogskin
and hurled it into the fire.

It flared up green, a rush of flame
like a squall tearing through reeds.
O, I didn't know the shape of her need.
Weeping, she left me. Now I search
through all the swamps of the world.
And every human face
croaks out at me
its dumb reproach.

Letter from Another Country

Not knowing who will read this
or whether the censor will see fit to let it pass
I write once more to report to you.
Because I can imagine (just) your hand
touching this paper, I can hope
someone may receive this message.

The Country.

After six months the strangeness only grows.
Of course, the season changed. I had been warned
but nothing really prepares one for such cold.
At first I thought I'd understood
how it all fits together: climate, landscape
figures in the foreground giving proportion.
But now the patterns more and more elude me.
Maps don't contain the logic.
One is easily lost, and lost again
at turnings that had seemed familiar.
Landscapes change, or else my sense
of what they mean is altered. And then
they tell time differently here.
It's awkward to be always either too soon,
too slow, too distant or too quick.

The People.

Curious at first, eager to help me,
now bland and friendly, they come and go
as if this house were theirs.
The habit of touching hands and smiling

of which I wrote you, is not to be interpreted
quite the way I thought at first.
Yes, they mean well, but something else is meant.
At times one has the sense of being watched
like some sort of child, or god, or animal.
And it isn't clear what they expect.

The Language.

There is nothing now I cannot express.
Words and their rhythms come easy to the tongue.
The syntax is delightfully regular. Still
a kind of hunger haunts me
for richness, ambiguity or depth.
So much significance remains unsaid.
You wonder if the natives
speaking to one another
use a different dialect.

Daily Life.

The house they gave me is large.
A certain shabbiness prevails
and there is that smell in the corridors,
odd but not unpleasant, like old tobacco.
The rooms are cold at times. Things leak
or creak. I would have them fixed
if it were clear what is the landlord's business
and what's mine. Mealtimes are brief.
Although the food is palatable
I often feel a sickness much like hunger.
Work keeps me busy. I'm told I do it well.

In Closing.

I do it well. But ask them at home
to state again the purpose of this mission.
It grows less clear after these months
why I am here. What is the meaning of my task?
How long shall I be prepared to stay?
The messages I get are so obscure.
Tell those in charge to write more plainly.
Tell them I will do my best.

                      Remember that,
and try once more to find the books I asked for.
In exile you forget so much
you once knew by heart. Faces saved in memory
begin to blur . . .

                   I will not sign:
my name in this place has a different meaning.

Lincoln Park Zoo, *Thalarctus Maritimus*

Viewed from the ramp, these spacious cliffs
and generous feast of water offer
Arctic nirvana. Off in a corner
the solitary polar bear
is making a sort of backward somersault
in ice-green sheets of spray.
               Below,
through plate glass observation ports
one sees how he does it. Again!
Again, that tumbling circle! The amazing
bulk of him sailing by in his mantle
of bubbles, the huge paws thrusting off.
The ecstasy of that creamy fur
as it billows past, revealing at belly's
root the neat rosette of his sex.
The priestly head is bowed in a nimbus
of foam. Eyes shut, he does not notice
us. Children, awestruck, then bored
begin to bang on the glass. Parents'
cameras dangle: there's nothing here
for a snapshot. Nothing to watch except
compulsion's endless arc.
               They leave.
The acrobat goes on with his ritual.
Working to get it right? Each turning
your try for the perfect dive? Or have you
become a prayer-wheel, repeating
some mantra ice-floes chant
into the polar darkness? There is no
ice here in your private ocean.
They gave you artful rocks, azure
lagoon, a black hatchway that leads
indoors.
         All night, I hold against my body
the curve of your body's journey.

Waking Some Mornings the Mind

gets up in time to look down
at the body still cocooned
in sleep   leans down to observe
this apparently simple
collection of folded parts:

this arm that lies like the root
of a tree   small grasses grow
out of its smooth freckled bark
hand curled up like an infant
smelling gently of itself
breath moving mindlessly in
and out   as waves that keep on
telling their names to the sand

this moment before it wakes
I watch my body the way
God might watch a trout at rest
in its river bed   shining

Geraldine Zetzel

My mother, who was Austrian and came here after her marriage, wanted very much for her children to speak her mother tongue, so I was brought up bilingual in English and German. When I was six we moved to Switzerland and French was added on. I look upon language as a source of richness but also of much confusion – I had a time when I didn't know which was my real true language. My experience as a child was of always being a foreigner and always being told, "Gee you have a funny accent, where do you come from?" People continue to think I come from somewhere else – and maybe they are right!

My father was a member of a well-to-do German-Jewish family. He was a real oddity, the black sheep in his family. His family was delighted that he played the cello but when he said, "I want to be a cellist," they had a fit – musicians were sort of déclassé people. But he went ahead and became a professional musician, playing the cello, doing some conducting and a little bit of composing. He was not wildly successful, partly because he didn't push himself in the professional things you have to do, such as touring and playing in little towns and working terribly hard. But that was his profession.

My parents were divorced when I was six. I lived with my mother and spent time with my father every summer; once we came back to the United States I was with him on vacations. He had many friends who were musicians and artists and his second wife, my stepmother, was a good amateur painter. They weren't language people but there was a lot of exposure to art.

I changed schools five times, five very different settings in different parts of the world. That was pretty tough. My mother remarried when I was about fourteen and we moved to the Midwest. For one very horrible year I went to a girls' school in the Midwest where I didn't fit in in any way – I was just hopeless. Then I went to boarding school in Connecticut for two years before college. I liked school, I did well, I cared a lot about doing well. Oddly enough my family were not so particular. They wanted me to do well but they didn't know what it was about. Less so with my father – he and I had a lot of rapport around a lot of things, especially when I was an adolescent.

As a child I was a big reader; books were tremendously important to me. I immersed myself in them – it was one way to shut out the world, that was clear. I was constantly being told to stop reading and do something else. I loved language. I have a poem from when I was ten or eleven that I wrote in response to an English assignment. It is a real sonnet, very stilted and childlike, but it says, Here is something you can do in language. I have a feeling that was close to the time we came back to live in the United States; maybe I finally got grounded in English as my primary language. I got a lot of excited attention from some teachers and that was very encouraging. I continued in a sporadic way to write poems in school and later more privately. In adolescence it became something I did occasionally because I was moved.

As a child I got a lot of help and encouragement from teachers. I had tremendous crushes on them; they were very important adults in my life and offset a somewhat conflicted and meager home life. The folks in my family were not so easy to be with or gratifying or supportive. My father was probably the only family member I ever showed any writing to. He was not a reader of any depth and he certainly wasn't a reader of poetry, but he was responsive and encouraging in a general way. From time to time I showed some things to one German great-uncle who cared a lot about me and took me seriously. He was a very cultured man, very loving. He was the one person, I think, outside of teachers that I had that kind of contact with.

My writing was precious to me. I can tell because I have the notebooks in which I inscribed the finished poems. They are very slim – I may have a total of fifteen poems from all of childhood and adolescence – but I remember thinking as a teenager and as a young adult, If the house burns down what am I going to take with me: those two notebooks.

English was my strongest subject. I was on the literary magazine in school and at one point in college was co-editor of a literary magazine that we rejuvenated. One winter I wrote a column for the college newspaper that was modeled on the *Spectator Papers*. I was, obviously, reading Addison and got very taken with the sort of essayist who comments on the passing scene in a somewhat distant and humorous way. I submitted a few poems to the magazine and some were rejected. That was one of the first times I felt, Oh, oh, maybe if you put yourself forward as a serious writer, not everyone is going to fall over in a faint of admiration. To the extent that I wrote, which was always very little, I didn't allow myself to be up front enough or try hard enough to feel all that rejected. It was as if I put a toe in the water, it was cold, I pulled it back and stayed there.

In school and even more in college, writing poetry was a kind of subversive activity for me. I did most of the actual creative writing when I was supposedly taking notes on a lecture on something quite different, say philosophy. It was as though there were two streams of consciousness – I was taking notes with my rational head and the irrational or unconscious was meanwhile jotting down some quite different stream. That persists to some extent; often if I am working on one poem, another one intrudes and that one is usually deeper and comes from a different level. It's as though there is something that works better if I don't put my total attention on it.

Until I was in my twenties I secretly defined myself as a writer, but one who was not writing much or seriously or doing anything to become more of a writer. By the time I was getting toward the end of college, I never thought I would do that as my life work or that it was anything but a private dream, a private world I was not going to expose. I think I used writing partly to try to figure out what I was feeling and thinking, a way to sort out very intense emotions. I can hardly bear to look at those old poems now; they are pretty awful both aesthetically and as reminders of some pretty awful times, usually acute confusion or pain. In the better ones the confusion and pain were very veiled and very whispered, but I know what is behind them.

In college I had a terrific affair with a much older man, European, a professor. He was a writer himself, a deeply literate person. He was German speaking, which may have been part of the attraction, and he too was a wanderer and exile. He thought I was very good but of course he was also madly in love with me. It was heady stuff and while it lasted, it was tremendously encouraging.

After college I took a turn towards a much more outward kind of life. Since I had always been very interested in children, I went into teaching, initially into a teacher-training program. That is what brought me to Cambridge. I taught a peculiar brand of English lesson that had to do with the school I was at. We did English and social studies as one and I integrated that with art, drama and a few other subjects, a curriculum that I helped devise. A lot of my creative energy went into that work; I liked it and was very good at it. And it was some kind of lifesaver since I was pretty spaced out and disconnected from people and very scared.

On and off from the age of about sixteen I was in therapy, which helped me stay glued together at times I might have come unglued. I was in a lot of anguish a lot of the time, very dislocated. The intellectual life of school and college gave me an anchor and I used that, but emotionally it was very hard for me to be close to people and yet I needed people desperately. I was desperately lonely, frightened to death of relationships and constantly on tenterhooks. Things got steadier when I found my profession. It gave me something to go on, something I knew I was good at. Being able to build connections with kids grounded me in the world of human relations and I had colleagues, a setting, a whole context in which to be effective.

After I got married I continued to teach for a year – my first child was born just three weeks after school ended. I had two kids very close together so it was an extremely busy time.

The writing seemed to have largely gone underground. When there was an occasional burst, it was usually because I was experiencing a lot of emotional turmoil – not because I wanted to communicate something as much as that I wanted to understand it for myself. Arthur, my husband, was not very encouraging about that or about other things I did that were creative. He didn't mean to put me down about it, but he did. He had very, very high standards and didn't like the idea of people fiddling around in an amateurish fashion. And I was very easily deflected.

The exception was when we decided to go and live abroad for a year, the four of us, when the children were three and four. The idea of that year was that he would pursue some research in mathematics which was his field and I would write. Arthur gave up his job and I had just finished graduate school, so off we went. We lived outside of Florence for a year; it was the perfect setup – I had a lovely study looking over Italian gardens, I had help to take care of the children, I had a cook. He had a piano and his math. We both had in common the most tremendously unsuccessful winter in terms of work. I thought, At last I have my chance to become this writer that I think I secretly am. And I had nothing to say. It was acutely painful; I sat in that study every morning with a nice little Olivetti typewriter and nothing to say. I came back feeling, That is that, it was a youthful illusion, I am not a writer, I can't write, I have nothing to say, forget it.

When we came back I became engaged in a lot of serious volunteer work for five or six years until the children were older. Then I worked, first part-time and then eventually full-time, as a school administrator in the same cozy and very nice private school that I had taught in originally. And there was always this trickle of poems, one or two a year, or one and a half. When a poem arrived on my consciousness doorstep I was very excited. I knew enough to get it down but I never knew enough to do anything with it – I couldn't in any way rewrite or work on it. Pretty much all the poems I have from those years are what I would now call a first draft. Occasionally I would write anecdotal stuff, observations about the children. A sort of observer thread has been with me ever since the beginning: to stand back and look very carefully at what is happening. But that was very sporadic; I have only a few folders. For example, we had "adopted" children through Foster Plan and when we were in Italy we went to visit both of them. I wrote about those experiences because they were tremendously exciting to me. There is one short story that I tried to get into some known shape with the help of a few friends, but I never sent it out, never did anything much about it.

I was not reading any poetry. My idea of a modern poet was e e cummings who was considered avant-garde in the 1940's when I wrote a college paper about him. That was the last time I checked in on who was writing. Writing was a tiny piece of my life, always back in there somewhere but not much was going on. And really not much did go on until the time of Arthur's illness. It was only a year and half from the first symptom to his death, which is unusually rapid for Hodgkin's disease. The expectation was that he might do very well and he might even be cured. It was very shocking to everybody because it all happened so fast. There were a few letups when he went into remission but that was very brief. Except for that it was just straight-out crisis.

The force behind the first poem that came out of that situation was the sense of fragility, of life endangerment. It was a poem attempting to seize the moment of experience we were currently having together and came out of a very different place from anything that had happened before. Its tone is different, its language is still somewhat poetic, somewhat forced and fancy, but I was struggling toward saying it plain.

At the same time that all this was going on, I took up pottery purely as a way to get away from the difficult situation of having a husband ill with cancer, the outcome so uncertain, things so difficult and his being home a lot. I loved ceramics, loved the struggle of it. Technically it's difficult as hell to learn to throw on the wheel. That was a kind of risk taking and, of course, I defined it as, I am just doing this for fun, so who cares. That made it easier. It was fascinating to me because it was without words, without punctuation, without thought, without analysis. It was the experience of creating, minus all the difficulties of trying to be articulate. It was a great relief and I became totally absorbed when I was doing it, which was perfect for that time and perfect later in other ways. I have been a somewhat precise and fastidious, fussy kind of person. But you can't be that if you are going to be a potter. I liked the mess, the slop, the wet, the clay and the stuff all over the place. It was a release, but it was also good creative work. And then, in my somewhat rigid fashion, I thought, Well, maybe poetry was something I was attracted to when I was young, and now in this stage of life my creative energy needs to go into pottery. For a while I thought, That's it, *pottery* not *poetry* – as though it had to be either/or.

After Arthur died I wrote poems which were not directly about him or not directly about death but they were certainly triggered by all that. Among them was "Letter from Another Country" which dates almost exactly from six months after his death. I feel it is a seminal poem for me because it is the first time I discovered you can just *say* it, you don't have to disguise it in pretty music or make it "sound like poetry." Just say what you mean and what you feel. That poem made me think, Well, maybe I can't dismiss myself as a writer, maybe there is something there that has to be pursued.

It was some time around then that I signed up at our local adult education center for a course in poetry. My idea of a workshop was essentially to go there and have my poems admired, so that when I was given suggestions or criticism, I was totally baffled, I didn't know what to do with any of it. Even the hint that one could work on something didn't penetrate; I had no idea how to do that. I felt held up to some standard I didn't understand, criticized for some things I wasn't trying to do anyway, told to do something totally different. I think that retarded me because I wasn't ready to fight back, I didn't know how and I only felt put down. If a teacher is trying to make you write like himself or pegs you as a certain type of writer, when you are really beginning and fumbling around, or seems to be criticizing aspects of your work while missing the main point or is essentially not respectful, that is not useful. I think that respectfulness is what makes it possible for people to get on with their own development. It certainly was for me.

A year after Arthur's death I took my collected works from

that era – I may have had ten poems – and submitted them to Breadloaf Writers Conference. They accepted me, which I now realize is no great accolade – they are happy to take paying customers! It was a very "groupy" kind of experience; you are thrown into intimate closeness with a bunch of people you have never seen before. It is very intense, there are a number of egos clamoring, a lot of people who are very fragile, a good deal more fragile than I was and I wasn't in tremendous shape. The teachers, in addition to John Ciardi who was running it, included William Meredith, Robert Pack, Maxine Kumin, Diane Wakoski. There were lectures and talks and seminars; I made some contacts with real poets which was pretty exciting. Meredith gave me a formal critique but I couldn't make much use of his help because I really just wanted him to fall over and say, "Wow!" And of course that is not what happened at all. It's a setting that tells you there's a hell of a lot of competition, shows you there's a whole world, "po biz" as some people call it, that has its own ways and that you clearly don't belong to yet. At least I didn't. I think it was not discouraging and I remained basically glad that I did it, but when I look at what happened next – which is that things kind of petered out again – I wonder if it didn't set me back some. I went through another period when I thought, That's it, you wrote when you were young because you were in a muddle and you wrote in these years because you were under this tremendous stress and grief, but now that you have gotten all this out of your system, it's gone again.

I turned seriously to pottery and that was what I did for a number of years as my main creative work – I enjoyed it and got pretty good at it. The next real change was an extraordinary week at Pendle Hill, a Quaker center outside of Philadelphia that gives various short-term courses. I took a week's course given by M.C. Richards, who has written several books, the most known called *Centering*. She led us through a week of fascinating experiences in clay; and after we had worked in clay on an exercise, we would reflect and write in response to the experience. The writing that came together for me with the pottery made me sure that I still needed words as well as clay to complete things. It was as if this voice said loud and clear, "The hell you can give up poetry, here we are!" It wasn't immediate, I didn't come back all fired up and sit down and write poetry, but it was a clear turn.

In that same period Lou and I became involved. We got married in the winter of 1972 and I was occupied with changing houses, getting a whole new family, new relationships and obligations. I continued to work at school administration full-time, but I decided, for various good reasons, that I had come to the end of the satisfaction I could get from that work. I had been affiliated with the school a total of seventeen years and it was very, very hard to remove myself. I could have stayed till retirement where I was honored and loved and had community and plenty to do, aspects of which I loved. For a couple of years it took most of my energy to decide to leave, to leave and to figure out what next. I paid attention to what my inner feelings and needs were and what I wanted out of work in a way I never had. To accept that I might end up working as a volunteer instead of a paid employee took a while to sort out.

I now work as a child advocate and mediator, which I do as a professional who volunteers her services. The discovery of the freedom to be ignorant, to be a beginner, to ask and not present myself as so competent was a great relief. I was asked to write two manuals on mediation, a much more serious kind of technical writing than I had ever tried to do. I did it with tremendous effort. I am now a paid consultant for a pilot project using family systems intervention to try to prevent teen-age pregnancies. My task is to write training materials so that this program can be replicated.

In the middle of my work transition I bumped into an old acquaintance, Nina Nyhart, who was just starting up a course called "Writing with Your Eyes" which was based on visual imagery. I enrolled in her class for a term and it was then I began to feel I could do something with my poems besides write them and have them just sit there as they had happened. When I became able to define myself in writing as a beginner, in spite of the number of things I had attempted over the years, I became able to learn, and that's mattered a lot. I could look at my work objectively, the way a painter stands back from the canvas and says, "Now, is that really where I want that color?"

And I could listen to what other people have to say. I had developed enough confidence and understanding of the process to be able to do something like a revision once in a while. It wasn't that long ago, around 1983, and from then on I've kept moving.

A week-long workshop with Ruth Whitman here in Cambridge in 1984 really gave me another big shove. I found that week immensely stimulating; I liked the company and the writing exercises. But the thing that sticks is that in our conference she looked at me with her big brown eyes and said, "You are an accomplished poet." I thought, Here is a poet who says I am a poet! I had not heard anything so resounding anywhere before. And I could identify with her personally: she is very female, connected with the world of family and bread and daughters and objects, down-to-earth and rooted, a particular kind of intellectuality. I felt safe with her. She knows what she's doing, she is not going to ask anyone to do what they can't do, she is not going to put anyone on the spot, she is respectful – all the things a good teacher ought to be.

It was a big push and it coincided with a certain amount of freeing for me, that I had different kinds of things to say. Possibly what happened to me with the Whitman workshop, and before that with Nina's class, is that I felt I had a wider range. For example Whitman asked us to write a poem about apples. I was still caught in a high seriousness that came from way back. You can be serious about apples, God knows, but I hadn't known that I could be serious or funny or anything else just about an apple. I felt, I can compose in different keys, I can do things that are lighter and heavier, and I can use a much wider range of subject matter too. I have had a very rich life with lots of experiences, a lot of images, a lot to remember. I have a very acute memory that is kinesthetic too, not just visual. There is a lot of stuff there to use if I can just zig-zag around the barriers I put up: You don't want to talk about that, you don't want to talk about this. One of the things that stops me again and again is my perception of myself as essentially a very melancholy poet. There are times I cannot stand it, when I think if all I am going to hear from underground is these depressive noises I am not going to write. The censor gets louder than the impulse and that stops me cold. Other times I can say, So okay, I am a melancholy poet, what's wrong with that? It's not so bad to write about loss all the time, that's one of the themes. I have a feeling it's going to come and go like that.

And in that workshop I had the company of people somewhat like me in life stage and in writing-life stage, serious but not famous yet. My work was pretty good – it wasn't the best, it wasn't the worst – but I could see it in the context of other people's work and see, Yeah, this stuff is all right. That was very affirming and enabled me to stop being what I call a closet writer, to expose myself to criticism and rejection and other things which I haven't found that horrendous once I decided to do it. It just took so long to get there.

I've gone now for four terms to a workshop run by Kinereth Gensler at Radcliffe Seminars where my poems get read and commented on by very intelligent and thoughtful people who have been at it for a long time as both writers and critics. The teacher keeps a good grip on the process so things move along, everybody gets their fair share. The limiting thing for me is that there is a core group of people who continue term after term, and we get to know each other pretty well and what each one is going to say – or we think we do. And we get to know what the group likes, which is really dangerous because it is so seductive to write what you know is going to be liked. I set myself the task this summer of writing things that I would show to nobody for a while just to get away from all that. There would be a good deal of head-scratching about "Difficult Balance" and I think, Well thank God, I finally managed to get around that. I wrote something and *I* know what it means and *I* know I want it that way and, yes indeed, the group will say, "What are you doing here?"

One of the things I've learned most from being in this workshop is about critiquing poetry. I used to sit there itching for *my* poem to be read. Now I think I almost learn more by participating in this thoughtful reading and criticism. I begin to understand why something works the way it does, from titles to line breaks to diction to point of view, without their being discussed in an intellectual manner but just by using the material that comes.

The next chapter for me, in regard to writing, has been to become much more committed, systematic, aware and ready for the impulse when it comes, to do a number of things that are profoundly symbolic. One has been to set up a real work-room. For the ten years I have lived in this house, my work-room has had a temporary worktable: the typewriter had to be moved on and off it, it was at the wrong height, the light wasn't really appropriate, there was no place to sit, and, guess what, there were no book shelves. I had been working in and out of folders which were stacked here and there and usually out of sight. It was just a question of getting organized and doing it, but I have only just completed it.

I've done better about making *space* than I have about mak-ing *time*. I think I am still in the stage I was at back in Italy: if I'm *there* and *now* is when I have to work on it, I choke, as they say in sports. Having a room to work in sometimes seems to raise more barriers than it lowers. I can sit there if I'm just doing revision but if I am thinking at all of something new, it doesn't work out that way. An example is the poem, "Difficult Balance," which came after a very dry period. One day when my husband's secretary couldn't come in, I sat in for her. As I was fiddling around answering the telephone, letting patients in and out and occasionally reading the newspaper, I started writing an extremely deep poem. It was as if I had to be dis-tracted at the surface for this other thing to come in the back door.

As far as process is concerned, I rarely know what I am writ-ing until it is on the page. I know where it begins but I don't know what it is. But now I can look at it on the page and say, Ah, this one is basically trying to do this. That's what makes revision possible. And I have gotten bolder and bolder. I even get quite easy with saying, Of course *that* is where it started but that's the wrong phrase and it's in the wrong diction. It doesn't have to be in the poem just because it came to you when you were in the bathtub. I have gotten to be a terrific reviser. What I can't do as well is to stop revising and let it go and say, All right, this is version number twenty-three, I think we've got it as well as we're going to get it and let's go on to the next. I keep all versions of everything. I am not quite sure why, but once in a while there has been a big pay-off – I go way back to the beginning and find some word or phrase that seems right that I had discarded many versions before. Usually at some point in the writing, I read the poem into a tape and listen to it. If there is an awkwardness or some stumbling, that is a sign to me that something isn't working in my inner ear.

I get it down in a much looser way than I used to – in lines or phrases or fragments or sequences. After a few versions like that, usually longhand, often with alternate words down one side where I think specific words may not be right, I begin to know what kind of line length, whether I want it to be less formal or more formal, whether it seems to be headed for stanzas or something else, whether it's going to have some metrical scheme. Most of my work does have a metrical scheme of beats though I have done some syllabic poems. I think all my work has an underlying structure and formality. I like the constraint of a certain amount of form because I find it makes me think very, very hard about what I mean. The economy, the discipline make for more intense writing. I have done some very formal poems, some villanelles. They are pretty terrible but I think it is a good thing to try.

I find I often write poems with water in them or about currents somehow. I used to fight that and want not to repeat myself. But one of things about finding my voice is feeling, These are my metaphors, these are my images, these are my favorite turns of phrases. So what? That's me, my language. It took a long while not to feel that as merely repetitive.

I have attempted other kinds of writing. I have written a few short stories, but I have never felt I had a grip on that form, though there are some wonderful bits in the two or three short stories I've written. I think there is a storyteller in me and that is part of what the more narrative work in my poetry is. I have a fascination with what happened next, especially in a slightly magical poem like "An Old Story."

I think I am still near the beginning of my serious career. My confidence is going to go up and down a lot. In periods when I haven't been able to write or what I've written has been unsatisfactory, I have had sinking feelings that maybe again this was just a rush and the rush is over. I've thought, Who do I think I am, what is this? Here I have in the cellar a lovely work-shop in which to do pottery and I'm not doing it, and now I have a lovely desk on which to write poetry which I am not doing. But the thing that is clear to me is that I have gotten much better. I have made steady progress and that is a thread of gratification that keeps on. I haven't ever felt in the last few years that I have made some false turn. I feel that I know what my voice is and that actually there are two different versions of it, one the very lyrical, small, simple kind and the other the more narrative or mythological kind. I am not distracted by thinking maybe I want to be some other kind of poet or write some very different kind of language.

Publication has been minimal. At times it's been depress-ing to feel that there is no audience for me – that's hampered me, slowed me up. I have a poem published in *Waterways,* which advertised in *Coda* for poems on a funny theme: worms, parrots, and something. I had a worm poem and they took it but it is not well-printed. And then *Sunrust,* a magazine that takes poems about rural America which I'd read about in *Coda* and *Poets' Marketplace,* took one called "Knobbed Whelk." *Sun-rust* looks more like a real magazine but I don't know who will ever see it. I also have a poem coming out in *Radcliffe Quarterly.*

I am of two minds: to have something published in a very obscure, not particularly well-done magazine doesn't feel very rewarding and on the other hand it is neat to have something in print when you have just been sending them out and getting them back. What I try to do initially is make up packets of two or three poems that represent a good balance and send them with the intention that as soon as they come back, I will send them out again to the next place. I am completely faithful about not doing double submissions, but it is a pain because your work can be out for months. The few times that I have had anything other than a form letter, I have been over-whelmed with joy, even with, "Of these, we have liked this one best, sorry we can't use them." Just the fact that there is some human element in the rejection helps. I don't want to get hooked on trying to get published but on the other hand I don't want to give it up, so I plug away at it in a somewhat erratic way.

Recently, I was invited out of the blue, by nobody I had ever heard of, to submit for a poetry reading in Westport Point, Massachusetts where I have a summer house. They picked four of the ones I'd sent. The reading felt a lot like my debut at Carnegie Hall and I had some trouble keeping it all in proportion. The feedback I got tells me that I do have a talent for this kind of presentation, a good voice, presence, a way of talking about the poems that engages people. And the poems themselves "speak well" in public. I long to do more of it but have no idea, really, how to go about this.

.   .   .

Although he has no experience of poetry and not a great deal of knowledge about it, my husband is immensely appreciative and interested. If I need to work or be obsessively engaged, it's all right. He takes it seriously, thinks it is a marvelous endeavor, is very excited when anything good happens. I show him almost everything. He often doesn't understand it, but I don't care; I just want to show it to him and he wants to see it. It's not that he is never critical; he will say, "I don't like this as much as I like some other of your things" or "I don't understand it," which is okay because basically what he is *not* saying is, "Why are you doing this odd thing, what is this odd occupation you are interested in, what does it matter?" I think there is always a problem for me in feeling that it matters. I feel my work in the world matters because I am trying to help other people, trying to fight inequity, injustice and misery. I can't imagine being a full-time writer because the other side of me requires action and seeing the effect of action. To spend six hours trying to get the metrical form of a poem just right, I have trouble sometimes justifying as a real occupation. But I don't ever have that question from Lou or my kids or my friends, the ones that I share poems with.

I don't feel hurried, I don't feel as if I am getting a late start on some huge body of work that has to be done before I die or before I run out of juice. I think part of the reason that I have found a language and a voice is maturity, knowing how I perceive the world, how I feel about it, what there is I want to communicate. I feel I am just where I ought to be given my history as a writer. Somewhere down the line, in a year or two, I will have enough good poems to start thinking about a chapbook. I am going to go step by step and if five or ten years from now I manage a book, that is fine. But I don't feel rushed and I don't feel it has to be. But there is one inner change. I used to think, After I am dead "they" will find the various folders with the various bits of writing in them and maybe they will think some of them are worth preserving and maybe not, but I am not going to do anything about it. Well, coming out of the drawer or coming out of the closet and saying, "No, I mean it, I mean it *now*," is different. I am not particularly hooked on the idea of immortality by my work, but I do feel, just as I felt with my children, that this is a way, however slight and tenuous, of contributing and making a mark, of having my voice heard.

Still if people say to me at a party, "Well, what do you do?" I say I am a child advocate, I do this and that and the other thing. And if it seems to fit in, I'll say I am also working on my writing. I used to never mention it – it wasn't real enough or I wasn't prepared to take the consequences of such a declaration. Recently however, when I was asked to talk to a group of Russian women about family mediation and they asked what else I did, I said, quite without premeditation, but with perhaps some faint consciousness of how writers are valued in the USSR, "I'm a writer. I write some technical materials. And I'm a poet." There it was, out at last!

Adele Bowers

. . .

The Hunting Season

Celia Hendricks was a widow sixty-three years of age. She and her four cats lived in a sparsely-populated area of New York state, near the Pennsylvania border, in a house they called modern when she and her husband designed it thirty-five years earlier. Before they built it, they spent a year of weekends looking for the right land. They wanted wildness, privacy, woods, flowing water. "And rocks," Celia would add, "we must have rocks." She was an amateur sculptor and was convinced that within every piece of limestone or marble a perfect creature waited to be freed.

After they found their land, one hundred fifty acres of it, the builder advised them to site their house near the road. "When the snow comes, and believe you me, it certainly comes," he said, "best let the county clear it away." Besides, it was just a narrow dirt road and not more than a half-dozen cars passed on any ordinary day. But Garson said to Celia, "I want to be able to piss off my own back porch and run around in my birthday suit if I feel like it." And Celia found a series of natural rock terraces in the woods and dreamed of herself and Garson eating meals there summer after summer, so back they went, a half-mile in from the road, and perched their house, a collection of cubes, on a concrete slab poured onto the rock outcropping which overhung a steep gorge. Garson used to love to stand visitors on the lip of the ledge and exclaim, "Five separate glaciers dumped their loads down there," swinging his hand over the ravine. Sometimes it was the hand holding the martini, in which case he would bless the scenery with expensive gin as he waved.

Far below, in its rocky bed, water flowed all year round, in springtime a torrent, a trickle in August. The slope was heavily wooded, many of the trees ancient, its steepness evidently having kept at bay the loggers who for a century at least had repeatedly cut over the surrounding land. The forest was a typical northeastern mixture: maples in abundance, birches, beeches, occasional oaks and, on the lower slopes, dark hemlock groves, in which animals took refuge against winter storms. Copper-colored dry leaves carpeted the forest floor; beneath them, springy leafmold nurtured a layer of ferns, ground pine, partridgeberry, mosses.

Above the ravine, before the land began rising again, were rough meadows in which a few rusty remnants of long-abandoned farm machinery lay among encroaching hawthorns and bramble thickets. Here and there, venerable white pines spread their powerful limbs over dozens of their seedlings, many nibbled into crooked shapes by deer. Among the pines, at the base of the hill, was a small pond. Its brown water was never more than a few feet deep and in dry summers a mere puddle, yet it abounded with frogs, salamanders, turtles and their eggs and larvae. Mornings and evenings, birds flew in to drink, bathe, feed. Many animal paths led to the pond; paw and hoof prints usually could be seen in its muddy banks. Between the pond and a nearby small hayfield grew many large, self-seeded apple trees.

"Hey," Garson said when they discovered this combination of forest, edge, water and field, "we got ourselves a wildlife sanctuary at no extra charge."

"Hush, Garson," said Celia, "let's keep it a secret between us and the animals. Say 'sanctuary' around here and you'll draw hunters like flies."

So starting in their first year, they posted NO HUNTING signs all around their land. And pruned and thinned the wild apples and set out seedling bushes for wildlife cover and food. And arranged with a nearby farmer to come each year in his off-season to mow the meadows and hayfield, keeping the forest from closing in on the wildlife browse.

"That's the animals' dining room," Garson would tell city friends who came visiting in the early years. "It belongs to the deer, the turkey, the foxes."

"And the woodchucks, Garson," Celia always added at this point, "don't forget the woodchucks."

"OK, OK," he'd answer, "and the moles and the mice and the chipmunks too."

"You bet," she'd sing back. Then she'd turn to their friends and explain, "Garson gives names to everything, so that's now the animals' dining room." And she told how he'd shoved aside the papers one Sunday morning soon after they moved into the house, saying, "Come on, Celia, put on your boots. We're going to church."

"Boots? Church? Garson, have you started drinking so early?" Celia often used a tone of feigned exasperation with Garson.

"Don't argue, woman, just come," he'd said. So she laced on the boots and followed him to the woods, along a tiny trail, up and down over rock ledges, and into a dim clearing part way up the mountain. "There." Garson swung his arm towards the massive, silvery, smooth-barked beech trees that encircled them. "Aren't those cathedral columns? And," he pointed to the leafy, light-speckled roof of the forest, "isn't that the Sistine ceiling up there? You may pray if you wish."

Then they sat side by side on a flat rock, the silence creaking around them until Celia sighed, "Oh, Garson," as though her lap had just been filled with rubies and diamonds. After that, for the next three decades, they attended their church many Sunday mornings unless it rained or snowed.

The very first Sunday after Garson died of kidney failure, Celia forced herself along the narrow trail. Soon a crackling sound made her turn. Emerging from the undergrowth was Oscar, the long-haired, strawberry-blond cat of whom Garson used to say, "That one belongs on a satin cushion in some boudoir, not in a wilderness." The cat's yellow eyes were huge with apprehension but his feathery tail was lifted. He jumped to the rock beside Celia and began to wash his pink nostrils.

"What a fine fellow," Celia said before her voice broke. She gathered the cat into her arms and let herself weep into his soft fur. But soon a sharp explosion, then another, shook the stillness. She lifted her head. "At least a mile away," she remembered Garson's saying of such shots, but she stood up anyway, spilling the cat onto the ground. As she picked her way back down the path, she thought, the hunting season must have begun. Then she whispered, "But it's not November." Dismayed, she tried to count the weeks between Garson's first, sudden attack and his death. Today's October seventeenth, she concluded. Not the deer season. Then why the shots? Birds, she realized. Grouse, partridges. Turkeys. She stopped walking. Turkeys. Garson's turkeys. All the past summer he had watched them feeding in the field, those great black creatures. "Twelve customers today," he'd call. Or, "Celia, hurry, the Honcho himself and the whole damn flock. Twenty-four!" Dizzily, she thought, his binoculars are still on the window sill.

In the weeks following, she thought, maybe I should go someplace as she and Garson had often done during the hunting season. But she couldn't mobilize energy to plan a trip. Instead, when the hospital where Garson had died asked her to volunteer as a nurse's aide, she said yes and spent three days a week shuffling up and down the hallways, arm in arm with stroke victims learning to walk again; or slowly spoonfeeding the senile patients, wiping their vacant faces, grooming their thin hair with a soft baby brush.

On the other afternoons, she fled her lonely house and went walking, at first only on her own property, then into the surrounding countryside. My widow walks, Garson would name them, she'd think while covering miles, for hours, until finally weary, she was glad to re-enter the silent house and sink into a hot tub. Later, in her robe, a drink at her elbow, she'd try to watch the evening news on television. But with no Garson pushing forward in the chair next to hers, arguing with the screen, soon she'd switch off the set. Oh, Garson, she'd think, you made so much noise and filled so much space. And came between me and the things in the world I can't face. Then she would busy herself fixing dinner, first for the clamoring cats, then herself. After cleaning up, she'd wander through the house. Sometimes she stopped in her studio and contemplated the finished pieces standing on the shelves or floor. One night she uncovered the stand. She looked from the self-portrait she'd begun last spring, into the mirror she'd set up behind it. Was my face so long and bony when he looked into it, she wondered? And my hair so dead white? She tucked the loose strands of hair back into her bun and re-pinned it.

Occasionally the phone would ring. Some neighbor or nearby acquaintance. Rarely, a faraway friend, for Garson and she had lost touch with most of these, especially after they retired early and moved into the house full-time. We didn't need friends, Celia thought, we had each other. But her brother's widow called regularly, every third or fourth evening from her home in a village sixty miles away. They'd talk for ten or fifteen minutes, about their health, their gardens, books they were reading, problems with their houses. Celia would tell Sarah about the hospital, the cats. Anything but Garson's absence. That she did not want to talk about. Nor accept Sarah's invitations or offers to come visit. Later, she told herself. Right now, another person's presence interfered with the past life she felt still vibrating about her. Made her lose touch with it, and that she did not want, even for a day. Nor to disturb the new silence massing behind the echoes of her past life; that she was also learning to listen for. Some poet had written that the answer to loneliness is solitude. Was it Marianne Moore, she wondered? No matter, she understood what was meant. I have to find my balance, she thought. Without the distraction of another person's voice, even speaking comfort. Maybe it would be different if they'd had a child. Or even a niece or nephew. End of the line for all of us, she'd think. Then open some book, always fiction or poetry rather than the history, current affairs or science Garson had consumed in great quantities. By midnight, she'd stop reading and walk through the house again, closing windows, putting out lights, patting the various cats as she passed them. One of them, the white-fronted stray who, gaunt and flea-ridden, had appeared one rainy night four years before and remained to become the dominant cat, would invariably lift his head inquiringly. "Yes, Mister," she'd say, "time for bed," and wait while he stood up, arched his back, stretched, and raced ahead of her to the bedroom. Later, pinioned by the four inert cats pressing against her, she'd wake, nudge them with her feet, push at them to re-position herself, grumble "Oh, you cats," and, companioned, fall back asleep.

But days she was not at the hospital, she wearied of her aloneness. One afternoon an old collie ambled from his porch steps to the roadside and stood wagging his tail as she walked by. Maybe I should get a dog, she thought. Then she pictured to herself the small, stiff, mutilated corpses deposited regularly by the cats outside the kitchen door which Garson had always removed before, but now she had to carry off into the woods. No, no more pets.

So she walked alone, even after winter hardened in, cold and windy. In mid-January, the first snow fell. By February, it was deep enough for her to trudge across the blanketed fields on snowshoes and venture into the woods, alone in the landscape except for animal tracks in the snow. Occasionally, she glimpsed a rabbit, a squirrel, or a deer. Once, on her drive home from the hospital, she spotted what she hoped was a turkey vanishing into the woods. Weeks later, as she was on her way to the pond to listen for spring peepers, she came around a blackberry thicket to be stopped abruptly by a wild commotion at her feet. As she froze in place, a huge turkey rose into the air, screeching, flapping and almost grazing Celia's face while, on the ground, a crown of poults flurried off into the bushes. The hen landed on a nearby limb and screamed abuse. Celia retreated to the driveway, thinking, that's where I belong, not where the wild ones are trying to live, meanwhile rejoicing that at least one of each sex had survived. In March, a blizzard kept her indoors but soon a succession of mild days cleared the roads of snow and ice and she was able to walk out again. By late spring, she was again tramping steadily for miles, even on the long, steep hills, her leg muscles toughening and her body, always thin, growing hard and sinewy.

When the spring freshets dried, sometimes she left the roadsides to walk cross-country. But now, remembering the turkeys, she forced herself to watch the ground ahead for movements or signs. In the woods, she practiced gliding smoothly in among the branches and stepping lightly on the dry leaves. Like an Indian, she thought, or a wild creature. One afternoon, she noticed a pile of fresh chips at the base of a dead tree ahead of her. She stopped and listened. Silence, except for the sound of air entering her nostrils. She parted her lips and stood motionless. In a few moments, a huge woodpecker flew in and landed just below an oval hole she now saw halfway up the trunk of the dead tree. As though she were not there, the bird reared back and began hammering. A pileated, she whispered to herself, exulting.

In May, early one morning while she was eating breakfast at the window, she noticed movement at the edge of the meadow. When she focused her binoculars on the spot, she saw it was a doe and two fawns. As she watched, one fawn suddenly stopped feeding, sprang straight upwards and landed stiffly on its thin legs. Then, leaping and landing, its stiff motions resembling those of a rocking horse, it raced along the edge of the meadow. The doe glanced up, its jaws calmly working, flicked its tail, and bent again to the grasses. Oh, Garson, Celia thought, how you would have enjoyed this. After that, most mornings and evenings the same trio came to feed and Celia watched the young ones growing day by day and their dam's rough, grey winter coat turning sleek and brown.

One evening, after darkness blotted out the view from the window, Celia drifted into her studio and studied a large stone Garson had brought home from a quarry months before. For the first time in almost a year, she took up a chisel. "I've begun a new piece," she told Sarah a few nights later. The next Saturday, Sarah appeared and handed Celia a book. The women sat side by side on the couch and looked at the photographs of whitetail deer. After Sarah left, Celia set the book on a shelf. I don't want to sculpt a photograph, she said to herself. Instead she began looking carefully for the living deer on her walks. She learned to recognize their bedding places by the pressed-down foliage; the narrow paths they made in the grasses; the triangular hoofprints they left in soft soil or forest debris; the piles of their dark, pellet droppings; their scrapings on tree bark; the frayed ends of twigs they had nibbled. One afternoon, Celia followed such a trail into a small clearing in the forest. There, a few feet ahead, face to face with Celia, stood a large doe. For a moment, motionless, they both stared at each other. Then the animal turned and pounded off, its tail up, the white underside flashing. Celia let out the breath she'd been holding. We were both curious, she marveled. More curious than frightened. Not enemies; almost like two foreigners, silenced by lack of a common language.

After that encounter, she went eagerly each morning to her studio to work on her deer until lunchtime, when she usually carried her tray out onto the terrace. As she was sitting there one day eating in the sunshine, she gradually became aware of persistent barking in the near distance. I wish they'd stop, she thought. The image of a dog pack running a deer passed though her mind. The fawns. She got up from her lunch, went to the garage and rummaged for the walking staff Garson had cut and polished for her years before. With it in hand, she set out towards the noise.

As she walked, she wondered what she would do if she encountered the dogs. Or came upon a wounded deer. But she kept walking. When she had just reached the edge of the wetland, the barking stopped. She continued to pick her way in. At the pond, she slowly began circling it, looking for tracks in the mud. Suddenly she stopped in midstep. A shiny thing lay at her feet, a steel bowl, about the size of a grapefruit. A heavy chain extended from it to a nearby log. She tapped the point of her staff into the bowl. The device clamped shut. My God, she whispered. She looked around, picked up a stone and knocked at the chain until it broke loose from the log. She lifted the trap. Whoever set this, she thought, had his dogs with him, running free, while he placed the trap. Right on the path where some animal headed for the water would step into it. And be held by the chain. Until when? She remembered reading how animals sometimes gnawed off a leg to escape from a trap. She sat down on the log.

Did inventors really plan these things? And workers in factories sit and assemble them, inspectors examine them, packers carton them? Fool, she answered herself, of course, like guns, bombs, missiles. Suddenly she remembered the Tower of London, she walking with Garson through gallery after gallery lined with glass cases in which, like works of art, axes, swords, fetters, torture racks were displayed. She gazed down at the mechanism dangling from the end of the chain she was holding. Here is where it starts, she thought, the killing. First the innocent animals. No. First the compassion in the human spirit. Then the animals. Then our whole blood-drenched history. Even here, on these quiet acres. Our peaceable kingdom. She stood up.

At the house, she dropped the trap in the driveway, and with a sledgehammer kept smashing at it until she managed to flatten it. As she tossed it into the trash can, she thought, at least that one will never be used again. Then she located the hunting posters they'd had printed years ago and lettered NO TRAPPING across the bottom margin of one of them. As she had often seen Garson do, she nailed the card to a square of plywood and affixed it to a metal stake. Then she walked back to the pond and pounded the stake into the earth at its head. That'll do it, she thought.

And for months, it seemed to. No one tampered with the sign at the pond. She found no more traps, no spent cartridges. Caught no sound or sight of trespassers. But one morning early in September, as she was watering late lettuce seedlings, again she heard a sound of baying. She twisted the hose nozzle shut and listened. Yes, dogs, and not far away, perhaps the hayfield. She got the same walking stick and started towards the noise. As she approached the field, she saw them, four, possibly five, dogs. They were jumping, twisting in the air, tumbling back over each other. She tried to walk faster.

Suddenly, the dogs stood motionless. Four, she could see clearly, all with their heads lifted, until, as to a signal she could not hear, three of them bounded off. The fourth remained and nuzzled something on the ground before he, too, streaked across the field, hurdled the stone wall and disappeared into the brush. Celia kept walking, her gaze fixed on the spot they'd been. Closer, she saw something white on the ground. Oh, no, she whispered and began to run. It was Mister, lying on his side, his eyes closed. Clumps of his white fur were clinging to the beaten-down grasses around him. Celia lifted the limp body. She thought she detected a faint vibration. Half-running, half-walking, she carried the cat across the field and up the driveway. At the car, she laid him on the seat and raced to the house for her keys. Before she started the motor, she placed her sweater around the unconscious cat. Then she backed and turned the car and, wheels screeching, sped downhill.

When she burst into the veterinarian's office, all she could manage was a hoarse "Please." The receptionist rose from her desk at once and led her to the inner room. The doctor appeared, leaned over Mister. Almost immediately, he straightened and pulled the stethoscope from his ears. "He's gone, Mrs. Hendricks," he said. Celia nodded, her throat full, and gathered up the body.

At home, she got a shovel and near a lilac bush under which Mister had often napped on hot summer afternoons, she began digging. Why am I doing this, she asked herself? Mister no longer exists. As Garson no longer exists. But she kept digging until she struck a rock, which she pried loose with the point of the shovel. Stiffly, she walked to the car, returned with the cat's body, wrapped in her sweater, laid it into the hole, replaced the soil and rolled the rock over the spot. Then she went to the house, washed her hands and telephoned for her neighbor's teenage son to come work with her. While she waited for him, she assembled nails and hammers and lettered NO TRAPPING on all the remaining posters.

As soon as the Johnson car stopped in the driveway, Celia began speaking. "One of my cats," she said, then stopped. "Tom," she began again, "four dogs running loose in the hayfield this morning killed my cat. The white cat, who used to wander all over."

"I'm sorry to hear it," the man said. Then he added, "I know the cats mean a lot to you. And to Mr. Hendricks they did, too."

"Yes," Celia said and blinked, thinking of that rainy night Garson had heard a noise outside, slid open the terrace door, looked down at the drenched, square-jowled, battered tomcat and said, "Well, Mister, come in." She started speaking again, "Tom, I think the dogs that killed my cat belong to the same person who set the trap. I told you about that, didn't I? Anyway, someone's wandering around here, with traps and dogs, ignoring the no-trespassing signs. Maybe most of them have been torn away by now. That's why I need Kenny, to help me re-post. Before the next hunting season starts. Tom, you know my place. Where do you think they're coming in?"

Tom pointed uphill. "Probably up there. The place next to yours, Cooper's, the man from New Jersey, it's not posted. Everybody hunts up there. Some of them probably climb over the wall onto your land and follow the trail down the woods to the pond, through the meadows, behind the pines. You'd never see them from the house."

"Thanks, Tom, we'll start there." She gathered the supplies, then turned back to the car. "Tom, I know you don't feel the way I do about hunting but I appreciate your help." "Mrs. Hendricks," Tom answered, "you pay your taxes and have the right to keep anyone off you want. Kenny's glad for the job." Then he nodded and drove off while Celia followed the boy uphill.

At the back line, leapfrogging each other, Celia and Kenny nailed signs to trees ten feet or so apart. Then they worked down through the forest, behind the meadows, into the ravine, along the stream and, in twilight, back up along the south line, completing the wide circle of the acreage almost in the dark. Then Celia drove Kenny home. When she returned, she fed the three cats, avoiding the corner where Mister's plate stood clean and empty. Then, not hungry and shaky with fatigue, she undressed, fell into bed and dropped off to sleep instantly.

Nighttimes after that, she'd walk quickly down the corridor where that squarish, white-and-tabby cat used to bound ahead, thinking, more absence in the house. More corners empty where life used to be.

Daytimes, too restless to work in the studio, when she did not go to the hospital, she stayed outdoors most of the time, keeping to the back roads again. As a large station wagon drove by her one October afternoon, she noticed three men in the front seat and five others in the back, all wearing hunters' heavy, bright clothing and visored caps, and with their rifles piled against the rear window. A few days later, on a rutted, almost impassable road, a man appeared over a rise ahead, his orange coveralls luminescent even at a distance. He was walking slowly, his head turned towards the woods, a rifle cradled in one arm. As they came abreast of each other, he looked towards Celia but, although she saw the smile starting on his lips, she glanced aside and passed him silently. Later, when she stopped to pay Tom for mowing the meadow, she asked him, "Why am I meeting hunters so early this year?"

"I guess, varmints," he said. Anger flashed through Celia. An ugly name justifies the killing, she thought. But Tom was still talking, "Getting ready for deer. Bumper crop this year, game warden says. Expecting hunters from all over. The county can use the business."

Celia thought as she walked home, yes, it was true. They needed the business. Big families, small incomes, most of the locals. And she, with her comfortable pension, her property paid up, what could she say? What had she ever been able to say? Like that time years ago, she had been following Tom's mother, helping her gather eggs from the hens' nests in the barn and suddenly had almost collided with the carcass of a large animal hanging from one of the beams, a deer, its body hacked open. Mrs. Johnson turned at what must have been Celia's audible gasp and said, gently but with assurance, "The Bible tells us, human beings have dominion over other creatures of the earth." Staring into the cave of scarlet, shiny flesh, Celia had countered hotly, "The Bible also says, Thou shalt not kill." That night she told Garson she would never eat meat again. "Maybe you're so sensitive about animals," he teased her, "because you were one in a former life." "Or will be," she remembered answering, "and want to defend myself while I still have words."

But what good were words between her and the man who set the trap? The hunters she met on the roads? Even Tom. He was a good man, she knew that, fair in his dealings, loving to his family, helpful as a neighbor. Even kind to his cows and chickens. Up to the day he slaughtered them. But that's their food, she argued to herself, the farm animals he slaughters and the wild ones he hunts. And the red fox? The one he told her he'd seen outside his barn, and later baited, and shot? And had had mounted to display on his mantelpiece? Perhaps the same fox Garson and she used to watch trotting sometimes across their fields. She sighed and bowed her head. I don't eat meat, she thought, as she looked down at her moving feet, but I wear leather boots. She sighed again, wondering, is it possible to be human without complicity? Snatches of a poem she had once read teased at her mind as she walked. At home, she dropped her jacket on a chair, and rummaged among her books until, in an anthology, she found a long poem by a Finnish poet, a woman she had never read elsewhere, Eeva-Liisa Manner. The passage she had tried to remember was at the end:

> *Oh darkness that swallows everything; the cries for*
> *   help of the animals*
> *that drag themselves slowly through the creation;*
> *what God created this unmercy? was it God?*
> *what God created these inhumans? was it Satan?*
> *men, greedy of mercy, cruel towards animals,*
> *great in reason, small in mind.*
>
> *Pray for the animals, you that pray,*
> *you that beg for mercy, for success and for peace,*
> *the immanent spirit has also been poured into them,*
> *they are also souled, more complete than you,*
> *and clear, brave, beautiful;*
> *and if we begin from the beginning, who knows,*
> *we shall have to share also these sufferings,*
> *simpler, more severe, more unlimited than ours.*

She was reading through the whole poem again when the phone rang. It was her sister-in-law. "Sarah," Celia said at once, "Tom Johnson tells me this is going to be the heaviest hunting season in years. After Mister, I'm afraid for the cats. May I bring them to you? Your backyard is safer than here." So a few days later, Celia delivered the cats, stayed through the weekend, and returned to her own house the evening before the season opened. With no cats leading her kitchenwards, she skipped her own dinner and instead, got her binoculars, and went to look at the sky. As she stepped outside the front door and looked up, she gasped. In the moonless, cloudless sky, Orion stretched across the blue-blackness, even the dim stars of its dagger distinct. She stepped away from the house, onto the lawn and, heading back, found the stars she knew and whispered their names aloud: Rigel, Betelgeuse, Castor, Pollux, Alderbaran. She focused the binoculars on the Pleiades and counted its six sparkling jewels. What a night, she thought. And what a fine day it would be tomorrow. Then she remembered the deer. She lowered the binoculars. Suddenly, the splendor was indifferent, chilling. She went inside.

Whether the first shot woke her or whether it was the first shot she heard after waking, she was not sure. But as she opened her eyes to the pre-dawn dimness, she thought, whoever fired is certainly pushing the legal definition of daylight hours. Maybe it was Tom or some other local, making sure of his deer before the hunters arrived. Barefooted, she went to the living room window. There they were, the five regulars, browsing, ghostly in the halflight. Oh, stay here, she thought.

The next morning all five were there again, the doe in the near corner with her fawns, now almost as large as their mother. The third morning, Celia rose late, saw no deer. The fourth was a Saturday. After breakfast, she urged herself into the studio, determined that today she would achieve the look of sinewy slenderness she wanted in her stone creature's flanks and legs, and somehow make its hooves look both dainty and strong as steel. For hours, she was unaware of anything outside the studio until an interval of particularly loud, prolonged firing made her put down her tools and go to the window. At first, she saw nothing unusual. Then, soundlessly, two deer stepped side by side up from the ravine, and stopped on the terrace. A moment later, singly and in pairs others rose into view, stopped and all crowded close together. Celia counted eleven deer, more than she'd ever seen so near the house or to each other. One animal turned its head and Celia looked directly into its large, expressionless eyes. Then the animals began to move, awkwardly at first, bumping into each other, until they fanned out across the hillside and streamed upwards towards the woods with their customary grace.

Those were the last deer she saw for weeks. Alive, that is. Dead ones, she saw every day she drove out. On the roofs of passing cars. Hanging stiffly from the porch beams of sportsmen's camps or outside the work sheds of deer butchers who had set up business along the highways. One afternoon, as she was headed home on an unfamiliar route, Celia drove past a sign, Deer Check Station. A few hundred feet later was an access road, then a large parking area crowded with waiting passenger cars, vans, station wagons and pickup trucks. Most of the doors were open. The drivers, dressed in bulky, bright hunting uniforms, stood outside their vehicles, talking and laughing while over their heads the dead deer lay on their sides, one, sometimes two, on each cartop, the necks frozen backwards, the eyes still open, white tags fluttering from the legs. My God, Celia whispered to herself.

Thereafter, she took another route. When she could, she abstained from driving; when she couldn't, she tried averting her eyes from oncoming vehicles to avoid the sight of the corpses. She also drove apprehensively, constantly watching the roadsides for movement and snapping on her high beam whenever she could, with the hope of warning animals away, feeling in herself the exhaustion and confusion they must be feeling, driven day after day from their regular bedding places and food and water trails. Nevertheless, one dark November afternoon, the season in its third week, she had barely a second's warning as a deer bounded out of the woods, across the shoulder and onto the highway just ahead. She slammed the brake, swung the wheel and swerved into the empty oncoming lane, yet the animal smashed into the side of her car and was flung to the shoulder of the road, where it lay, its legs thrashing. By the time Celia stopped, and burst open her door, the animal was getting to its feet. Shakily at first, then gradually trotting, it disappeared among the trees. Maybe, Celia thought, and the word was fervent as a prayer, maybe it was only shocked. But she could still feel the sickening impact. What to do? Get Tom. Then they could try to track the deer. If they found it injured, he could shoot it. Her stomach clenched. Someone behind started honking. She got back into the car, pulled it off the road, stopped again and slowly, searching for signs on the ground, walked across the shoulder, into the woods. Nothing. No blood, no sound.

She drove home, phoned the game warden. "We'll look

around," he said, his tone neutral. But what could he do? What had she done? That night, sleepless, she brooded into the darkness. Maybe she should give up the car. But without a car, how could she go on living here? Maybe she should move, go back to the city. No animals there to injure. Except stray cats. She turned to her other side. Leave this house, this land? Where, as long as she lived, Garson also lived? All those years of our talking, she thought, and I can't remember what we said about one of us dying first. And leaving the other one alone. In this solitude, this wildness we chose. Trying to defend that choice, the life we tried to make. Maybe ridiculous from the start.

Celia sighed, felt a dry ache in her throat. She tried swallowing it away, then rose and stumbled into the kitchen. She warmed some milk, drank it, lay down again. When she closed her eyes, she saw the deer rising one after the other onto the ledge, their huge, blank eyes gazing into hers. She got up again, swallowed two aspirin. Found a sweater of Garson's, pulled it on over her pajamas and, comforted, fell asleep. Woke an hour later, her face burning.

So it went, all night, the next day. Once she dreamed she heard Garson groaning alongside and woke groping for him in the empty bed. Another time, she thought she heard the telephone ringing but before it stopped, she sank back into her murky sleep until a convulsion jolted her awake. It was the trap; she had dreamed the trap had wrenched her arm. She turned her head towards the windows. Blue sky. Are the fawns still alive, she wondered. Tears stung at her inflamed eyelids but her arm was too tired to wipe them away.

The next time she woke, the room was dark. She got up, her dizziness gone, went to the kitchen, filled the kettle, spooned oatmeal into a saucepan, tea into the pot. While she waited for the water to boil, she quartered an orange and thirstily sucked at the fruit. The clock said one-thirty. But which night? The afternoon she hit the deer, she'd been driving home from the hospital. Thursday. That night she got sick. And the next day, yesterday, Friday. So now it was Saturday. The weekend. The closing weekend. The hunters' last chance. She ate her oatmeal, drank the tea, refilled the cup and carried it with her back to bed. Once there, suddenly exhausted again, she set the cup on the night table and fell asleep immediately.

The next time she opened her eyes, she came awake at once, her head clear, her mind made up. She glanced at the clock. Six-twenty. She swung out of bed, went to the bathroom, showered away the last of her stiffness.

Wrapped in a towel, she stood at her open closet, slid the clothes along the rod, lifted out a pair of chino slacks, a tan pullover, a hip-length brown jacket. After she dressed, she brushed out her long hair, and tied it back with a light scarf. In the entry, she drew on woolen socks and laced up her hiking boots. She chose a brown knitted cap from the hatrack, pulled it down over her ears, then freed her ponytail so that it hung down her back.

Outside, the air was cold and windless and the sky was lightening. Part way up the path, she stopped and turned. I left the bedroom light on, she thought. No matter. Her gaze followed the lines of the house. How snug it sat on its stone terraces. We did a good job, my darling, she thought, then turned back to the hill.

As she climbed, strength flowed into her legs. Rhythmically, gracefully, she swung upwards, slipping among the brambles, into the forest, through the church clearing without pausing and upwards again between the columnar beeches. Bluejays were screaming over her head, but she ignored them, her gaze on the rising trail of faint, triangular indentations and occasional piles of dark pellets in the duff.

She was approaching the stone wall when she heard the first shot. Her pace remained steady although her heart began to thud. Now she saw the posters gleaming against the dark trunks of the trees ahead. At the boundary wall, lightly grasping an overhanging branch, she stepped, stone to stone, up to the top and down on the other side.

Here she paused briefly and scanned the forest floor. A second shot cracked the silence, echoed through the woods. Then another, and another, but she paid them no more attention now than she did the squawking jays. In a moment, she began moving again on the narrow trail that wound through ferny ground cover, into a grassy area where deer had bedded recently, then again upwards, on thin, rocky soil; she following, climbing lightly, noiselessly, towards the high meadows, her clothes snug on her slender sinewy body, the long coil of her white hair streaming down her back, bounding gently, the light ends of her white scarf fluttering.

Adele Bowers

My father was fifty when I was born, a very old fifty. Life had been very harsh. In Rumania, he was apprenticed at the age of eleven to live with the family of a man who ran a hardware business. When he came to New York, he opened a hardware store on the Bowery, a long, dark place with the smell of rust and oil in the air. I hated to hear my father's stories because they were so sad, and I hated to hear my mother's stories because I was convinced she was pretending that she had been rich and beautiful and that everyone adored her; they were somehow against my father. I had a brother, twenty-five years older, who had left home before I was born and actually not communicated with my parents. My mother's favorite child was the boy who had gone away, and he had gone away not because of her, but because of my father. I looked like my father and it was conveyed to me that the beauty of my family was on my mother's side. In every respect I didn't have my mother's approval.

Rumanian was my first language. I have a very early memory of one of the first times that my mother permitted me to go out and play by myself. I was on the stoop of our building, surrounded by a ring of children who were laughing and telling me to "say it again" – my name in Rumanian. I backed up against the door of the building and just got deeper and deeper into the corner; I wouldn't say a word. And then someone opened the door and I ran up to my apartment. I know, partly from memory and partly from being told by my parents, that I came in and said, "I am not going to speak Rumanian anymore." Almost the next day I was speaking English.

I was a very early and ardent reader; books and stories fascinated me. I would bring new schoolbooks home and try not to read them right away, because then class would be dull. But I couldn't resist; I would read them all immediately. My whole feeling about books was born of my dependence on literature as a source of information about the world. I didn't get much from my parents; for various reasons they were just out of things. They were Rumanians and there weren't that many Rumanians in New York. Neither of them had a family, they had very few friends and they weren't close to their neighbors. They weren't particularly religious, so they weren't connected to a synagogue. Literature was where I learned about families and social life and a whole other way of life.

Very early I started to try to imitate what I was reading. The stories I wrote in elementary school were sentimental and about things I really didn't know, but I was proud of them. I remember one was about a religious conversion but my family was not religious, I knew very little about religion – I wasn't sure I had it right. I kept notebooks, ruled, with thin red crumbly covers, the inexpensive ones, and in them I would make lists of all the books I read and write little book reviews. And I would write little scenes of my own. I carried those notebooks around for a long time and eventually lost them.

But most of my writing was connected with school. The compositions intrigued me and I would do a lot with those. I thought writing had to be very fancy and elaborate; I tried to use long words. Sometimes I misused a word and would be told I misused it. And then I was mortified. I remember talking to a teacher and using the word "incorrigible." I noticed this flicker of amusement passing over her face and then being suppressed, and I realized I had said something wrong. I knew how to use the dictionary and I found out I had mispronounced it. Well, that paralyzed me – I was really terrified after that.

When I was eleven, we moved to East Harlem which at that time was an Italian neighborhood, immigrants whose children were first-generation Americans. I went to a really rotten school, old, decaying. Most of the students were kids who weren't encouraged to do well in school. I was one of the small group who did well in English. English was my life and the library was my companionship – I treasured every little word of praise from a teacher, every comment. Once, in junior high school, the English teacher wrote on a paper, "You write very well and if you work at it, you may become a writer, a real writer." I couldn't believe that. I showed it to my mother and she was very annoyed with it. She thought I ought to be a teacher and that is *all* I ought to do and any idea I had of writing was preposterous. My father wasn't that interested. I would show him my paper if I had a good mark and he would say, "Very nice." But he was tired, he was beaten down, his world was a very narrow place, he didn't know what I was talking about. The biggest fear they had was poverty; they thought this encouragement was turning my thoughts to disastrous avenues. So I became very secretive about my writing.

In junior high school, I wrote stories, poems and articles – pompous solemn articles that said practically nothing. I became the editor of the school magazine. The faculty advisor, who was my adored biology teacher, would say, "You come here after school and work on your compositions. If you want to write stories or work on a poem for the magazine you can do it here." "Here" was her classroom and storeroom of lab supplies and microscopes. She would be in the storeroom and I in the classroom. Sometimes she'd invite me to her apartment on Central Park West and make tea for me, and we would sit in her living room overlooking the park. I thought that was elegance, the very greatest. I don't know whether my mother went to my school and complained that this teacher was keeping me after school too much or what happened, but real opposition to my relationship with her developed. The school principal even became involved in it. It is funny how everything connected with writing got spoiled for me.

In high school in Harlem, I was again part of an elite of good students. A school friend lived on Fifth Avenue in the nineties and visiting her, I saw how people lived a totally different world. I remember telling her mother that I wanted to be a writer and she said, very kindly, "I am sure you can be anything you want to be because you are a very bright child." I was astounded at the different attitude. I treasured that comment but it wasn't enough to outweigh the rest of my life. I felt then and for a long time afterward that some curse had been put on me by my parents, that they had brainwashed me. That wasn't a word we used at that time, but that was really the way I felt. I was fearful of my own impulse.

Because I adored my teacher I became a super biology student. Yet I got a rotten mark on the Regents. Even though I didn't really like the subject, when I was admitted into Hunter College, which was the only college I had any hope of going to, I chose it as a major with an allied science as a minor. My first two years were a disaster because of all that damned science. The dean would regularly summon me to his office and say, "We cannot understand how someone in the 99th percentile performs in the lowest percentile permitted in college." My poor marks were a black cloud over my head for my first three years. Then I changed to an English major and did much better. By then my father had died and my mother and I were trying to run his business because it was our only hope for any income. I thought of myself as destined someday to be a writer, but it was nothing I even dared to think of doing when I got out of college. I took a lot of education courses and tried to prepare myself for a teaching career.

In my senior year when I was associate editor of the literary magazine, I wrote a very left-wing story called "And To Take Arms." This was during a period of idealistic political ferment and was about a young girl who worked in Macy's and hated it and had a terrible life. The story ends with her seeing that the way out is radical political effort. It was a convincing picture of an adolescent in a difficult period in the world – for most students, there were no jobs, little money, not much future. Suddenly I was a three-day wonder in the college. Outwardly I remained calm and dignified as people came up to me in the hall and said, "We loved your story." I'd say, "Thank you very much" and act very cool about the whole thing but every opportunity I got, I would sneak off somewhere and reread the story. I couldn't believe I had written it. For once I didn't feel that I had missed or that the subject was something I didn't know about. I felt then that I had a glimpse of what being a writer meant.

I graduated from college in 1936, right in the teeth of the depression. Then came the grim business of trying to find a job, hanging around employment agencies. I took the exam for teaching English and became a substitute high school English teacher. I didn't like teaching. Because of my love of literature, books, magazines, writing, editing, I wanted to go into publishing.

I got married in 1941. My husband was somewhat younger than I and although he hadn't finished college, we left New York City. I became pregnant, had a child, he was drafted. I had to go back to work; she went into a war nursery. I never went back to teaching. We lived out of New York for about four or five years, in Rochester, Detroit, Chicago. I worked on a few newspapers, writing community news, trying to write stories when I could, but very unsatisfied with what I was doing. I was trying to write about women whose husbands were drafted, women bringing up children alone, but I myself was alone with a very young child and we didn't have much money. I spent a lot of time trying to save money, walking around to look for cheap food, moving to shared apartments where I became the chief housekeeper, collecting the others' ration coupons and doing all the shopping and cooking.

When we came back to New York, I got a job as copywriter in the education department of Popular Science Publishing Company. Later I moved to the advertising department, then started wooing the head of the book department until I got myself a copywriting job there. When my boss died suddenly, they gave me his job of managing mail-order selling of books and subscriptions. When the Board of Directors told us to start a book club, that became my project. We created the Outdoor Life Book Club, the Popular Science Book Club, a Nature Book Club and a Women's Crafts Book Club. I was head of that operation which became bigger and bigger as the clubs grew, involving many millions of dollars a year.

Opportunities arose for me without a fight. The company management let me try new projects. I'd work very hard and be successful enough for them to let me rise as the job grew. I was the only woman executive in my company. The job was very challenging and I enjoyed it, but it took all my time, all my thinking. Business doesn't pay large salaries and give you positions of power lightly – they want your heart's blood and nothing less. And that is the way I worked. It was so beguiling that I couldn't think of anything else. I started to work for that company in the late 1940's and I left in 1980.

.   .   .

Somewhere in the 1950's, when we were both beginning to do better and my job hadn't yet become as complex and interesting as it did later, I remember saying to my husband, "How would it be if I quit my job now that you are doing better and really gave myself a couple of years to just see whether I could do anything with writing?" He said, "Well, we'll think about it," but never mentioned it again. I brought it up once or twice more, then I realized that it was not going to happen. Plus there was so much trouble in the marriage, I forgot about writing. When the marriage finally broke up in 1959, I went into a five-year profound depression. I tried to write during that time, to fictionalize my own experience, but I couldn't convert it into a believable story. I would cheapen my material, sentimentalize it, trying to prove my case, making the character an object of pity and reproach. As raw as my feelings were, it was my respect for literature that made me realize that there was something wrong there, the character wasn't true. But it was an attempt to console myself, and it helped me even though nothing very good came out of it.

Around that time, I did take a little workshop that was given in the Village by a woman writer. When a marriage breaks up, you are left with a lot of hours that were previously filled with household tasks, angers, fights. All of a sudden there is all this empty time – I was terrified of it. I was looking for help, for consolation, for distraction. She read some of my work and said, "No one in this group seems to be able to catch feelings the way you can." I thought, Well, that is something. I stayed with the workshop for perhaps a year, during which my job began to take off and some of the satisfaction I had been groping for began to come out of the job. Again the writing began to fade away. Jobs are easier than writing – you go to the office and work is waiting on your desk. You don't have to be your own starter.

After that, sometime in the 1960's, when my job got under control, no longer so demanding, I began to write poetry. I registered for Kenneth Koch's workshop at the New School. He was fantastic. One of his first assignments was to choose one of three contemporary American poets he selected, take his collected poems somewhere where you could be alone with it for the entire weekend. You were not to talk to anyone or use the telephone or go anywhere, but just read the poems, Friday, Saturday, Sunday morning. On Sunday afternoon you were to put the book aside and write a poem. I went with William Carlos Williams' poetry to a little cabin in Connecticut I had bought with my husband. Friday, I spent the whole evening reading; all day Saturday and Sunday morning I went for walks, came back and read. I talked to nobody. Then I wrote a little poem about dogwood trees. Somehow it reflected that conversational, unadorned tone of Williams, though without any of his great sudden flashes of language. The experience was a revelation for me.

Koch was very tough. If you wrote a poem that was ironic, he would say, "I don't want any irony in this class, I don't want any phony humor, none of that crap." And you sort of knew what he meant. Someone wrote a poem in which there were gray seagulls. And he said, "Gray! I never want to see that word again in this class. Gray is a dead word, especially gray seagulls. I want new things. If you can't come up with the right adjective, forget the adjective, I want a verb that says something, none of this dead language." I understood everything he said. I wished someone had said that to me twenty years earlier. My language freshened and loosened up during that period and for quite a while afterward.

I never even thought to do fiction during those years. I wrote poetry a little bit in the late 1960's and early 1970's, in periods of intense emotion of one sort or another. If I was in love, for example, I would drop into poetry. I would wake up in the morning with poems going through my head and on the way to work I would scratch them out on the bus, or if I was walking, I would stop and lean against a building. Then I would hit my office and within ten minutes the clatter of business drove the poetry away. At night I would try, but gradually the immediacy of poetry faded away. I lost the sense and grasp of it. Writing advertising copy is a different way of using language. I found it almost impossible to go from one to the other.

Then one day in January, 1979, I told the president and corporate vice president of my company, who were taking me to lunch, that I wanted to leave at the end of that year. I hadn't planned to do it; like many big decisions, I seemed to make it without thinking. During the course of that year, I kept getting small anxiety attacks. I remember walking on Madison Avenue one lunchtime, part of the bustle; I was going to meet people, everything was exciting. Suddenly I said to myself, Where will I be next year this time? I had to lean against the building until my dizziness passed. I thought, My God what have I done, what am I going to do? By now I was married again. I asked my husband, "What the hell am I going to do when I retire?"

In the month of November, I saw an ad for an intensive weekend writing workshop that New York University was sponsoring. I thought, What the hell, I can at least see what it is like. At the beginning of the workshop one of the leaders said, "I want you to write ten things you are afraid of, that keep you from writing." I don't know whether I got to ten, but the things I wrote were interesting. For example, embarrassment. Grace Paley is a very good friend of mine, a marvelous friend to me, the warmest, most lovely woman. Knowing Grace, how can I, inept, inexperienced, feeble, think of doing this? I wrote various things like that. Like the shame of being inadequate. I came from a job where I was an executive, people looked up to me, young women in the company came and said, "You are my role model" – how could I be a beginner again?

Then the workshop leaders sent everyone off in little groups to read their work. Mine was much better than the others. People in my little group said, "You must be a writer" and I said, "No, I really am not." One guy cornered me afterwards and said, "But you *have* been writing haven't you?" And I said, "No, not for a long time." And he said, "Well, something has been going on underneath because yours is not the work of a beginning writer."

The story I wrote in the workshop was much better than my earlier sporadic attempts. It had more sureness, more knowledge of the structure and tension of a story; it was more stripped and unadorned than my fiction used to be. The poetry writing was helping the prose. I was pleased that, without having written fiction for almost twenty years, there had been a change. True, I had been thinking, making little notes for stories I might some day write. I realized that the process can go on underneath.

So I said to myself, Maybe it isn't too late. I decided I would not pay any attention to age, to the unseemliness of a gray-haired woman taking a workshop, a woman retired from a whole professional career acting like a young beginner. Well, I decided, that was the way it was, that had to be the way I did it. I kept my city apartment and told my husband, who was going to want to live in the country, that I would stay in the city during the week. It wasn't what he had expected or wanted, but ours is a marriage that profits from time apart. I think he now recognizes that too.

I read some books on writing. One of them, mentioned at the workshop, was Peter Elbow's, *Writing Without Teachers,* in which he suggests very specific things, like free writing. Just write freely for ten minutes, don't censor yourself, don't even reread it, the point being to loosen up. I decided that I was going to sit down every morning and if I couldn't do anything else, I was going to do one of Peter Elbow's free writings. I did that for maybe two or three months, every day. And then I said to myself, This isn't necessary. I don't really need to free up. I can put words together.

The first few years I tried to suspend judgment on my work. I said to myself, I am like a beginning piano student, I am playing scales and one doesn't judge scales too harshly. I am not interested in publishing. I made a career, I got my approval; that is not what I am after. In two or three seasons I wrote about ten stories, my kind of exercise stories. One came off very well. I showed it to a friend of mine who was an editor and she gave it to the fiction editor of a new magazine called *Prime Time,* a sophisticated magazine for the fifty-plus group. It was published in that magazine in 1981.

At first I had trouble with discipline, constantly fighting against feeling, What does it really matter, why am I doing this. It wasn't only that I didn't think the writing was good enough – that is a constant struggle – but I began to feel that, to be a writer, you have to have a lot of hope for life and the world. I find the world pretty black and hopeless. I have gone from early political activism to total withdrawal – I find it a traumatic experience to look at the front page of the *New York Times*. My fears, my lack of confidence underneath my apparent confidence, my pessimism operate against writing. I have to push all that aside to write.

That period when I would finish one story, put it away and another one would come to me, came to an end. I made a lot of starts that wouldn't develop and I began to run into trouble. At the end of one summer when I couldn't get started again, I complained to a friend of mine and she said, "There's a women's writing group starting a workshop in the Village, why don't you come with me?" The leader was a wonderful young woman named Linsey Abrams who teaches at Sarah Lawrence, a novelist, very enthusiastic, very kind. Many of the women in the group were young, some of them quite talented. I brought in some of the stories I had been writing and read them aloud. The reactions got me back to a writing routine. At the end of that workshop some of the people suggested we continue as a support group. We have done that – we meet once every couple of weeks in the Village. I don't think I will ever take another workshop; I don't need it now. But I like to read to the support group. Although I read aloud to myself when I am working, I hear it differently when I read to a group.

I also get help from an editor friend, not a writer at all but a very close reader. When I feel something is good and I have taken it almost as far as I can, I show it to her. Her cogent comments are usually constructive and start me thinking. For example, in one story she just put her finger on a spot about a page before where I'd ended the story and said, "You don't need anything else." I took the story back, read it and saw she was 100 percent right."

. . .

When the support group began to talk about sending things out, I looked into the small magazines, got a subscription to *Coda* and started sending some of my stories. I sent "The Hunting Season" to about six places. It kept coming back with good comments and I kept reworking it. I probably should have sent the revised version back to *New England Review* which had liked· it very much, but when *Creeping Bent* took it, even though it was a small magazine, I was very happy. I wanted that story to be published. I have had several other stories and poems published, most recently in *Sunrust* and *Katskill Life*.

I keep telling my group that writers who want to be published have to be persistent. I've learned not to be bothered by rejections. A good friend has had stories published in the *New Yorker*, *Esquire* and other prestigious magazines and has won awards, yet she gets the same rejection slips I get, the same lack of comment that anyone else gets. So much of acceptance is accident – a story has to please a particular editor at a particular time. You have to keep submitting and hope for that accident. But trying to be published is a tedious business. I truly mean it when I say that publication isn't as important to me at this point in my life as the feeling that maybe what I am working on is good. I would love to have the sense that I know what I am doing and I could call upon it and get it working as a constant.

. . .

As far as routine is concerned, I am not a writer who can sit and write for hours. I usually write in the morning, but not exclusively. I think the books on writing that advise you to write in the morning when you are in touch with your subconscious or unconscious are right, although I have to go for a walk before I sit down at my desk. I don't write much in the summer. I stay in the country as a gardener, a subsistence farmer, an outdoor person. The first couple of summers I tried very hard to write, but in the country you have to work in the garden in the cool of the morning. So I just decided that I would have this part-time, winter writing life.

I am a compulsive rewriter. I almost can't get through a

page without starting to rewrite; unless the beginning is right, I can't go on. I tighten, cut, try to get it to flow more smoothly. After I have gone through that process and maybe carried it from beginning to end somehow, I begin to try to work with scenes. Although my tendency is to prune and shorten, the real rewriting that I need is to enrich. I want it stripped and I want it bare, yet there has to be enough. Sometimes, I let myself off too easy. There were portions of "The Hunting Season" that caused me intense pain – for example, when she hits the deer with the car. I didn't want to have that happen off-stage, but I didn't have it in the story for a long time because I couldn't bear to deal with it. I have to force myself to write at that intensity. I actually feel sick to my stomach sometimes because I don't want to confront, I don't want to look for meaning, I don't want to face hard truths, I want to turn away. Sometimes I play solitary scrabble for two hours, one hand against the other, until I get disgusted at my waste of time.

I have trouble objectifying, putting the distance between myself and my own experience that art requires, extracting from the mass of my own experience the moments, the incidents that become the story. I have written several stories from a male point of view. A couple of times I have written with one point of view and changed the whole story around to the other character's point of view, trying to get a tone I can carry through that sounds right. Usually I am sympathetic to my characters, but I play with the idea of writing from the inside of a despicable character. I want to write a story about a marriage breaking up and the man really being rotten, as I feel men sometimes are, and write it from the man's point of view. I haven't done it yet, but it comes and goes through my mind that penetrating that character would force me to be objective.

Sometimes I consciously try to imitate something I have read. For example while I was struggling with a story and couldn't get the tone, I read a story by Edna O'Brien in the *New Yorker* which had absolutely nothing to do with mine, but I loved the tone. I said to myself, I am a learner, I am going to copy the masters. I placed the Edna O'Brien story alongside mine as though I were copying it. Something in that story gave me the tone I wanted, though my story had nothing to do with hers. That's how Koch's poetry exercise worked – you got into a mode. Art grows from art.

I almost always have a model for characters. I find it much easier to get the tone if I have a real person in mind, although the story is not necessarily that person's story. The model for the character in "The Hunting Season" was an actual woman I know, though she doesn't have the character's life, ideas or feelings. The real woman gave me the start. But then of course, the feelings and thoughts of the story character became closer to me than to the memory of the real model.

.   .   .

When younger people tell me that they want to write, I urge them to structure their lives so they can be writers as soon as possible. Perhaps not much is lost by postponing, perhaps it is possible to pick up at any point and reclaim early talent, but I don't think anything is gained. If I could live a second life, I think I would make much more of an effort to have a half-time job and try to be a writer. I certainly have not altered my feeling that that is what I want most to be able to be. I wish I had seen my life that way earlier, if only because I think younger people, not knowing as much greediness, as much tragedy as happens in a lifetime, are more hopeful, take more chances. On the other hand, I tend to be very optimistic about aging in general. I think it is overrated as a destructive force. I think people tend to let themselves off too easily on the grounds that they are getting old. I don't think the mind deteriorates or the memory or even the body all that much if you don't let it. The important thing is to keep words flowing, coming, to keep the energy up. Writing comes with the doing. When I am not writing or working on something, I feel rotten, I feel a sense of something missing in my life, I feel closed in, as if my mind isn't working and everything is sluggish and inoperative. I don't like that feeling.

Why do I write? I had a friend who answered that question in a way that has always stayed in my mind: I have to give something back. Literature was really life for me, my entrance to the world, my foundation in life. It set the world straight for me. And now I come to that time when I have to return something to the stream. I have to take the final test: okay, now you have got all this, you do a little bit of it. And also one has to have some work in the world. I don't want a job, I don't want another career, I don't need to make a living, fortunately. I did that and I am able to live on what I made, so I don't have to work to earn. This is the work I choose to do at this time with whatever energy and mind I have.

And also I write because it is a way of making sense of experience. It is an amazing organizer of experience and fact and observation. I have a great sense of order in life generally – I am neat, I like to organize things. Writing fiction is, in all its ambiguity and all its suggestiveness and free form, a way to impose an order on experience, although consciously I am not doing it for that reason. I think some of the pleasure that comes from writing, when it works right, is that somehow in that mysterious and elusive series of words there is some kind of shape, there is some sort of meaning.

Given that I have been doing this now for six years, I wish I had gotten farther, but that is the way it is. Whoever said life is short and art is long was dead right. Art certainly is long. It takes a long, long time to create a little bit. I fight the idea that one loses energy as one gets along in years. I am going to be easy on myself in the sense of not asking myself the big questions, Is this really worth it, is this really good? I try not to compare myself with accomplished writers of great talent or with some abstraction or say, Where do I dare? I do the best I can.

Sadie Wernick Hurwitz

One Minute Play
about an Old Woman Discarding

Act 1 -
Scene 1

more of his old business papers
and still unexpired credit cards

and finding among them his new 1979
driver's license, good for another four years

She drops it in the rubbish basket where
it falls stubbornly face upward as if she'd laid

it there, upon a crumpled PAID
mortuary bill.

Observing that it was a
really nice picture of him, she lifts it

out of the trash and puts it back
into the "gold box." Then one-by-one

she breaks the credit cards and
mutters reverently *damn*

Curtain

Duet

Why I've got to move out	*Maladie a deux*
She has her antennae up	I have my antennae up
and she's on fine tune	and I'm on fine tune
and there's nothing – nothing	and there's nothing – nothing
I can hide	she can hide
I have grabbed the	she has grabbed the
phone too soon	phone too soon
and if I shut the	and if she shuts the
door I'll still	door or brights
ignite my voice and	her voice
she will hear my	I'll see her
pride explode and	turned buffoon
catch the shattered	and I will bleed
splinters in her side	from splinters of
and what I want	her shattered pride
to do is slam the	and what I want
damn receiver down	to do is smash
and crash her	into her tortured
sound-track room	room and crash
and scream	the damn receiver down
for God's sake	and scream
Mother, love affairs	for God's sake Baby
end all the time	love affairs end
it's not	all the time pretend
as if I died!	the bastard died!

all the shirley temples

It was time, time enough to have long forgiven,
but the poem, unforgiving, bitter as the stubborn

memory, cold as a decade of suppers waiting, had
won for me Recognition,   a prize in fact and I

was ego bound to read it all aloud to him
And he asked the white plastic bag inside the

basket by his chair, "Why do you write only
about the bad things." And he reminded the

morning paper "How about all the Saturday night
reservations at *Rene et Jean's* when we dressed

the kids and ourselves up to the teeth and we'd
let them walk in ahead of us   watching people

smile at them   and then at us   and the
Maitre d' would bow us to the table and the

head waiter was already chilling the sauterne in
the ice bucket and even before we ordered they

served up shirley temples for the kids . . .

    Once a thousand years ago, with the shining
    evidence of what was still between us tender

    touching, before he brought a vandal to my door
    before I saw me old in a shattered mirror on

    walls that almost fell apart, I unlaced to him
    forever my self in welcome wide, as even now

    beside the spit bag I bent gentle to the
    hawking old man with the new leg prosthesis.

    Slightly, ever so slightly, I felt the grey
    stubble scratch my mouth and smother my apology

    "I had forgotten all the shirley temples" I said

Tsivya

I

As in Scylla and Charybdis

Tsivya
Immigration changed
Her name to Celia
But Papa, simple
Gentle soul,
In his ignorance
Pronounced it Scylla
When I was twenty-two
I chose the maelstrom

II

Circe's Daughter

Included in my dowry
Was the knife and skill
To slash and cut
But each time
At the sight of Blood
I winced, and
Waited for the night
To find his mouth
Then pressing hard
My nakedness
Against his wounds, I
Seared them shut with
All my heat to make him
Animal again.

III

The Maelstrom – and After

The money fights
The money fights
The foul words
the ugliness
The wishing, "Die!
Why don't you die!"
And then the
Goddam bed.

Down-soft and warm
In all their suckling needs
Each one in turn
Dug tiny fingers
In my breasts
And gave me *meaning*

IV

The Better Part of Valor

I thought it was for me
The children wept
You came
At me with a club
And I was fighting
For my life
And didn't know
That in my hand
I held the knife
Or that my mother
Put it there

What kind of special skill was this
That fought to kill
Yet sought to kiss
What instinct fed survival into needing
What blade that slashed out at the air
What fury fighting off despair
Dissolved – for fear
I'd find the children
Bleeding

V

Polonaise

There were daisy fields in Bialystok
But were there never roses?
Never summer gardens – only restless springs?
Springs recalled – where Polish girls
Slipped through German borders
To return at dusk, darkness making
Logical sudden full-blown pregnancies
Conceived by yards of fine silk
Wrapped around slim waists under
Billowed skirts and blouses – and one
No more than twelve, too young, too fast
To fool the gendarmes – Tsivya.
Feet flying, leaping for the moving
Train, racing through the cars
Scrambling under benches, then suddenly!
Hidden and protected by the young
Baker's apprentice, with his heavy coat
And his respectable train ticket.
"That was when we fell in love,"

Papa would say. She waved
Aside his reminiscences, *"Liebe!*
Liebe! Fool! I wanted to see America,
So I ran with you from the *pogroms,"*
(Then – to that distance,) ". . . leaving
>   my little sisters
>   and my little brothers
>   and my mother
>   and my father
>   to the Austrian . . ."

>   (Love was not for speaking
>   Even tenderness was in a foreign tongue
>   *"Mihr fa dihr"* and only then
>   In whispers to her young.)

VI

And Honey Wild

That year with Papa gone
And you alone, and I
With all my children nearly grown
You and I, Mama, awoke,
Both of us to what we were
And what we never spoke.

>   The old man sleeps a philosophic
>   Calm – while I toss fitful in the night
>   Where Tsivya's truant soul must see
>   How Tsivya's fire smoulders low
>   And courses slow in me.

Note: *mihr far dihr* is Yiddish for "me for you"

High from a Haven Window

Here   in California's December   on the
Venice beach front   this is a truant wind
a careless runner   at first kicking aside

only the lightest things in its path   a
cigarette stub   an empty matchbook   some
kind of dry leaf from a tree on a walkstreet

but soon a quickening pace   a mood turned
surly   a whipping up of sand into low brown
clouds   then with new force abetted by a

rabble rain   the truant turned vandal
now   against the surprised beachgoers
a sudden outburst   as of a temper   a

sweeping and a swirling and tossing around
of beach garbage into the angry grey air
broken junk food paper cartons   muddied

cola cups   a newspage become bird   frightened
into flight   from somewhere that low whistle
and the full storm something to run from

> But you can stay inside   you live here
> protected by walls   that brisk walk
> in the open air to maintain the heart
>
> and the arteries   can wait another day
> depositing the pension check can wait
> another day   no need for you ever

to be out in that again   only the
postman must be   but somewhere
between those two worlds   the postman's

must   and your   no need   comes the
stubborn nostalgia for the arrogant
way you raced the runner in March

and laughed as you passed him

Patronage, Recognition, and Celebration

Yes, sweet beach person
I can spare a quarter
No need for thanks
Besides, it very well could be
We share a world in common
Within our separate worlds

In your body, aging perhaps a little fast
 (no offense intended)   as in mine, already old
The heart persists. As your blood courses
Stubborn   so does mine
And here.   And now.   Within our
Common separation-in-common
From where we are
And where we once dreamed of being
In that sand-eating compromise
Between feasts we envisioned
And crumbs we hold
We somehow breathe this day's
Clean fresh morning in
And you   and I   Good Buddy
Survive

Sadie Wernick Hurwitz

When my mother, who had five years of education in Poland, came to the United States, she somehow taught herself to read English words. She had a feeling for language and for litera- ture, an utter contempt for the uneducated. She was quick to call people fools. My father, in his world view of people, was her exact counterpoint. He never judged or condemned anyone. He was gentle. He was good. And he was giving. Once when I was sixteen years old, he took my sister and me on a day's out- ing for the express purpose of getting me away from the house because my mother was preparing a surprise sweet-sixteen party for me. He had just had an ingrown toenail removed and was walking around with that terrible pain just to make it easier for my mother to get the party ready. Both of them, in their respec- tive ways, were highly supportive parents, always making us feel that we were talented and special – when we were small, show- ing us off to their friends, encouraging us to dance, to sing, to perform. My mother insisted she had no favorites but I think I was the one she boasted about most – "my Sadie, my Sadie."

My mother's sister, my Aunt Jennie, reinforced my feelings of security as a child. I remember once – I must have been four or five – I was on a beach in Connecticut with her and noticed the way the spray caught the sunlight. "Jennie," I said, "look, there are diamonds dancing on the water." And my aunt exclaimed to all the people around her, "Do you hear what this wonderful poet is saying? She sees diamonds dancing on the water!" Between Jennie and my mother there was this tremendous feeling that I was something marvelous. And along with this was my father's approval of everything that my mother said about me and my sister and my brother who was born sixteen years later.

Long before my brother was born, we moved from Connecticut to Long Beach because my father was a baker and my mother was afraid the flour would get in his lungs. She wanted him here in California where the sun is shining all the time. He became a baker when we came here anyhow.

Here for the first time – but only for a brief time and it didn't come from my parents – I discovered disapproval. I encountered anti-Semitism on a Long Beach grammar school playground. A small group of kids, led by a vicious twelve-year-old boy, began to taunt my sister and me for being Jewish. The little monster would hold his open palm under his chin, emulating a beard, and yell, "Ay, Ay, Ikey! You killed God!" I went home crying, told my mother and she gave me a song to sing. "Tell them this poem," she said, "I'm a Jew/you could be too/even Jesus was a Jew." I did that and these kids were impressed. Then I started showing that I could do other things. In my heavy shoes I could stand on my toes. And my sister and I would do a song and all the kids would gather around on the playground and listen to us.

In Long Beach, my mother took us to dancing instructors and singing instructors, gave us piano lessons and wrote us little scripts so we could act them out. We danced at performances for the Jewish clubs that my mother belonged to. My mother never had to do any pushing with me, I was an outgoing show-off.

·   ·   ·

Somewhere in those lower grades I must have done some writing or she wouldn't have always said, "How smart my Sadie is." And somewhere in junior high and high school I became aware of the fact that I could write. Teachers read my essays in class. In high school I was one of the feature writers on the school paper. I think I wrote poetry in my column. Another teacher wrote in my annual, "To Sadie, a promising young writer – may she fulfill the promise." That was encouraging enough to lead me to dream I could someday get a job on a newspaper.

After I graduated high school, I went to the *Los Angles Examiner* in the innocent hope that I could get hired. I was eighteen and a rather showy girl. I came in wearing a suit with a purple skirt, purple shoes, purple hat – the only thing that wasn't purple was my veil. But I was scared to death, so scared. I walked in and said to this tall woman they finally brought out, who wanted to know what I wanted: "I'm a writer, I'm looking for a job on a newspaper." And she said "We don't hire women." Hedda Hopper was the only woman there. So much for confidence. That is where I decided I had to do something else.

Law fascinated me in a way. But to study law, you've got to put in a full twenty-four hours. It's not like speed-reading *David Copperfield* two days before a high school literature test and conning the teacher with a glowing essay on Charles Dickens. My mother was very supportive, but she was one of those concerned Jewish mothers who wants her daughter to get married. So I divided my time between getting a husband and speed-reading everything from Blackstone to case law. I was married in July, 1933 and took the August bar exam. I was already pregnant. But it wasn't that early morning nausea that made me flunk. You just don't bluff away a bar exam the way you do *David Copperfield* in a high school test.

Nine months and ten days after I was married, my first child was born. Seventeen months later my second child was born. I got pregnant fourteen months later and had an abortion. Ten years later, I got pregnant again and had another abortion. Then I started dreaming at night that I was holding a child and once, when my daughter got very, very sick and I couldn't get the fever down, I prayed to God, "Please God, save her for me and I will have two more children to make up for the ones I aborted." And that is what I did. There are ten years between the two spans.

·   ·   ·

The minute I was married and started having children, I started writing about my children, sending little fillers into magazines. I wrote a filler called "In a Little Boy's Pockets." Then once when I was riding in a car with my husband, there was a radio announcer saying, "I've got to read something to you that impressed me very much." He read my "In a Little Boy's Pockets" and surprised the heck out of me.

Writing became a compulsion. It took care of every problem I had. It could be a release from every tension. Or something impressive would happen and I'd decide it had to be written down. I remember winning some kind of recognition with a story poem about a bridge game, "Shoot the Card to me Pard." I kept on submitting fillers to magazines. I got a lot of rejections but every once in a while I'd get printed. But I had to confine my writing life to fillers, because I couldn't devote all my time. The business of life was interfering.

I kept projecting my own ambitions onto my kids, gave them music, gave them art, gave them dancing, gave them singing, gave them all those things. Then I started writing songs. Sometimes I wrote with a musician, sometimes I just made up lyrics to a melody that came to my head. There was a man in our neighborhood who heard that I had written a song, that I was a writer, and he would come to me and sing tunes. I would say to him, "Mr. Laub, Beethoven wrote that tune a long time ago." He would say, "What's the difference, if he wouldn't have written it, I would." But Mr. Laub did bring me some old folk tunes. One was an old Yiddish melody to which I wrote, "Mama, Mama, Mama, there's dancing in the street." That song made it on Capitol Records.

For a while I would go to any one of the numerous hungry musicians in town, pay between seven and ten dollars, sing them my lyrics and they would write the lead sheet for me. Then I'd make a demo to promote the song. I sold songs as my children grew up. I got two or three songs recorded. I was so happy with even getting recognized I didn't sign contracts, I didn't protect my rights, I didn't collect royalties except on that one song.

When the children were in college and I was close to forty, I wrote a college production, *Heads I Win*, a musical about Henry the Eighth. My children had told the drama department that their mother wrote, so they came to me and asked me to help them with the script. My son Richard was the conductor; his friend, Bob Bowers, a very fine musician, wrote the music. I also have a play called *The Bareback Writer and the Clown* that I wrote during the hippie era. I interspersed it with my songs and sent it to somebody who was very much impressed with it and wanted me to send more. She produced it in a different city and I never had a chance to see it. Once someone asked me to write a series of dramatic tableaux and I tossed them off. When they were produced, she took credit for them. I called her to ask how she had nerve to take credit for my work and she said, "I sent you a box of candy." As a matter of fact, she didn't even do that. The man who ran the neighborhood fruit stand heard I was a writer. His wife, he said, was a member of a theater co-op group and needed someone to help write songs. I met her, and with her I wrote songs for a musical of the old melodrama, *Murder in the Old Barn*. This woman is still my friend.

I did things without getting anything, that other people were getting paid all kinds of money for. That was the pattern of my life. I didn't move with writers. There were my children and my husband and friends. I just wrote a lot of things and occasionally gave them to others.

.   .   .

I didn't work at all until my husband went broke and then it was either going on welfare or going to work. Working and leaving the children alone, to me, was a terrible thing because I was so much the mother. Worse, having recognized the need to get a job, I couldn't get one. I tried at the *Los Angeles Times*. Now newspapers were taking women, but they gave you a kind of written psychological test. I was quite naive, I answered the way I thought it *should* be answered and didn't realize it was a much more sophisticated world, that the truthful answers would have passed. I came home and said, "I flunked the test" and my husband said, "Forget it, kid, you are not good for anything, forget it."

That did it. I went back to the work market, took every test I could find, the city, the county, all the civil service. I passed every single one and became a municipal court clerk. I went to college at night and for almost ten years I worked in the municipal court. I wrote a musical about the courts. I used to sing my songs to the kids in the office: "They will put you in the game/if your minister's the same/and if you play with the guy/who calls the plays." I was complaining about the games that were going on at the municipal court. You could get a high grade in the test, but if a boss had relatives that he wanted to get in, you got a lower rating on the oral and the other guy got a higher rating.

Because of my legal background I worked for a year in the District Attorney's office in the "Failure to Provide" division, where they were getting after fathers who weren't providing for children. I wrote about that – powerful stuff, but then I've read that social writing doesn't sell.

When I graduated from college with a degree in social science, I took a test for social worker. Again there was a good God watching me – I passed. A few decades earlier it might not have happened. It was hard to get into social service. It was hard to get into government service even if you tried coming in through the back door on a lesser job. I was a woman. I couldn't type worth a darn. And I was Jewish. There was quite a selective thing there.

I was a social worker for ten years. The second half of that ten-year period, I was a children's services worker. The children on my caseload began to occupy my mind all the time – even at the end of my day's work. When my younger daughter, Andrea, became a meditator, she encouraged me to do the same because I was under such terrible tension. But I'd meditate and those kids would still come into my mind. I wrote pieces about them.

.   .   .

I began writing poetry after my husband went broke again. It took less time. I had learned that the best writing was to say the most in the briefest words. You could do that with poetry. At first I was just tossing it off. Later I realized that it takes just as much effort to write a good poem as a good essay. When I went back to college to get a couple more degrees so I could earn a decent living, the poetry began in earnest. Almost every semester I took a course in poetry. In Henri Coulette's poetry class at CSULA, I remember one day after we all submitted poems for criticism, he said, "My situation with Sadie's poetry is like that of a lover; he can't see anything wrong with the beloved." I entered contests and felt guilty when I won because here I was, fifty, competing with kids. I won speaking contests, I have a gold cup somewhere in my basement that was a first prize – I felt guilty about that. I turned in a story, "Sins of the Mothers," to a short story writing teacher who evidently told others, because other professors seemed to have heard about it. He just kept shaking his head back and forth and saying, "Wonderful, wonderful – it just needs one more up and down." I have short stories all around the house. I have one that took some kind of an award, a love story. I don't know if I ever lived a love story, but I always dreamed a love story.

It was then that I really started submitting things and began to get comments and little notes. The editors at *Ohio Review* told me if I would just tighten up "Tsivya," they would like the poem. But nobody told me how to tighten up a poem. I never really got constructive criticism about poetry. I had to learn for myself. If a poem came back three or four times, I figured it wasn't somebody's cup of tea. But even then I found that somebody might just rave over something that had come back four or five times. I joined the California Poetry Society and entered contests every year. If I didn't win a first or second, I always won third or fourth place. Recently, I became a member of Poetry Society of America; I tried many years ago and they told me my work was good but I wasn't there yet.

Then postage went up so high that I couldn't afford to send out hundreds of submissions with twenty-two cent stamps. I read in one of the writers' magazines that if you are a good writer and you self-publish, there is more valid approbation than for books that come out from the vanity presses. I thought, This is the time I have to publish my own. I followed the article step by step and published seven hundred copies of *A Kind of Attachment*. It has about seventy pages of poems. It cost me less than five thousand dollars.

I wrote a news release. I called *COSMEP* to give me a list of names that would be good contacts. Because I didn't specifically ask for reviewers, they gave me a list that included a certain amount of libraries where I got some wonderful responses. I sent out some publicity flyers, but I didn't finish because again the cost became almost exorbitant. I went personally to local libraries. Wherever I went they bought my book. It's in Small World here on the Venice, California beach front; it is in a place on the Santa Monica Mall; it is in a wonderful bookstore, The Bhodi Tree, right out of Beverly Hills. But that isn't enough. A book sits on the shelves and won't sell if you don't promote it. I have failed to follow through on enough reviewers. You must get to the reviewers because reviews have a wide circle, they can touch the entire world.

I was reviewed in *Poetry Flash.* A friend of mine had a reading for me at her literary group. An *L.A. Times* writer sent me a personal letter with comments. One man, a reviewer to whom I sent a book, wrote about four or five months later and said, "It is as rich as a good plate of matzoh ball soup." Why people identify my work with a feast I don't know. I have letters: "Dear Sadie, this may seem a silly thing to do, but I just had to write and tell you I picked up your book and it was so wonderful, I found so many things that I warm to, I loved it."

.   .   .

I find myself going to poetry workshops when I have something new, to see the kind of input I can get from some of the young kids. Even when I was living in Los Angeles, I would come all the way out here to "Beyond Baroque," a well-known poetry center. You just go in on Wednesdays and hope there isn't too big a crowd so you can read your poetry. We've had classes where sometimes there were only five and other times when there were fifty – it is seasonal. We sit in a circle and a commentator introduces herself along with three or four other people who work there, and tells the group, "We are not concerned with content, what we are here to do is to work on the craft of the poem."

No one else who is seventy-five years old comes to that Beyond Baroque class. There may be a few in their sixties. They are nice about my age, except that I think they don't understand my world. A poem of mine doesn't reach their world.

There may be a quiet respect for my stuff but often it is not their cup of tea. If they were publishers, they wouldn't buy it. And this is what I think is happening in a lot of poetry publications. There is a generation of such young poets who probably are not into the kind of thing I write. One poem I thought they would like ends with kids cowering "frightened in the gore-soaked corners of our lives." I was showing children suffering from the infighting of parents. They missed it completely. And yet I know a lot of them have suffered. On the other hand, I have had things published in college publications by very young people. "all the shirley temples" was in a college publication.

I think they are very tired of hearing me say I like a poem that is accessible. I think that the more people who find a poem accessible, the longer the poem will live. True, there are some very sensitive and fine poets who are not eager to expose themselves to the whole world, only to those who will recognize what they are being so elliptical about. On the other hand there is an arrogant kind of elliptical poet who says, "If you don't understand what I am saying, that's *your* problem." I choose not to be that kind of poet. I don't think I could be. I look for truth in everything I write. My criticism of much of the poetry that comes to Baroque is that it is neither truthful nor honest but is there for effect. On the other hand, there are some things that are very truthful and very honest but so lacking in skill you just see somebody vomiting out an experience. That is not poetry.

I have learned to cull out unimportant criticism and the criticism that works. I went to one class run by Holly Prado who occasionally reviews poetry for the *L.A. Times Magazine.* Her comment about my poetry was, "It is like a good table wine." I was not satisfied with that criticism. I want my poetry to be better than good table wine, I want it to be good vintage wine. After that class was over, one of the students sent me a letter telling me how much she loved my poetry. It depends on whom you reach. I have not been discouraged by what anyone said. I never had a chance to be sensitive about anything because I had harsh critics all around me, a man who criticized my writing, and children, whose opinion I respected, who criticized my music. Rejection never stopped me because I knew I was good,

but to this day I don't know how good. I think that if I played
the publicity game, which is so important, then what I do that is
good would be much more widely recognized.

.   .   .

In regard to process, I compose poems when I walk on the
beach, when I drive the car, when I am making dinner, when I
am talking to somebody and the thought comes. I write in the
course of my living, in the course of anything that is traumatic.
I write it in my head and do a lot of revisions in my head. I can
be driving the car and say, Now Sadie, be careful how you drive,
you can't write poetry while you drive. I have three poems in
my head now, but because I haven't finished them I haven't put
them down. The typewriter is the last place I go to. And when I
put it down, I remember it. I look at something over and over
and over again. The structure grows. Sometimes I will write a
poem, two lines and a space, two lines and a space. The poem
makes the breaks. Sometimes after I have rewritten and rewritten and rewritten, I say, Damn it, I have got a poem here. And
if I send it out and it comes back, I think to myself, Dumb,
stupid editor, he doesn't know anything. But if it comes back
four or five times, I read it again and say, Wait a minute, what is
wrong with this poem? I find myself being my own harshest critic, which is all right except I don't know when I have made a
good criticism. I have one poem in three or four versions and I
still don't know which is the best. I wish I could put my finger
on it and know. The consolation for that is, a lot of poets go
through the same thing.

I am the world's worst typist so it takes me forever to type,
but I am very precise about the right presentation. When I
come into the Beyond Baroque class and see kids bringing in
pencil-scribbled stuff, I think to myself, This is not those
ancient times when a prisoner had to pick up a piece of brown
paper and write something with whatever mark he could make.
Give people the dignity of presenting a poem that can be read.
So even when I come into the poetry class, I have my name on
the upper left-hand corner, I have my address, I have the
amount of lines on the upper right side of the poem, I put my
name on the bottom of the poem. Darned if I didn't get one

comment from an editor, "Don't tell us how many lines you have in your twenty-line poem. We are not that stupid."

. . .

Once when I was busy publishing my book, I met my sister near the printing office in an eating place where she had invited me for lunch. And she said, "Sit down and eat, what you're doing can wait." I guess I came on pretty dramatically. I said, "Ethel, this is my life, I have got to do *this*." Actually, I have never made my writing the kind of driving force that shoves everybody out. The other things that are a part of my life are as integral to me as my genes. They *are* my genes, my children, my seed. I can't say to anybody, "I have things to do, stay away." Because everybody and everything is a part of my life. It is in the very first poem, "Of Bondage Made Aware," in my book, where "a bud-woman coming upon/a stumbling/bumbling, green fellow . . . offers up her shoulder/and encircling with her arms/his flinging out . . ." My life is always full, there is no such thing as being alone. One day I came into the poetry meeting and they asked me, "Have you written anything?" I said, "No, life got in the way." Everyone began to laugh. And someone said the obvious, "Well that is what poetry is about, why didn't you write."

Do I think I would have done it all over? Well I would have done it differently so I could have done more. Everything is poetry now. I think it is my form, the form I have crystallized on. There is a kind of aristocracy in being a good poet. I think that is my weakness. I shouldn't need that. Success for me would be, if someone I respected, whose work I admired, were to read my work and say, "This is good." Money is always a nice thing, but then I think that even in winning a big prize, you don't know who the judges were, what appealed to them. But if someone who is respected in literary society as a fine poet says my work is good, then I know my work is good.

I will write as long as my mind is working. I always repeat the story of John Adams who prayed before he had his final stroke, "Dear God, let my mind go last." I will write as long as my mind is there and I have the capacity to hold a pen.

Erma J. Fisk

. . .

Excerpts from *Parrots' Wood*

Day 1. Early morning

A gray, lowering, late January day. I am lowering too. I stayed
too late at last night's party? Somewhere in my subconscious a
warning stirs? I should be joyful, setting off on an adventure. I
am too hurried to wonder about the implications of this, for as
usual I am late. Munching a piece of toast I look about my living room with its many big windows – more of a bird blind than
a room, my nonbirding friends tell me, laughing.

"Keep cool," I bid it. "Wait for me." I always wonder if I will
get to come back to it.

Twenty-five miles north I catch the small plane that will
ferry me to Boston. "Catch" is an old-fashioned word for the
orderly filing by numbered boarding passes through carpeted
corridors that lead you onto today's huge buses of the air. It still
applies to a small-town airport when you arrive tardily, have to
run out on the field with the ticket agent in the hope the pilot
will see you and let down the steps of his small vehicle.

I am starting for Belize, a country in Central America. I
told you this so long ago I'd better mention it again. Sleepy, but
well ahead of time at Boston's Logan Airport, I buy a chocolate
bar, a whodunit to pass the time, scrub my mind vacation-clean.
While I am in the LADIES (only these days they call it less ele-
gantly WOMEN, and graph a triangular skirt on the door.

Don't complain, Mrs. Fisk, you've often been where a bush was all there was. Count your blessings) I hear my name urgently called. I react with alarm. My connections are tight. Our group is to meet in Belize City. From there we will be transported, I don't know how. By small plane? Airboat? Decrepit truck? I've used them all in that country. Sixty miles inland the dozen of us – biologist, volunteers, some with training, some enthusiastic tyros – will settle in for a week, two weeks, in my case a month of study. I know I keep repeating. Please ignore it. Don't I tell you something new each time?

I join an equally alarmed huddle at the reservation desk. All of us are tight-lipped. I storm at myself. *"What are you doing here?* Why are you always getting yourself into these situations? Last year you *promised* yourself you would never go south of Carolina again, don't you remember? This year you can't even get out of Boston!"

.   .   .

"Why are you going to that funny little country again?" friends had asked a few nights ago. If I were going to London or Vienna they would understand. Nice people. I enjoy the contrasts they offer to the woman I have become, widowed. They disapprove of the way I live, scold me, are sincerely troubled when I elect to stay in remote areas miles from help, from conveniences. Helen tries to keep me properly social, invites men she considers suitable to have dinner with me. Joe knows better.

"What would Brad say?" Helen asked, fretting. "Suppose something happens to you, like last year? What medical supplies do you carry, will there be a doctor in your group?"

I had laughed. Neither of the two doctors on my last trip to Belize had even had a Band-Aid with them. A scraped knee had become infected, brought me home finally in an airport wheelchair.

I hugged Helen affectionately, selected another of her decorative hors d'oeuvres, accepted another glass of wine from Joe. I wouldn't look at the picture of Brad they had conjured up, sitting in one of their comfortable chairs as he so often had, in their pleasant living room. That part of my life is gone. I try to look now only at whatever project I have managed to get involved in, which some researcher has offered, which will lead me away from that life. But it isn't easy.

I had walked to the windows to hide my face, stood with my back to them, sipping my wine. Turning –

"Don't you two scold me," I begged them. "I need you. I know I'm crazy. I suppose it's not knowing what I am getting into that attracts me, really – having to cope when I find myself in jams. So far I've been lucky. You would hate the discomforts, often the food" (Helen winced), "but I don't mind. The people are interesting, someone always takes care of me. I must look helpless . . ."

"Orders up a wheelchair for you?" Helen asked sarcastically. "Gets you a bed in that Boston hospital?"

I had prowled their room, restless. Unexpectedly, we had reached a deeper level. Their concern, the wine had broken through the tautness that sustains me. We were all aware of Brad, his presence in that big wing chair. Listening also, wanting to help me.

"I have to try things that are too hard for me. I don't have many friends left from the old days who put up with me the way you do; I've moved too far away, geographically and otherwise. I live in two worlds, not comfortable in either. I don't know where I belong."

Joe offered to refill my glass, but I shook my head. I was trying to think.

"Here with you I am comforted, coddled. Out with those researchers who use me I am an amateur, not yet at ease. It's like living on a seesaw. I have to learn to balance in the middle. I don't know where – or who – I am. I'm someone I have yet to define. Is this too much for you?"

This time, passing, I let my glass be refilled. The sound poured clear in our silence. Their faces were turned up in understanding.

"I've no one to straighten out my values. When you live in a family they let you know. Every day! They criticize you, tease you, love you. Tell you what you are doing wrong – or right. You have a man to do your thinking, open the mayonnaise jars, find your misplaced keys, slap you into bed at night.

"Now I have to make all the decisions. How do I know if

they are right? Should I stay here, having friends for lunch, reading, hiring a neighbor boy to shovel the snow? Shovel it myself for exercise? Or do I launch myself out into chiggers, discomfort, food I wouldn't tolerate at home? Do I pick safety because I'm older now, or adventure?

"I work with men in their thirties and forties. They live in a different world than we do. They grew up during Vietnam, during the protests, the sexual and women's revolutions of the sixties. If I want them to like me, to earn their respect, I must adjust to attitudes very different from ours. It is a challenge. It keeps me on an edge. This trip to Belize will be easy. The group is mixed, I don't have to worry about being older. I've been there five times, I'll know more than most of them.

"I come back to you each time for TLC. I know I can count on you. You scold me – I love it – but you never let my seesaw down with a thump into the mud of my new playgrounds. There are plenty of others to do that – you had a few of them here this afternoon – Ted, Mary. . . . When *you* say something I can trust you. We all live on bases of shifting sands, need trust.

"You didn't understand that article I'd written." They laugh. "But that scientist you asked to meet me did. He knew what it means to an amateur to be published in such a journal. When someone of his stature says what he did to me I put it under my pillow nights, treasure it until it is worn threadbare. Praise from the others, like Ted, is just fluff, cotton candy."

At the moment, standing at a reservation desk in Logan Airport on this raw, gray, winter day, even a handful of cotton candy caught on my coat would comfort me.

A harried young official tries to soothe us. Our plane is grounded in Providence. We will be accommodated by another line, if we can get to it in time. He herds us to a bus where – equally soothing – I sight my luggage wedged on a cart. I don't travel with much, and after experiences we won't go into I am careful always to carry in hand my binoculars, sneakers, toothbrush, notebooks. But I need what I take.

The bus is held up in traffic. My anxiety is compounded by a meager breakfast gulped long ago, before reaching that small plane that brought me to Boston. But all goes well, we are delivered in time, led aboard, a motherly seatmate shows me my seat belt, my flotation pillow. I told you I look helpless. (How many countries did Brad and I fly to after he retired into the Commerce Department? Forty-one? And how many have I been in since, on my own?) I thank my new friend. While I eat every scrap of breakfast that arrives, in case of no lunch, she pulls a ball of virulent green wool from her knitting bag and casts on stitches. A sweater for her latest grandson, she informs me proudly, and tells me how cute he and his brothers are. . . .

I have given myself over to the lift and sway of our ship. I love planes. (Or did before the seats became smaller and tighter, as I have become larger.) Someone else does the driving, pours the coffee, serves the meals, hands me a napkin, offers a magazine. I can become as excited as I used to be fifty years ago when on a voyage through the sea of air, lifting, swelling to a crest, gliding down – planes were smaller, more responsive to air waves then – you were aware how thin the metal skin was between you and the winds that roved the skies. Outside my window would tower a shifting wilderness of shadowed canyons, changing pinnacles of gleaming white, sunlit glory, threatening depths. Suddenly, frighteningly, a jagged mountain peak – this would be in Peru, where the pilots threaded their way adventurously through continental ranges; suddenly a forever expanse of ocean where miniature boats sailed on a frozen sapphire surface; or the random tracks of ancient rivers marked geological ages of our own country. An infinitude of space below me.

My first flights were two-dollar barnstorming ones from a grassy airfield in Buffalo, while the three men of my family, aged four through twenty-five, watched nervously from below. My first transcontinental flight was to Seattle as representative to a Junior League Convention. On the way we were attacked by thunderstorms. The plane pitched and moaned, as did the passengers, except for an interested man who helped me toss airsick bags along the rows, the stewardesses having cravenly strapped themselves into their seats. Lightning exploded on either side of us. I thought all flying was like this, a war with the elements to end, as that one ultimately did, in a calm and rain-washed sunset, the slopes of the Rockies instead of thunderbolts flaming below us.

On my return I came to a choice of roads. My seatmate was a man of my own age, attractive, impeccable in clothes that spoke more of ranches than of cities. He recognized me by the sweeping black pirate hat that had marked me in a newspaper line-up splashed on the front page of the newspaper the day of our arrival. (We were displaced, the next day, by Hitler's invasion of Holland.) Finding that my acquaintance with western life derived only from Zane Grey, he urged me to break my journey at his stop of Pendleton, to spend a few days on an authentic western spread. He was open, friendly. His eyes twinkled as he sensed the shock of this proposition to my New England upbringing. He had a sister, he offered; she would chaperone us. It would be a shame for me to return east (he did not consider Buffalo west as I did, having been raised in Boston) untutored in what our country had to offer. He could provide a gentle riding horse. Why not?

I was sorely tempted. How easy it must be for women whose love is not securely rooted, who are not anticipating the welcome, the man who will be waiting, to slip briefly from the commitments of marriage, to forget or ignore the promises they made before the stresses of daily life obliterated these. As our plane refueled we walked along the chain link fence, he outside, me within. A desert wind lifted the wide brim of my hat. The land stretched limitlessly in beauty behind him. I was sure I wouldn't change my mind, he teased? What about those two small boys, I countered, running about at the airport gate, their father? My fingers and his eyes went to the flowers pinned on my shoulder, fragrant and visible sign of the love awaiting me. We parted with mutual regret.

But you see I still remember. Over all the years the temptation, the beckon of that other road has not faded. I wonder if he is now one of those cattlemen overgrazing the land I am always trying to save?

Long ago. Perhaps it is the happiness reflected in my face that catches the eye of a man balancing his way down the aisle of this plane forty years later. He stops to chat over the head of my seatmate. Considering me her private property she sniffs, then accepts the situation. When this new friend passes, the Atlantic is obscured by gray wool, our ship drones on flatly. I am shortly asleep. The whodunit can wait.

I awake to peanuts and orange juice, to the serene blue skies, the blue sea off Florida. We circle far out across the Everglades, where I used to be flown in a little Park Service plane to make surveys of eagle nests, of thousands of the wading birds that existed then, of rafts of white pelican, duck, coot. We circle over the square-mile agricultural fields about Homestead, which provide winter tomatoes and potatoes and beans and mangoes and limes and huge avocadoes for the nation's dinner tables. Being displaced now – the fields, not the tables, which may some day be bare as fields – by square miles of trailer parks and condominiums. . . .

We swing in finally over busy boulevards where racial violence is commonplace, over the Perimeter Road where I used to park to birdwatch. I notice a lack of grackles and gulls on the grass between the airport runways. So the Port Authority has finally found a way to be rid of its animal life? In my day there had been jackrabbits and prairie dogs and other escaped fauna as well as birds, although these exotic hazards were not publicized. Somewhere inside by the central escalator used to be an Audubon plaque proclaiming the airport a sanctuary for burrowing owls. If it is still there it is not visible among the jostling lines of travelers, families spread out on the floor with babies and paper bags and stuffed animals and lunches. There can be no owls outside either in that jostle of international planes coming and going. Back when it was emptier the Miami Airport was my Club; I constantly encountered friends from past years. Once, unexpectedly at 3:00 A.M., my elder son and his wife – both of us setting forth on Christmas trips to Peru, but separately. Once, equally unexpectedly, my daughter. I hadn't known either of them would be there. As my son pointed out, do you write your mother that at 3:00 A.M. you will be changing planes at an airport thirty miles away, why doesn't she drive up and say Hello? I had to agree with him.

Our children! During those years, distant in Florida, the thought of them was like the bugling of geese skeining against my horizon in an affirmation of life, of continuity; like the half-remembered music of spring peepers when dusk settles among the trees of a swamp. Like the soft fall of snow outside a window reflecting firelight inside. Like music spilling through an open doorway, across a lawn I used to pass walking home at night. Only I couldn't listen to music in those days. It cut too deeply through the protective layers with which I struggled to mute my loneliness, into a quiet desperation that could seize me unawares.

I had separated myself from our children. I hadn't dismissed them, just set them aside until I had learned to stand by myself. It wasn't that I didn't still love them or, I suppose, they love me. At that stage of our lives they were building their own families. I was trying to build a life among people who didn't know if I had children, if there was a "Mrs." in front of the nickname they called me by. I was building with tools foreign to my hands, in a land and a culture strange to me.

I used to send the children my itinerary whenever I went out of the country, "in case they needed me." Later I realized I was doing this not for their security but for my own. I was clutching, trying to find a place where I belonged, was needed. I couldn't emotionally accept that I wasn't. If I returned from Costa Rica they might call and ask cheerfully, "How was Trinidad?" . . .

At last our plane taxis in. At one extreme of the airport, I am to leave from the other. If it is not already too late. I am first in line to disembark –

"Run," bids my stewardess. "Don't worry about your luggage, it will get there before you do. But run!"

Why don't they send me perched on the dolly with my bags, I wonder? It would be quicker, easier. Hurt the airport image, I suppose. Start a trend.

"Don't run," my doctor has been telling me all winter. "Don't get excited."

I run. The Miami Airport has been home to me for too many years, it won't let me collapse with a heart attack today. I can rest on that flight to Belize, which is further in sitting time than it looks on the map. How long had it taken Gene and Sandy and me to fly there from the Keys the year we made a wading bird survey around the Gulf of Mexico for National Audubon Society? We were in a little plane, a Cessna. As always we were grounded in Lafayette by rain. (Rain, rain, does the sun never shine in Lafayette? Not when I am there.) I hurt that knee, counting martins. The doctor's pills made me sleepy, I had slept the whole length of Padre Island, one of the famous bird spots I had wanted for years to see. We must have been a week and more reaching Belize, held up at each stop by Mexican officials who coveted our emergency supplies and our rifle Ah, that rifle! Gene would never tell me how much it cost in bribes to keep it. I guess you can't compare the trips. Even in a jet today's trip will be long, broken only by peanuts, the lunch and liquids stewards dispense to ease monotony and keep us in good humor.

Midway through the airport, panting, backpack askew, I am advised by a bulletin board that my departing plane has been delayed. So I pause, as always, to greet my husband where he had stood by the Pan Am desk on our last trip. After twenty years his presence still is there, in that green shirt and madras hat, his hazel eyes warm with affection, laughing at me; saying – Off again? Saying – I love you. I stand, heedless of the people that push around me. Slowly, eyes focused far away, I too push through the flow into a drugstore and concentrate on buying another whodunit, anodyne for sleepless nights. Then again I set off to meet the friends of my current life, with whom I am about to embark on this newest adventure.

·   ·   ·

Still Day 9. Evening
Letter to My Children

Twenty-one years ago tonight. So long ago now that perhaps in another foreign land, a full moon reflected again like an elongated lantern in water, friends about me, finally I can take out those days and look at them; perhaps even write about them so their weight will not so heavily lie inside of me any longer. They are not a cancer – just a weight, a sadness, a wonder, lying leaden. So long ago that that woman with the dancing feet skipped her way each evening between the flower beds, across the wooden walk that led to a dining room where a marimba band played gayly. There is no guilt – we do not dictate the way we are made, the astonishing actions that spring from our subconscious. Half a dozen of us were birding at Lago Atitlan, a small, shining expanse of blue in the Guatemalan Sierra, green-clad mountains steep about it, volcanoes at the far end. Reeds edged its shores between the Mayan villages. Mornings no wind ruffled the blue surface. The primitive boat of a fisherman drifted here and there, a waterbird trailed its wake, ducks swam below the balconies of the Hotel Tzanjuyu for pieces of a breakfast roll tossed to them. In the afternoons the chucomeel wind blew in from the Pacific, carrying moisture, swirling a doughnut of cloud around the tip of the highest volcano, breaking waves onto the pebbled beaches; fisherboats were drawn up into the reeds.

In the tower room of the hotel, carried there by the Guatemalan servants, shoulders strong under their woven jackets, their eyes soft with sympathy, your father lay dying. Oxygen tanks sent over the mountains from the Embassy in the City stood by his bed. His mask . . . his heavy breathing. . . . His hand – that beloved hand – lay slack on the bed cover, reaching out to where I crouched on the floor beside him. There was no question about his future. It had been in the eyes of the two American doctors – fortuitous arrivals at this highland inn. As a favor to our leader they had examined their countryman. Now they stood outside in the corridor with me, hesitant to speak.

"Tell me!" I think I beat on the chest of the nearest one. Surely my voice did. "I have to know! I can't stand this, tell me the truth!"

They told me.

"How long?" They told me.

The mountains between us and a hospital were too high for his transport, and even if they were not it was useless. Perhaps now, with all that is known about hearts? It might have been different? They stood with me. Decent, kindly men.

I had to eat. If I were not to break I had twice a day to leave that tower room, for however short a time. Your father understood. He was conscious, just . . . far away. So in my pretty vacation dresses at breakfast and at dinner I crossed the lawn to the dining room, people smiling at me, inviting me to sit with them. I smiled back and passed on to sit with the manager's young American wife, who knew my circumstances. Each evening as I crossed on that wooden walk the music of a marimba band would drift through the lighted open windows to meet me. My world collapsing, the rock on which my life – your lives – is founded drowning in a steadily rising sea, my feet would start tripping. They danced on their toes. My skirt swayed and lilted to the music like a girl's. The day's new crop of tourists smiled at the happiness of my feet and I smiled back – two women in one body. One dead, frozen, numb; one a girl gay, alive, *dancing*. How do you explain that?

The night your father died the band did not play, the manager had known more than I did. My feet lifted on the boardwalk, stuttered, stopped in puzzlement.

"That's funny," I said to our son, who, no passport, no money, no ticket or time when my appeal reached him, had arrived. "A marimba band plays every night for dinner. It's marvelous. I wonder what has happened?"

My feet queried me again. I learned later that the manager had canceled the band out of respect. I wish he hadn't. Your father would have liked leaving to music. Silence is forever.

Twenty years ago. I could never tell you about it: you could never ask me. The weight of our silence lies within me again tonight, sitting on a porch so far from you, in a rain forest. Just as on our pond here, the lights there had shimmered on the still waters of Atitlan. The clouds there had been pink and gold in the afterglow. Our feet had rung hollowly on the boardwalk.

That night I slept across the hall in the room our leader had used. It had not been made up. He was a good friend, but there was no comfort in his cold bed. In the dark, on the fringe of consciousness, I woke to a deliberate, synchronous tread of feet in the corridor; passing with heavy finality, fading into the ultimate silence.

Years later, in Washington, sleeping in a row house with brick walls ordinarily soundproof, I was wakened, heard in the night that same heavy tread of feet. I didn't need to be told next day that my neighbor was gone.

Twenty years ago tonight. A lifetime. It has taken me a lifetime to be willing to listen again to that silence, to lake waves lapping on shale, to that heavy tramp of feet in the corridor. There is more you might ask me. You can read between the lines, but this is at least a beginning. I have lived through these years like a tree that appears normal, standing straight, its roots deep, sheltered from the wind by others growing around it; but inside hollow, burned black and dry by lightning. Tentatively once or twice I sent out green shoots, but they withered.

Over the years two men you don't know helped me. One brutal, refusing sympathy, roughly taught me to be tough, that no one helps you but yourself. He forced me to stand on my own feet. The other, meeting me later, took for granted that I was alive, and normal. He was sometimes rough too, but he nourished me, pushed me into accomplishment. I had to feel that if he believed in me I must have value. He died. He and your father would have liked each other. I think of them somewhere in that airy expanse of sky where the spirit goes when the mortal body releases it. They are sitting about a table, one with his pipe, one with a cigar. Your Uncle Jack is there, too, and Gramp, highballs in hand, looking down in amusement at my efforts, pleased with my small triumphs; waiting for me.

.   .   .

Day 30

My roommate has a heart condition. Often in the night I wake to worry over her heavy breathing, to wonder at the curiosity and restlessness that has brought her here. But tonight I lie awake trying to dissipate a nightmare.

From the room above a woman picks her way down the stairs. Her flashlight throws monstrous shadows on the wall as she passes. My night already is full of monstrous shadows. When she returns I pull on my clothes and go out to pick my own way, on the path that leads to the Western Road with its broken pavement. I think better in motion, and I have a lot of thinking to do.

I have been lying to myself these weeks I have been here in Belize. Determined not to face truth, I have been sitting about reading, totting up figures, editing Diane's manuscript, writing bits and pieces of one of my own, baking bread. I haven't jumped eagerly out of bed each morning as for the last twenty years I have so happily done. I have explained this as the need to stand aside so others can learn, be able when I am gone to carry on the research and conservation activities that matter so much to me. I have made a big thing out of my smug generosity. It has been a fat lie.

What I am trying to cover over, what I am refusing to admit, is that I can no longer do what I wish. I no longer tell my body what to do; it is telling me. I resent this inevitable fact so much that I have been papering it over with every noble excuse I can dream up, instead of facing it. I tell myself that I have been banding birds too long, I am tired of it, I need a new career. Well, I am not tired of being up when the sun blazes orange through the leaves, of working outdoors until a great moon splashes white across my path, or hangs in a pendant scimitar as finally I close my nets at night. But my bones *are* weary; I *do* need a new career. So I am going to have to find one, or carve one out. Or quit.

Ever since Brad left I have said – and meant – that when I can no longer do what I want, live the way I want, I will quit. I am responsible to no one.

"Whose decision is this?" I had argued with a doctor. "This is *my* life, *my* body!" We were discussing the life-support systems that keep you technically alive when what matters to you, to your friends and family, has disintegrated. . . .

Knowing I can quit has been a comfort to me. Several times I have seriously considered it but delayed, been grateful as new adventures, new people, new twists to living unexpectedly surfaced. (I suspect I have also delayed because I lack the character to get my scattered affairs in order.) If the decision were clean-cut there would be no problem. My life is my own, to live as I wish, to dispose of when I wish. But is it? Or have I painted myself into a corner?

Yesterday when I walked past the pineapple farm with its guinea hens I had stopped and talked with the woman there, interested in her life, in the robust attitude she showed toward it. This is what I have done these years I have been alone – worked myself into other people's lives for my own selfish reasons, to keep myself going. Until, even if I didn't meant to, didn't realize what was happening, deliberately I acquired an extended family scattered from California to Florida, from

Louisiana to Maine. I have made myself into a surrogate grand-mother, a friendly aunt or cousin to whom its members may come – this year, next year, sometimes it is long before they sur-face – for comfort and care; to borrow money, to be spoiled for a few days; to be loved. In need of someone who will listen (and try not to advise). They *do* surface. They pay me back royally in filling my loneliness, in giving *me* comfort and care and spoil-ing, letting me borrow warmth from their lives.

So now, because my knees are old, I no longer see or hear as well as I did, my fingers have grown gnarled, I am bored and discouraged, I should turn on them? Say, in essence, "You have been useful, thanks. But the humiliations of age are more important to me than our friendship, I am quitting"?

Can I callously withdraw like that, reject them, let them know I never really cared about their concerns? We learn to lose our friends. Rejection is something other. Am I so badly off that I can deliberately do this? I love these people, or at the least I respect and am fond of them. I worked my own way into our friendships. And like love, friendship carries obligations. My father wove that into my childhood, made it a tenet of my philosophy.

Or is this false pride, and I am fooling myself again? Mak-ing another excuse because death is final and who knows what tomorrow might bring? Where does truth lie? How do we know what motives really control us? Why do the elderly and ill keep on living, clutching at life? Out of fear? Curiosity? The happy ones are rare. I have to decide, to think hard about all this. Unwilling to face up to how my next few years (if I have any coming) must be handled, is why I have been complaining here all month about the climate, the mud, the lack of fresh adven-ture. I have been morose, critical instead of merry, surly: have lost myself. Perhaps the others have been too busy to notice. I have a few days left to make up. I don't need to be so down in the dumps; you choose your paths in this world. Well, I'm not sure about this, but at least you can try. . . .

I have recaptured my serenity. With departure imminent, a lot of recapitulation and merry talk has been going on. I have been thanked, and genuinely, for my contribution to the pro-ject – not for that staff of life, the bread loaves, but for the staffs of knowledge and helpfulness. I find this embarrassing but of course gratifying. So my bouts of self-pity haven't been as apparent as I feared, everyone has been preoccupied with their own concerns and self-doubts. It is only reasonable that I should be slowing down. Our table even listened to, and laughed at stories I got into telling at breakfast. Maybe I haven't lost myself after all. Or am refound. Everyone's life is filled with ups and downs. . . .

I'll be glad to go home; this climate saps my energy. It is true I have been banding birds for too many years. It is time for me to take another road. Thirty years is a generation; I need regeneration. What motivates me is challenge, something new to deal with, the nervousness that comes from feeling inadequate, the learning, the triumph when something succeeds, the people who teach me, the new friends. Even when I can't do a job well it leads to something else; another door opens. My past is strewn with attempts – and fun.

I will return to a carapace I had built to store my books and records, pots and pans and paintings, furniture that came to Boston in sailing ships, which I should take better care of for my grandchildren. When I unlock my door that house will be empty, cold. And quiet – so quiet. . . . Those first minutes I will stand, my heart constricted, crying What am I doing here? There is no place, no one to run to for comfort. I have a sister with imagination. When I still lived in Washington, in the Georgetown row home where Brad and I had been together, whenever I returned from a trip she would have a bowl of flowers on my – our – hall table; something alive, glowing to welcome me, speaking of love. The house on Cape Cod is silent, although from the pines a chickadee will pipe an inquiry at my presence.

Brad is not in this house I had built. He is a photograph, a citation on the wall. Because you cannot see wind, the sun's energy that lies in golden light upon the grass, does this mean these don't enfold us? It is odd that he has come back to me so rarely in all these years – he himself, his hand closed on mine. Once I was lying on a hospital cart, awaiting a verdict from men who moved about me. Once I had fallen from a boat, was treading water. Once . . . I was at my desk in firelight, my head in my hands. For a long moment his shoulder comforted me, my panic subsided. Then slowly, like the ghosts in stories –

"Don't go!" I had cried wildly. He was wearing a bathrobe his grandson-namesake now takes from the closet when he comes to visit. "Don't go!" My voice had strangled in nightmare. He was gone. Death I can accept; there is no choice. Absence is something else. . . .

Across the verandah I see Steve watching me. He knows I am far away. He came up the stairs a few minutes ago, settled quietly with his own book. We didn't need to speak. We don't see each other often, we live too distant to work together, but there is understanding between us, a solid relationship. What will he go back to? His marital life is not easy. He has passed often through that door I will unlock on Cape Cod. He is there inside, as well as here across the verandah.

For I will go home to that house I built. The door will stick, as usual, need the pressure of my knee. It will be, as I said, cold and silent inside. Then, as I hang up my coat, bring in my luggage, slowly my house will come alive. It is the people who have entered, the people who have been happy there, who make a home out of whatever shelter you have, be it a house, a tent, a van, a boat. If they are fond of you, they leave a piece of their heart behind, an ambience, a ghost of spirit at ease. My heart – fortunately it seems to regenerate – is scattered all up and down the Atlantic from Trinidad to Hilton Head: to a Jersey marsh, to Vermont, to Maine. A piece of it is in an Adirondack boathouse, in rooms looking out on Pacific surf, on a Kentucky crabapple tree, on an Arizona desert. You will find me at the window of a New York apartment where finches peck at a frozen winter windowbox. I walk into these rooms as into happiness, knowing I am welcome, belong. As these people in my home belong.

This isn't memory. Some of my visitors I have never met – they were here in my absence, knowing which rock the key lives under. Here a child is curled up in the big chair by the fireplace, his book open beside it. On the bathroom shelf is a lipstick left by an unknown woman: pretty, my neighbor reported. Someone is brewing coffee in the kitchen. To them too this house has been a home, and now, when I need them, they are here, like bright sparks from the fire I light. Someone has built me a fire to light, knowing I would be cold, need the cheerful blaze to warm my spirit as well as my hands.

"When I look around," wrote a man, leaving his thanks with the key "in an odd way it is as if you are here." He sounded surprised.

But of course I am here, it isn't odd at all. And now, to my pleasure I am aware of him looking into the fridge, mending the troublesome lock on my door: his hand is on my telephone. The ghosts of those who have crossed my threshold wrap me in cloaks of many textures. Their voices speak in my cold rooms. . . .

People give me worried looks when I talk like this. Why is it queer? Chan hears bird notes none of us do. Musicians play symphonies and sonatas in their heads, tea and wine tasters use senses you and I lack or have never refined. The Dobermans tell us when other animals come into the compound. Can't you easily go back to a scene where you were among friends, smell perfume, pipe smoke drifting in the air of years ago? My mother had strong extrasensory perceptions, I can't compare with her. But I often know – if my senses are open – who is on the other end of my telephone, whose letter is lying on my hall floor below the postman's slot. There is a letter there now of importance; I can see part of it clearly, slipped out between junk mail. Will it be one that will trigger my future, once I am home?

The world is full of currents we can't lay corporeal hands on – trust, faith, gravity, magnetic fields, love. . . . They add richness to all our hours. Even if, as scoffers warn me, I am as often wrong as right. I don't mind scoffers. They must have something that sustains them equally. I just wish they would be willing to tell me, so I might tune in on their frequencies too.

I wonder about that letter, seeing it again on the rug of my hall. I never have to plan What To Do. Life picks me up by the scruff of my neck, not always gently. But I need a future to look forward to, to bring that glint of adventure to my eye.

There must be someone who can use me, I think, as I wash my mixing bowl and clean the mahogany table for the last time. In spite of my creaking joints. I am cheerful. I am willing – if not eager – to mend bird nets. I am an excellent packer of luggage into cars, a good bread baker, good at picking up what has been left behind. I like people and will usually do as I am told. (Usually. I also have a full quota of faults, but I prefer not to list these.) While I talk a lot about being adventurous, there has always been someone on my ventures to run the jeeps and boats, repair temperamental equipment, clean the fish, do my arithmetic.

I will leave a piece of my heart here at Parrots' Wood. Where? By the pond? In my corner of the Common Room, coffee drinkers chatting around me, a pile of unclaimed laundry under my arm?

The martins have left my slice of sky. Those two women are at the gate, a walk having sharpened their appetites, no doubt. I am in charge of lunch – bananas and cheese and the last of the peanut butter. My bread is ready to bake, which means another argument with that oven, seated on the floor, my leg propping the door open, my thumb aching on the button until the balky mechanism decides to function. Diane is better at this than I.

In my desk drawer at home, faded and thumbed, is a quotation from Sigurd F. Olson I copied, I don't know from where, twenty years ago. I was looking for a way to live. His reach toward the future, the road he set me on, seems as good a way to end this journal as any.

> Life is a series of open horizons, with one no sooner completed than another looms ahead. . . . Penetrations into the unknown, all give meaning to what has gone before and courage for what is to come. More than physical features they are horizons of mind and spirit. . . . And when there are no longer any beckoning mirages ahead a man dies.

Erma J. Fisk

I grew up in Brookline, Massachusetts, the third of four children. My father was an insurance executive, self-made, a workaholic. We children all sort of grew up on our own in a big house with a cook and a maid and a man who noisily shoveled coal into our big furnace and kept our gardens. We were loved but Mother went about her pleasures, my father went about his business, we were left to work out our own occupations. I read a lot and played the piano, not well but with enjoyment. Mother's motto was "Let the little flowers blossom." Later in life she said that if she were raising us all over again, she would certainly have handled us differently. I guess all parents feel that way. They pretty much left my time open for me to do what I wanted, but I didn't know what I wanted. I wasted a lot of time and have been making up for it these last years when once again, widowed, I have been left to find my own occupations.

I was athletic, not an intellectual. My mother hoped I'd play golf. She was a minor champion. Because of that I suppose I had a block against it. In those days skiing and camping were not yet on the horizon. I skated, played tennis, went to summer camp, rode. All the outdoor experiences were important to me. I enjoyed using my muscles, using my body. My greatest frustration these days is that my body tells me what I can't do. Every day I have to accept this, resentfully. I talk instead. I say I am going back to my piano but I don't have time. I'm always writing letters – I answer a letter the day it comes in or the hour it comes in.

I enjoyed school but was never taught the importance of thinking. I learned by rote, had good marks because I could read something the night before an exam, parrot it, then wipe it clean out of my mind. I did the same at Vassar College. I think I must always have been attracted by words. At Vassar there was a woodsy path at one end of campus – I used to walk there reading aloud Vincent Millay, Swinburne, Chaucer, the King James version of the Bible for their sound, the music. One summer, I think I was in high school, I remember, vaguely, that I took a public-speaking course that taught me to reach an audience not by declaiming or being pedantic but by talking with enthusiasm about a subject you know. Sixty years later that's what I am doing, lecturing about my books and conservation to raise royalties for the Nature Conservancy and Manomet Bird Observatory, to whom I have given my contracts.

I was the only one of our family who went to college. My father was really extremely pleased. I enjoyed Vassar to a certain extent but at sixteen I was socially too young; I didn't know how to handle myself except in sports. I limped along and didn't really get any place. I had friends but no goals. When I was a junior, at eighteen, I fell in love and that was it – forever. In those days a long-distance call was a great luxury so I wrote letters to my love – a lot of letters. I still write a lot of letters. Maybe my tombstone should say this.

I finished college, married right away, had a baby right away. We lived in Cambridge. I used to push my baby carriage up and down the Charles River. I wasn't allowed to push it in Harvard Square because in the 1920's nice girls didn't walk about Harvard Square. These days you see many nice girls but no baby carriages. Emancipation has brought changes.

I was busy being a domestic wife and mother to three children. I always took care of them and our home. When we moved to Buffalo I made small gardens to keep me busy outdoors, was den mother to the many children on our block. I planted about six times more shrubs and flowers than could be taken care of. Years later when I was well into my forties and had become aware of birds, I planted berry-bearing shrubs close to our windows so I could sit inside and observe these denizens of a world so different from ours. I worked for the Scouts, the Mother's Council at the children's school, did the usual volunteer work suitable to a "young matron" with my friends.

During the Great Depression, in the early thirties, I wrote occasional small anecdotes for the *New Yorker* and sent them to E.B. White, a man I knew then only as someone my husband had been at summer camp with. He was the editor of the "Talk of the Town" department. Some little thing struck me and I would send him a paragraph. Andy, as his friends called him, would take it and print it just the way I sent it in. He would send me checks for two dollars for each one, advising me to put it into canned spinach. I guess he was living on canned spinach at the time too. I met a man and wife, out-of-towners, who worked for one of the newspapers. They had me write book reviews for them. It was fun but I was aware I had an inadequate background and that they were terrible. Then my friends left town.

In the 1940's I became editor of the *Buffalo Junior League Newssheet* because I could type and could take a wordy article, edit it to size. Being editor, I knew what everyone was doing but didn't have to be responsible for it. I was sent to conferences in Chicago and Seattle, my first independent, exciting trips in the early days of plane travel. Eventually I became president of the League, but I was poor at it. I didn't like being an executive at all. From that I moved to being a speaker for the Red Cross during World War II. The woman who was running the Buffalo office of the Red Cross was overworked, glad to have me take her material and deliver it. Very bad for my ego, very good training for what I do now. I talked for them and also for the Community Chest in industrial plants where no women worked. At one big ironworks, Dorothy Lamour was the only woman who had set foot inside (except for secretarial help) before me. The next year when I returned, half the work force were women. In those early days, sometimes the man who introduced me would apologize that the only speaker he could obtain was a woman. I talked to Curtiss Airplane Company

through a battery of loudspeakers with many hundreds of workers below my balcony. I was excited doing this, being successful.
My family never listened to my exhortations and stories – not
willingly anyway. The war ended, my sponsors tried to get me
into administrative work, but I'm no good at that. I went back
to being a housewife and became a bird-watcher.

In 1955 my husband, a retailing executive recently retired,
was asked to initiate and manage the United States participation in International Trade Fairs for the U.S. Commerce Department. We started in Karachi, Pakistan, were back and forth
to India the first year. It was too hot in Karachi to do more than
just exist (for me) but in New Delhi I started writing home
about what we were doing, how I spent my days, what I was seeing that was so extraordinarily different from our life at home.
I was given the various errands to run, with a driver whose
misfitting name in English was Lovely the Lion-hearted. He
wanted to show off his city so always took me the longest routes
to our destinations, explaining what I was seeing, taking me
into temples. International travel was not all that common
then. My vision was fresh because I was ignorant of foreign ways
and cultures, very excited about what I was seeing. I wanted my
family to see all these things too. I borrowed a typewriter and
wrote great long letters home, sending some of them to the
Buffalo Evening News. I expected they would edit them, I didn't
know what they would want, but they printed them as they
came. And writing was an outlet for my boredom, having to sit
about in hotels, as years before in Cambridge I couldn't roam
about the streets by myself.

We would be abroad for a few months, come home, then
be dispatched again, staying briefly or for a month or more in
European cities, Japan, Colombia. I didn't know enough to
appreciate what I was seeing, I never had the background I
needed, but I saw a lot. One summer when we were home our
daughter was in a motorcycle accident in Italy. We lived in a
hospital in Verona for six weeks, nursing her in her own language. I used to sit by the statue of the Virgin Mary at the end
of her corridor, praying for her recovery, laying flowers at
Mary's feet after my excursions to market. I wrote in detail
about everything to her grandparents. It was an emotional out-

let for me, she had been seriously injured. These letters and the newspaper accounts are in my files for her or her children to read someday. I have never been able to go back to them, it was too painful and difficult an experience. Our second son, a mountain climber, was in an accident in the Swiss Alps where two of his companions were killed. I have the newspaper accounts of this too. It's odd how in my books I can refer to my husband's death but I can't write about our children.

I don't remember writing letters when we were stationed in Europe or Colombia, perhaps because we moved around so constantly. I spent my time walking, looking, eating, wishing I could be in the country. I was poor at the languages, so when we came back to Washington, D.C. to live because Brad continued in the Commerce Department, I was always put next to foreigners at diplomatic dinners because I was so sympathetic to their language problems. I did volunteer work, helping foreigners – meeting them at airports when they came to this country under government sponsorship, helping them until they were safely at their destinations. I taught English to foreign doctors at a hospital – I wish I had taken notes; their backgrounds and stories were fascinating. To satisfy my craving for being outdoors I went out for the day with Audubon groups. I gave talks here and there I called "Birding in Forty-one Countries." It was terrible because the only birds I had seen abroad were in city parks. I was asked to write for a popular magazine but then they turned my efforts down; they wanted more scandalous material than I could offer. I was, after all, just a housewife.

None of this was training for the activities I plunged into when I was widowed. I became an amateur field ornithologist, wholly ignorant but enormously enthusiastic. I learned the trade of bird-banding through working during fall migration at two important stations on the East Coast. Bird-banding is a research activity done under license to the U.S. Fish and Wildlife Service as a way of studying the migrations, longevities, food requirements, habitats and habits of wild birds. When I moved to Florida to work as a volunteer with the biologist – in those days the only one – at Everglades National Park, I started my own fall migration banding station. It was then the only one south of Virginia and the only one on the East Coast operating in winter. I learned by doing, by being instructed by men who took me on expeditions that needed a bander. I worked in the Caribbean, in Ecuador, in Mexico and British Honduras (now Belize). It was wonderful. If I had thought in terms of writing, I could have written half a dozen books or articles. I did write small pieces for a few ornithological journals. These brought birders to unspoiled primitive areas that eventually tourists spoiled. In Florida I lectured on birds to schools and Audubon groups. My first published "story" was for Florida Audubon's magazine, an account of a baby barn owl a policeman brought me, thinking it a vulture. I raised it to flying over a period of two months, feeding it its natural prey of mice and rats that friends and school children brought me, taking it to schools to display it as a beneficient denizen of our world rather than as a target for a gun. Actually my story was a journal, as my two books *Peacocks* and *Parrots* have been. I wrote it in the fall of 1970 when I was 65 years old.

In the fall of 1978, the then head of the Arizona Nature Conservancy asked me if I would be willing to document the bird life, by banding, of a ranch the Conservancy had bought and had not yet had time to study. It was remote, there was no electricity, no communication, I might be alone some of the time living in a small cabin, but there would be researchers coming up frequently to study the soil and grasses and botany and the animals. Hikers would be there weekends to climb the trail up the seventy-five hundred foot peak of Baboquivari Peak, sacred to the Papago gods. I had been to Arizona several times years before, and forgetting that winter is winter wherever you go, I delightedly consented. A "one-hundred-year rain" washed out the access road and I had few of the promised visitors. In the five months I was there, I went out for mail and supplies and company only five times and I had to leave in January as snow and cold made bird-banding impossible and living difficult. The small stove that kept me and my two kettles warm took only three sticks of mesquite at a time. I had an absolutely wonderful time that winter, having to be resourceful, entirely independent for the first time in my life. I loved it. It was a tremendously liberating and maturing experience that I wish I could have had when I was in my twenties.

Several months after I had returned to Cape Cod, where I was now living summers, studying terns on the beaches, I read a journal by a writer of mysteries, Dorothy Gilman, who had moved from New York City to a Nova Scotia fishing hamlet. Implicit in her pages were changes that had come in her values, which I recognized as the changes that had come in mine. I thought, I'd like to do that about my mountain.

I think of my first book as an unplanned pregnancy because I had no intention of writing a book. I hadn't even kept a diary after the first few days on the mountain. I would write for two hours and still not say what I wanted to say. I thought, What am I doing this for? I want to go to bed. But I did have access to letters I had written that friends had kept. It is just like talking. And of course I had my daily ornithological log with its factual data.

I couldn't keep from writing that book, it thrashed around inside of me demanding to come out. I worked on it happily every chance I could get and in several months had something to send out. A friend who ran a small publishing house read it, sent it back with suggestions for revision, then died and his firm closed. A friend of my daughter heard about it, offered to edit it for me for a publishing firm he was starting, so I sent him the revised version. Many months later it came back, unsuitable for the type of pictorial coffee table books he was doing, with the suggestion I send it to a press he thought would be interested. By then I hadn't seen it in so long that I wanted to revise it again, and did. This new press accepted it immediately, sent me a contract, and then proceeded to rewrite the whole book, taking out all that mattered to me, substituting gray words for my more colorful ones. I was furious. We wrangled all one winter, then I broke our contract. I'm sure they were glad to be rid of me.

I took the original version I had sent them, went through it, revising again. When I read it even now I still see sentences I'd like to change and guess an author is never satisfied. I showed it to a friend here on Cape Cod, Robert Finch, who had had two fine naturalist books published, and asked his opinion. By then I felt my pages should go to the town dump, but I was being stubborn. Bob had helpful suggestions, encouraged me, had me send it to his editor at W.W. Norton & Co. who, some months later, read it and accepted it. Three years after I started it! But as I say, I hadn't meant to write a book. I didn't have the great desire to be published that many writers do; I was writing to please myself, enjoying the re-creation of a powerful experience.

I didn't know anything about the publishing business, so I had a dandy time working with this editorial voice over the telephone. And I think he was amused by my innocence and excitement. We became firm friends He sent my manuscript back with little stickers on the pages, "flags," he called them, indicating where a sentence needed to be clarified, expanded, deleted. When I went through the manuscript, here was somebody talking to me all along the line. Every once in a while, to keep me going, he would say he liked something very much. It was companionable, it was a new world. Norton has a toll-free number, so when I didn't understand what he wanted, didn't agree with him, I could call him up and he would explain. Even when he had to persuade me out of my stubbornness, he was gentle, patient; eventually I would accept his judgment. That's why I like editors – with just a suggestion, a stimulating sentence they send you off in new directions, change your horizons. Unlike that other press, he never revised, just made suggestions for me to follow in my own way.

I loved all this. I had a new friend. I could call any time I had a problem, he would call when he had a problem. We worked together all winter. I learned about designers and copy editors and occupations I had only vaguely known existed. Now that I was accepted I could let my family and friends know what I had been up to, hiding from them. They were as impressed as I was. And so, in 1983, at age 78, *Peacocks of Baboquivari* was published; I became an Author.

It was terrific. It came just in time to save me. My joints had become creaky and cranky, which was making my disposition cranky. I couldn't do the field work I had so enjoyed, I had to step aside for younger people. Who likes to do that? But now I was being asked to give talks on how I had come to write a book, how I had become a field ornithologist instead of acting my age. Program chairmen are often desperate for speakers and soon I was talking from Maine to Washington, D.C. to Buffalo to universities, community groups, libraries, men's Pancake Breakfasts (60 men all to myself for a whole hour!) I loved it. My ego became enormous. *Peacocks* was reviewed first in the *New York Times*, then in many other papers. I thought I had written a bird journal but no one else seemed to. This puzzled me but not to the point of being indignant.

There was one hitch. Once my book was out in the shops I was losing my constant connection with those new friends in New York. By then I had been to Norton's offices, met them face to face, eaten and drunk wine with them. I didn't want to lose them. All this talking I was doing to sell the book (because I wanted there to be royalties for the Nature Conservancy) was all very well, but I missed the comradeship we had established.

The year after *Peacocks* came out, I went down to Belize in Central America with a research group from the Manomet Bird Observatory to study our migrant forest birds in their winter habitats. We were there a month and because there were really more of us than were needed to do the work, I spent some of my time writing. I didn't have a purpose, I was just enjoying myself. I've been allied with the Observatory since their beginning and one day soon after, I thought, You know, if you could string these bits and pieces you've been writing into a book, you could keep on working with those nice people at Norton and you could give the royalties to Manomet, which would be grateful for any sum you might raise for them, however small. I hadn't meant to write one book, here I was considering a second. I thought this hilarious, but I became intrigued by the idea. I called Norton and my editor said, "Why not?" So I wrote *Parrots' Wood*, basing it on the ornithological work we had done in Belize, but bringing in pieces of my life.

A book is like a child, it doesn't turn out the way you plan, it develops a will of its own. And it is also like producing a child in that while you may have a conceptual partner, you do the work, you are the one who must carry it to term, who shapes and gives it life. A publishing house has to wait until you bring it in its basket, done up in ribbons, before they can start counting the fingers and toes, check on its heartbeat, decide whether or not they will take it in. When I sent it to my editor, he was delighted. I don't think there were ten flags on it; I didn't have to leave anything out. I started *Parrots* in the winter of 1983 and it came out in 1985.

That summer my editor asked me if I would write an essay on bird-banding, perhaps twenty-five pages, for him to use for a nonprofit organization that taught publishing to minorities, helping them get employment. It wasn't to sell, it was a teaching device. I'd been banding birds by then for thirty years and giving demonstrations as well as illustrated lectures on banding, off and on for nearly as long, so I knew the questions people asked, anecdotes that might interest them. I did a hasty job. If I had known that six months after my new press – which I established for the purpose – had this essay, "The Bird with the Silver Bracelet" paperbacked, I would have distributed over twelve thousand copies to Audubons, Conservancies, nature centers, and environmental groups to sell for their own profit, I would surely have paid more attention! Perhaps it's just as well I didn't. As I said, a book runs away with you. I had to become a one-woman press, I had to become a business woman. At my age? My lawyer offered to be my assistant secretary. "You can't be," I told him. "I don't even have a secretary." I have a lot of trouble getting the State of Massachusetts to understand that I am not withholding employees' wages, not needing to present quarterly profit-and-loss sheets and all that. An author should stick to writing, not branch out so lightheartedly.

This year my editor honey-tongued me into writing another essay for the Coalition of Publishers for Employment. Another writer had failed him at the last moment, could I whip up "a bird-watcher's cookbook?" "No," I said firmly. "I'm no cook. I haven't had to cook for twenty years and besides, all bird-watchers eat is peanut butter and apples. They're out with their binoculars and telescopes and cameras . . ." But he was in a jam and we are friends, so I ended up obliging him with twenty-five pages for the Coalition.

The next thing I knew I had a contract for a full-scale cookbook to be built from those twenty-five pages. "Never mind the recipes," he told me, "just write a lot of chatter." To my amazement, and I am sure to Norton's amusement at my grumbling and mumbling about the distances between a freezing Arizona mountain on the Mexican border and a steaming stew, I have delivered them a manuscript. It occupied me during the winter doldrums. I am sure my friends wince when they see me coming with yet another experimental dish wrapped in a kitchen towel. Trying to assemble the book in some sort of order was hard on my disposition, but it is done, probably because it kept snowing and I couldn't get my car out my long driveway. It is a journal more than a cookbook, I fear. As I say, a book goes off in its own directions, thumbing its nose at its mother.

.   .   .

How do I write? That is the question I get most frequently. What is the actual process? I use a typewriter mostly. I don't use a word processor, I'm too old to conquer its mechanics. I like to look out my window when I am writing. I see, not a piece of paper, but my garden or snow making a filigree of the bushes or birds that come and go at my feeders. I note their dominance or nod at a neighbor's dog that comes to see if I have tossed out burned cookies. I can't write when there are interruptions. If I start working and the telephone rings, it interrupts my thinking and when I come back, even when I'm revising or proofreading, it takes me an hour or so to get inside what I'm doing again. On the other hand you can't turn your telephone off. It might be something exciting. I don't write well at night, almost always I have to rewrite the next day. So I do my tidy copying at night, the mechanical work. Although sometimes, rarely, when the hours stretch quiet and limitless and there is nothing to distract me, I could write all night. If I get hungry the spell is broken.

I think I see my world in words the way an artist must see it in designs and colors. I translate what I am seeing, what I feel, into words to make my vision real to me. I am always stringing words together, hunting for just the right one. And for some reason my creative self functions best when I'm surrounded by chattering people. What they are saying isn't important; they are telling stories and laughing, I don't really need to pay attention. Something that is said, or something in the atmosphere, or somebody I am looking at quite casually triggers something inside of me. Or is it a way of withdrawing from the group? I don't know. I can be sitting with people who are eating and talking and something I want to write, something I must write flows through me. I don't know where this demand comes from. Or if I am driving a car any distance, relaxed, seeing what is on the road, aware of the cars ahead and beside me, another side of my brain suddenly comes to life. I can't make it happen, it just does. I wrote a lot of *Parrots* in a room full of people or pulled off to the side of a highway. But if I don't catch the sentences flowing they are gone; often I can't even remember their subject. I may wake in the night, my subconscious ordering my thoughts, dictating two and three and four pages that I could never reproduce in the morning. The best parts of my books have come this way.

Finally when I have a sheaf of these random writings in hand, I have to find a way to weave them together. Writing them is fun. But trying to put them together in a rational way, that's work. I believe that whatever degree of facility I may have, it is necessary to pare and polish, revise and revise, then polish and pare some more until each sentence says not only what I want it to, but has made my meaning crystal clear to my readers. And it is necessary not to care about having readers. It is myself ultimately I write for. I have to satisfy myself before I can go public.

When I read, months later or years later, what I have put into one of my books, I am astonished. I wrote *that*? I know the paragraphs practically by heart but where is the woman who wrote them?

I think age is an advantage to a writer because there is a great pool of living to draw from. Both *Peacocks* and *Parrots* reflect this. It was unintentional, but my past lives, my emotional life surfaces – the reviews claim – through what I thought I was simply describing. I'd say my chief obstacles are not my age or lack of experience in writing but the lack of a definite goal. I need to be triggered. Also, I lack judgment. I can look at paragraphs, at whole pages and wonder, Should I leave these in or take them out? That's where a good editor is so important, to stimulate and reinforce as well as to be critical. I do know that what comes across the best is what has given me the most pleasure – or pain – in writing it.

Arlene Swift Jones

With Apologies to Blake and Exxon

Tiger, tiger, in your cool
night forest, come down out
of that burning bright
and fill my whatever-is-

the-equivalent of tank:
my sinews, my teeth . . . my nails,
to make me a burning
red dread. She-devil, if

you like. Come into my
smoldering and make my
brain, each innard flame.
No blame, my tiger.

I will be no lamb.
Burn me right up to the
last detail. In short,
immortalize my poetic

nights and in the day
just lay those velvety
stripes and tawny touch
right over my symmetry.

Poussin's "The Martyrdom of St. Erasmus"

The Vatican Exhibit at the Metropolitan Museum, NYC

The real crowdgatherer is
Poussin's bloody martyrdom
of Erasmus: his back on
a bench, his hands tied

to a block behind his head,
torso stretched drumtaut.
Attached to a rope, a hook
obvious in its intent,

gouges inwards to entrails
which will be pulled out
by a wheel. It will un-
ravel Erasmus: stomach

squashed, his intestines
will wrap like rope
on the spool. All will follow:
the hooked liver, the found

lungs, bursting their air.
Erasmus' eyes are paired
agates circling the small
rooms of his skull: his

teeth grind the red of his
mouth. All watch: the helmeted
soldier as witness,
the man at the wheel

to turn it, two angels
to place laurel on the
remains of his body. We, too,
wait – to catch the heart

still beat on the hook,
see the last silence sweep
the failed hands, the stilled feet,
be in the just-quitted rooms.

Rheumatoid Arthritis
for Drs. CLS, CSR
(The Hospital for Special Surgery, NYC)

Parts of my hands, my left
knee, are dust. They were
incinerated in the hospital
dump. Ashes already.

We work together, decide
which bones have expired
their use, talk about them
like old friends now dis-

tanced by their going off.
Now the shoulders' turn: their
sockets once so gleaming
remarkably like giant pearls

in their oyster cases,
the bluebone now bruising
as beachstones with the sea
gone, leeched away. Its

synovial sheath corroded, it
scrapes the pearl metamorphosed
into sponge gone fossil-rigid.
We talk about them as though

they are a raspberry garden
brambled by overgrowth, by
canes which must be thinned
to save the strength of berries,

to fatten the purpling mass,
sweeten juices; as though they
are bittersweet gone beyond
into a neighbor's orchard,

climbing trees, choking apples.
It is easier to lose parts
bit by bit than have the earth
greet you whole, and suddenly.

Silences

for Tillie Olsen

There are graves all around me
            of poems.
They are my own.
            I have walked over them
An insult to the dead
            my mother said
to walk on graves.

            I walk on them.

They are untended –
            aborted –
            a tear in the grass.

My mother was right
            because the graveyard
talks, walks, follows me
            everywhere
reminds me of hulls, husks
            skeletons, shells.

I have tried to fill
            that emptiness in me
with womanly things:
            jars of pickles
letters, cookbook meals.

The graves stalk me;
            the graves have eyes
            arms, legs
pickaxes, shovels;
            they would bury me.

Going Home to Iowa

I meet the land in my throat,
its small mounds rising; I have
known each one in particular:

wet creeks crevice into throats
and rise with rain from the sky,
blurring the hopeless lilacs;

the black walnut trees
slip like apparitions
out of dark solutions.

Presence was all: it was
the white leaf of love,
my absence unredeemable,

black as the loam of the earth
now covering rowed graves
with names deep in stone,

names once my own.
I look for me everywhere
in dry grasses, in spines

of burdock which cling to me,
milk pods spewing down,
the insisting thistle,

purple-flowered – its thorn
touches my reaching hand.
I know each weed, where it grows

as I know that the latch
on the door rejects me, rusted
and closed to me, from inside.

Lumbar Fusion

for Dr. Leon Root
(The Hospital for Special Surgery, NYC)

My bones spout blood, mopped by sponges.
Ears not mine hear the sizzle
and know the stench of cautery.

In this sleep without dreams,
my body "n-shaped" on the Wilson frame,
my dorsal landscape is devastated.

Skidders plough through the terrain,
stripping my spine. Bone is bulldozed,
timbered, peeled clean as a pearl.

They are *harvesting bone in standard fashion.*
My iliac crest is scrimshaw,
is cut into matchsticks, stacked,
bridged, to buttress my spine.

II

I am a white spider,
my eight legs tubes;
inside them, blood, air, water, life
scurry like ants: carry, return, carry;
each journey is a satellite tracing
of friendly or enemy craft.

The dials of my heart hold steady,
indicators count each lost cell.
The seismographic screen
writes the thunder of my lungs.
Breaths are black ink.

My face is nothing. A nose, a mouth
with antennae that bypass the scrape.

III

Rubber hands recover the landscape,
close fascia, subcutaneous intracuticular
layer on layer locked, wired shut.

I am a delivered cocoon
brought forth from a frozen landscape.
The suck of pump prods ears
beginning to hear.

My eyes tear
at the first
felt touch of a hand.

Symbiosis

Roots of the trailing arbutus live in a partnership relationship with a fungus. The plant is difficult to cultivate.

— Columbia Encyclopedia

The snow has rotted –
I stagger out, light-blinded –
my foot makes a black hole in winter.

I see a white trail, jet-iced in blue sky,
of people going somewhere,
to another country, maybe.
Darkness is where my feet go.

Black trees shiver. Shrug.
They tell me nothing.
I stand here,
all motion frozen,
my foot in the black hole
of what I know. It is easier
to stand still than go anywhere.

But my feet are impatient with me.
It is too soon, I tell them,
to lay bare my gloved fingers
and move their cold touch
under the curled needles of pine.
The sodden oak leaves still carry their heaviness,
my feet their own unleavened weight.

Still, there is no stopping either of us:
the stirred ganglia trailing each other
through moss, soft on these unforgiving rocks,
among patches graced with earth warming, sharing
the leftover leaves.

We go creeping, sending out
last year's messages to each other.
My hand obeys, naked, feeling its way,
runs along hairy, wind-toughened nerves,
finds the cow-tongued rasp of survived leaves:
the soft, first cry speeds up my arm,
informs my eye, my nose,
of the at-last-found pink-white
pungently-singing-breath of the
trailing arbutus.

Arlene Swift Jones

I grew up on an Iowa farm four miles from the nearest village, on which my father raised corn, oats and legumes on three hundred and eighty acres. My mother, who was educated up to ninth grade in a Quaker boarding school conducted in Norwegian, was a very religious woman, a serious person of quiet nature given to much introspection. She was an unlearned poet who wrote mournful poetry and family sagas and memorized long poems, including "The Vision of Sir Launfal." Had she been educated and trained, I think she probably would have been a fine poet.

I was a great tomboy, very much entertained by nature and animals. I rode horses, I swam, I went hunting, I was very, very physically active and strong. I enjoyed the strength, the movement of the body. I really competed with my brothers and wanted their approval and recognition as an equal, which I had for quite a while. I recognized that men had a more interesting time than women. In fact when I was a very small child, no more than three and a half, I wanted to be a man. I told my parents that I wanted to be called Johnny and when I grew up I wanted to be called John. I was always called Johnny by my father and mother.

I loved horses, I think, from the moment I was born. Before I was four years old, I could take my father's gray horses when he came home from the field, unhitch them and climb up on them. Once they were in the manger, I could take off their heavy bridles and feed them and lead them to water. I always had to make sure I kept out of their way because I was always barefoot, but I was never frightened of them. I loved every horse, every dog, every sheep, every cow. When I was twelve, I raised a calf in the boys' 4-H. The most terrible thing was knowing I was sending it off to slaughter – it was almost unbearable – yet I realized that farm animals were raised to be killed. That was the way farmers lived.

I hated to work inside. I helped my father and my sister helped my mother. When I was nine or ten, there was a threshing run comprised of many families and on my pony I carried water to the men in the fields, filling up the jugs, dumping them out, filling them up with fresh water and going again, all day long. Later I drove the horses when the hay was carried load after load to the barn, and I drove the tractor for my father when we cut the grain. I was very much a part of the seasons. Yet I always knew I would go away. I remember, as a small child, counting out-of-state cars, looking at people in cars going somewhere and saying, "I want to just get in a car and go." It isn't that I didn't love my home. I was very attached to it, to my mother. But I wanted to see the world, I wanted to understand what it was like beyond where I had grown up. My mother recognized that the best way she could help me was to let me go. I think that was quite remarkable.

As a child I read everything I could get my hands on, which wasn't a lot. The library that I had access to when I was in grammar school was open one day a week; I would take out four books, read them in two days and then have to wait until the next week. If I didn't have anything else, I just reread my books. I would even read the dictionary. I remember writing poems for my brother's school assignments when I was in third and fourth grades. He always got "A's" for them. I suppose I wrote them for myself too, but I don't remember. I know I always *wanted* to write. But I would tell my sister and she would laugh at me, so I kept it very quiet. I remember once dusting the upstairs and looking out at the sky and wanting to write: I didn't know what to do, how to do it, but I just felt the need so much. Once in high school, after we read a war story, "Fourteen Men from Company K," we were asked to write something ourselves. I wrote a story about an American and a German encountering each other at the front: I gave them one moment of recognition and an attempt to extend a hand to each other, as if to say, We're men, we're brothers. And then one was killed by the other. I remember having a lot of pleasure writing it.

I chose to go to Cornell College in Mount Vernon, Iowa because one of the faculty members had won the Pulitzer Prize. That was so impressive and exciting that there was no other place I wanted to go. It was one of the earliest colleges where writing was taught. In my freshman year, I took writing as an additional course by permission of the teacher, a man named Toppy Tull, who was a friend of Carl Sandburg, Edna St. Vincent Millay, Robert Frost and other writers who came to the campus. There wasn't anything structured about his class, you never had assignments, you just wrote what you wanted when you wanted. That's when I really started writing, both poetry and short stories, always out of my own experience. Toppy Tull liked what I wrote; I seemed to be the star of the class as I recall. Some of my friends complained about my working all the time. They would sit in what they called the "Cole Bin" and smoke and chat away or go to movies. How could I say I'd rather write a story than sit and talk to them? But, in general, that's the way I felt.

In my freshman year, I had two things published in *Husk*, the college literary magazine – which was really like a small university publication. The first was in an issue with an article by Frank Lloyd Wright. It was a story about a colt, born to a mare I had, that died five days later of a malformation of the intestine. That was the greatest tragedy that had happened to me – imagine that! It was told in first person and was a very straightforward, honest and rather passionate story. After it was published, my Shakespeare professor stopped me on the street and said, "Miss Swift, that was the most beautiful story!" I was so excited. The next day he stopped me again and said, "I'm still thinking about that story, it was really beautiful." I also had a poem published, called "Not Pain Alone." It suggested that it isn't just pain which gives things value, but good feelings too. I think that was a rejection of the religion under which I grew up: you're supposed to suffer here, so you can have the next world full of bliss. Well I was beginning to think that was pretty stupid. *Just* beginning to.

I got some thing in *Husk* in my sophomore year as well, a story of prejudice against an adopted boy in the small town in which I grew up. People always pointed a finger at him, that he was illegitimate, that he was going to be like his father. The whole thing intrigued me, but I didn't presume to answer the question of which came first, the prejudice or the fact that the boy was lazy, that he was not well-mannered or well-disciplined. That story was listed in Martha Foley's *Best American Stories of the Year* as "Distinctive." There in the list was John Steinbeck's name and after it, Arlene Swift. The recognition made me feel a great responsibility and, at the same time, it made me feel unworthy. If I could have gone home and said, "Look what happened to me, isn't that great!" and they had said "That's fantastic, you must continue!" perhaps it would have been different. I remember receiving a letter from an agent who said that he handled the work of Somerset Maugham, among others, and would like to handle my work. I never responded, I never even showed the letter to anybody. I was embarrassed. I thought, If he ever knows I'm only eighteen years old, he would never want to represent me. So I won't tell him.

Then I started working on my thesis which was about Robinson Jeffers. I chose him because the first poem of his I read hit me like a thunderbolt. It had to do with nature, the recognition of its beauty and cruelty as well. Then I stumbled upon "The Roan Stallion," just the right stuff for somebody eighteen years old who loved horses. I spent hours and hours reading and studying his work and really imitated him for quite a while. I wrote quite a fine poem about a horse that was published in *Husk*, called "The Star Fell Cold." I think I was prouder of that than anything I had written up to that point. Somehow I had reached a condensed and compact language, perhaps from the great amount of reading that I had done.

Toward the end of college I fell madly in love with a young student who was going to study medicine, and he fell madly in love with me. His parents thought that I was the most wonderful thing and almost, in a way, pressed an engagement. I suppose that always causes people to rebel. In short, he walked away and I felt devastated. I was lonely and lost and miserable for awhile.

I think the world was permeated with the fact that what women did wasn't that important, because eventually they were going to get married and not use what they did. That's what my father said all the time. What was different about me was that I was going to find a man whose career was sufficiently important that I could aid in his career. My mother said you should marry by the time you are twenty-four. I suppose that's what I expected and in the meanwhile I could do what I wanted, which was to go out and get a job.

I went out and started teaching – it was 1949 and I was just twenty-one. I was hired in a Cedar Rapids, Iowa school system as a "floating teacher" for six months, and then I was to be a regular teacher the following year. I loathed the whole thing, the teaching, the classroom; I felt I'd be there the rest of my life and I hated it. I was saved though, because I got a fellowship to Columbia which I had applied for because the professor who had won the Pulitzer Prize had had the same scholarship. It paid my entire way, including my fare and pocket money. The letter came in April and when I had to break a contract, the superintendent practically swore at me and said he would see that I never got another teaching job as long as I lived. It was hard but I think he succeeded in making me all the more determined to do it. If he had been nice and reasoned with me somewhat more, I probably would have reconsidered.

I didn't do any writing at Columbia because I completed a master's degree, including a thesis, in nine months. My teachers were some of the major people that were ever at Columbia: Lionel Trilling, Mark Van Doren, Joseph Wood Crutch, Marjorie Hope Nicholson. I thought about writing; I would sit in class and get ideas for poems or stories and write them down, but I never really finished anything. I did, however, see a lot of New York: I went to the theater, to the opera for the first time, I talked to a lot of people. I lived at International House and my first group of friends included an Indian, an Englishman, a man from Texas, a girl from California, a Swiss. No one was from an Iowa farm, so I was as unique as they were.

Quite soon, I recognized that I'd better figure out what I wanted to do or I would be teaching again. I applied for a Fulbright to England and a scholarship to the University of Oslo. I got the scholarship to Oslo for the summer, got on a boat, went to Europe and stayed for four years. After the University of Oslo, I traveled by bicycle through northern Europe, England, France. Eventually I had to get a job to stay in Europe. I traveled through every city in Germany where the U.S. forces were, looking for a teaching job because it seemed the most suitable for me. But I wasn't qualified because I didn't have two years' teaching experience. Eventually I got a job in Salzburg as an administrative assistant. There I met the man I married. There it was, I got married at age twenty-four. Ten months after I was married I had my first baby. And within three and a half years, I had three.

My husband worked for the Central Intelligence Agency and we were undercover as foreign service, living and traveling in Germany, Poland, Cyprus, the U.S., Norway, Switzerland. It was often a tense situation for him, for us; I had three little girls on my hands. It would take me six months to get the family settled in a country; for the children, home became where I was. I entertained a great deal. In fact, until the late 1960's every foreign service officer's efficiency report included a report on his wife, how she fit in diplomatic circles, how she entertained.

When my youngest child was four months old, I said, I have got to get a job. I couldn't wait to get a teaching job. The big problem was I couldn't get a job until I had someone to look after the children, and I couldn't pay someone to look after the children until I had a job. Eventually it worked out, and then – pack up and leave and start over again in another country. I taught in every country where I went, either in diplomatic schools or in a local school. I taught high school seniors and freshmen, I taught first grade in Poland and was later headmistress of that school. I lectured in universities, as guest speaker, on American literature, theater. Teaching kept me out of all the tea parties, the bridge, the social engagements, things that I hated, and it gave me a feeling of doing something worthwhile other than entertaining myself and the community at large. I led this life for more than twenty years, from 1952 when I was married until 1975.

I didn't write after I got married, but I always wanted to. I still have masses of notebooks with jottings in them for things that I wanted to write. The reason I didn't just sit down and do it, I think, is that my life was so fragmented. It seemed so presumptuous, somehow, that I would set aside time and that everyone who needed me could not come and make their demands. I am at the service of everyone, available to my community, my family, my children, everybody. I always was. I just couldn't say, Okay, this time is mine, don't bother me. But when we were living in Switzerland in 1970, I met a young woman who was a writer. When it came out that I had written, wanted to write, wasn't writing, she said, "But you *must* do it. Next week, I want to see something that you have written." I sat down and wrote a short story in one day and sent it to her. Then I did it again. She really got me started. I needed someone to say, "Why don't you *do* it." Or just someone to imitate. *She* did it, *she* set aside her time, nobody bothered *her*, no one was allowed to intrude on *her* life. She had a very small child and I didn't have anyone at home. Two of my girls were in prep school in the United States and the youngest one was fourteen. I thought if she can do it, I ought to be able to do it. And then I sat down and wrote quite a few more stories. I would send them to my friend, and we would get together about them. I started writing poetry in there as well, but I didn't really concentrate on it.

When we came back home in 1975, at the end of foreign service, I spent about a year and a half redoing our house, which was built by my husband's grandfather, and then became the assistant academic dean and college counselor at Ethel Walker School. At school I was always busy interviewing, counseling, running winter sessions; at home I wrote all of the girls' college recommendations. I worked eighteen to twenty-hour days. One day, when I had been there three years, I sat down and said to myself, Is this what you want to do? And I answered, No, I don't. I want to write, but not this. I was in my early fifties. I have been writing full-time since then, mostly poetry, but also prose.

I've written a book on Cyprus where I lived during the time

the Greeks and Turks started fighting each other. For three years I sat there watching Greeks and Turks locked in a need to confront each other; I watched people march over a precipice with their eyes wide open, knowing that nothing would ever be the same again. I learned a lot there. I took the book to a friend of a friend in Washington, D.C. whose work was to aid people in how to approach publishers. I saw him for an hour; it cost me forty dollars. I sent that book out to twelve major publishers with a cover letter written as he suggested I write it and I used his name. I heard from every one of them. Several said they would like to see more of my work. I rewrote the book, sent it out again and it was rejected with high praise. It has been sitting in my desk more or less ever since. Now, with advice from my teacher, Dick Allen, I am preparing to revise it again.

In 1979 I started a book about four generations of women. I had spent some time in the Quaker library in London, researching how Quakerism arrived in Norway and found that very fascinating. I had been to Norway again to visit family. The novel, which I call, *Four Horses, Four Riders*, concerns the breaking away of women from a very traditional role and a very religious upbringing. The first generation totally accepts tradition, the second has problems but is not questioning, the third has no problem until the teens or early adulthood, and then lots of problems and, finally, rejection. And her children have been brought up with no religion whatsoever. The question of what you substitute I leave unresolved at the end of the book. I am now revising it and have an editor waiting to read it.

.   .   .

I feel especially isolated from other writers because I lived out of this country for so long and then returned to my husband's birthplace where I had no connections. I live in a small town twenty-five miles from Hartford, an hour to Yale in New Haven, about forty-five minutes to Trinity College. I drive to these colleges for poetry readings and have tried to get into workshops, but they take only full-time students. I have looked for groups of people who share writing around here, but the ones I would like to join do not want an extra person. I was talking to a friend of mine who belongs to a group here and he said, "I wouldn't think of sending a poem out without running it by a group." And I said, "I have to, I don't have any choice."

One summer I went for a ten-day writing program at Duke University where Marvin Bell and Dave Smith were teachers and where I thought I was going to be part of a select group of experienced poets. There were some very nice people in the class, but many of them had never read a poem in their lives, much less written one, or they wrote a jingly kind of love poem. I don't mean to say that they are never going to be poets. Maybe they are. But I went to that workshop for tough criticism, and it turned out that *everybody* was wonderful, *everybody* was encouraged, *everybody* got patted on the back. When I said something critical about a poem, I was rather slapped on the back of my hands because it wasn't nice. In retrospect though, it wasn't a waste of time, because the workshop put me a little more in touch with the field of poetry and also taught me something about the system. Two years later I went to Bennington for a month-long writing program, though I couldn't remain for more than two weeks because I had to go into the hospital to have my knee replaced. The seminar met for an hour and a half every other day; nothing was scheduled in the afternoon so that people could write. Well that is all right for many people, but not for me since I live in a fair amount of isolation. I wanted things going on, more lectures, more contact.

What I have found is, if you are aggressive, you can just take your poems up to a teacher and say, "Would you read my stuff?" or "Have lunch with me." Poets seem to like it. But I am not that sort of person. I just can't go up and say "Hey! Read this poem. What do you think about this? What do you think about me?" I don't think poetry is a community experiment, I think it is a very private thing. But I go to workshops because I need some kind of professional contact, and I tend to believe that since these guys are poets and published, I should listen to them. But sometimes I sit back and say, No, I don't agree with that, that is *not* my poem.

I have been persistent in looking for contact. Once, after reading an inspiring article called "The Passion of the Modern Poet" in *The Writer*, by the poet Dick Allen, I found out where he was and got in touch with him. He took me on as an independent student at the University of Bridgeport which is an hour and twenty minutes from here. I go every two weeks and find it very, very fruitful. It's the contact, it's discussing poetry with someone.

. . .

I would have stopped long ago, I think, if publication were the only goal. You write because you need to, because you want to, because you have the ego to think you have something to say. It sorts out the world, keeps you sane, keeps chaos from your door, tells you what you think. Publication has come slowly though I send out and send out my poetry. I have received four hand-written notes from the editor of *Poetry*, notes from the editors of *NERBLQ, Ploughshares, Prairie Schooner, Shenandoah*. And not one of them has taken one poem! One of them said they are not personal enough. One said they were prosy. But I consider my work very concentrated and not prosy. I have encouraging personal letters from two university presses. One said my poetry manuscript was very worthy work which would be rewarded, and another wrote that among the seven hundred or so manuscripts received, he wanted mine, but the board didn't agree. I feel encouraged, but as Mark Twain said, "There is quite a difference between a cat and a catnip." (I'm not sure those are his exact words, but that was the intent.) There is quite a difference between being published and not being published. The first thing people ask you is, "Are you published?" It doesn't mean you are good, but it is a general acceptance. It makes you feel that somebody else believes in you. It is contact with the world of poets.

Rejections don't surprise me anymore. What surprises me is acceptance. I have three poems published in *Calyx,* Fall, '85. I have a poem in *Tar River,* one in *Calliope.* When I sent three or four poems for consideration by *Chowder Review,* the editor, Ron Slate, wrote back and said he would be happy to read a chapbook. I sent him one. Mine was selected to be published, but then they didn't have the money to publish it. I think I was more disappointed in hearing that the money had been withdrawn than I was elated with the fact it was selected. But I am

happy to say, my chapbook, called *The Insisting Thistle*, is about
to be published by Andrew Mountain Press in Hartford.

I have read my poems at libraries, in high school classes,
for a Unitarian group meeting, in a New York loft for a group
of friends invited by an artist. I enjoyed the readings because I
like the contact with people and I think I always interest people
with my poetry. My poetry is not obscure, you do not need a
dictionary for it, but it also is not simple. I like to think it
deserves many readings. I want my work to make people realize
the moment in which they live, what it is, the feel or the taste of
the air around them, the things that grow. Nature is very
important to me, though except for animals, it didn't used to
be. I marvel at the eternal spring that keeps coming, the
extraordinary tenacity of life. I am not a person who wants to
write about the hopelessness of the human condition. I am not
a pessimist.

Although some editors say my work is not personal enough,
I never want "me" in my poems. What I object to in much of
the poetry I read is that the little tiny thing that "I" did, along
with my lover, becomes significant in itself without being
attached to a larger meaning. I don't care about those poems,
because they are not telling me anything which is original or
interesting or different – they are just whining. I think I am
probably old-fashioned. The kind of short story I wrote when I
was eighteen would never be listed as distinctive today. It is a
very honest, passionate story, the kind of stuff I still write.

.   .   .

In regard to process, I start a poem with a line or phrase. That
line or phrase often comes to me at four o'clock in the morning and if I don't write it down, I won't have it. I write things
down in the dark, or if it's not freezing – as it usually is in the
winter – I get up and go to my study. A few words are enough;
the phrase makes me build the whole poem around it. I jot on
a yellow pad, not in order but as they come to me, all the
thoughts I have on the subject of the poem. I put them in some
sort of shape and write it out by long hand until it begins to
look like something. And as soon as it does, I put it on my word
processor; I like to see the shape of it physically. Sometimes I

get, not the line or the words, but just the idea of a poem I want to write. I can describe the idea on a whole page but I don't have a single word of the poem. Then I really just have to think about it intensely until it somehow takes shape. Sometimes, and this is pretty rare, the poem just writes itself. Most often I rework and rework and rework. I change a period. I move a word to the next line. I really try to get myself inside that poem so intently that the shell of the poem is around me and there is nothing else in my world but that poem. When I think I've finished a poem, I leave it for three or four days or longer and then go back to it. Then I see things new. After that I like not to go back to it, because I can linger and linger over it instead of going on to something else, and that is always a temptation or a problem.

I am often inspired in museums and have written a number of poems on medieval manuscripts. I often stand in front of a painting, as I did with "Poussin's 'The Martyrdom of St. Erasmus,'" and write the whole poem on the program, around the edges. That poem is really about people watching other people being cruel, not about saintdom or martyrdom or Christianity at all. It started out with three verses preceding the way it starts now, and halfway down the poem I said, "But the real crowdgatherer is . . ." I made that line the beginning. I reworded the last four lines endlessly.

. . .

So much of my life was jobs and children and responsibility. I didn't ever regret the teaching jobs. I learned a lot, I had contact with people, I made a lot of people love literature and taught them how to write a straightforward, honest sentence. I do feel that I have community responsibilities – I was just brought up like that. Since we moved to Connecticut, I served six years on the regional school board for a high school, with weekly meetings and committee meetings lasting several hours. I was on the search committee traveling around to all the schools, interviewing candidates for superintendent. I spent a lot of time improving the local library. I also am still the hostess and mother of my house, even though my children have gone. That is something I choose to do – they are my family, I love them, I have good relationships with them. I have three daughters: one lives at home and is in medical school, one is an artist in New York, and my eldest lives nearby and is a real estate dealer. Other things that keep me from writing are certain physical problems I have. I spend a lot of time in the hospital.

Yes, I regret not writing all those years. I sometimes wonder how would I have handled a particular topic thirty years ago. It would have been different, of course. And I wish I *had* said it then, that I considered it important enough, that somebody had given me some encouragement. If I had read Dorothy Brande's book, *Becoming a Writer*, thirty years ago, it would have made a lot of difference to me. She said, You have *got* to practice. Take yourself seriously. Call yourself a writer. Do it. But really I couldn't with small children. My husband thought I could take an hour here, take an hour there, but I can't write like that. It's not like crocheting, you just don't turn it on and turn it off – it requires long preparation in your mind and self-examination. I regret all the years I didn't write, but I keep saying, It is past, forget it, do it now, don't waste your time. So that is what I am trying to do. As an older writer, you really sift out things that perhaps are more trivial. What I mean is, there is a certain urgency now which I wouldn't have had thirty years ago. There is nothing wrong with a certain urgency.

Naomi Feigelson Chase

. . .

What Can You Do about Love

"Nobody sleeps together anymore," Jerry said when I told him Lucy and Jim hadn't slept together for a year.

"But they've only been married two years," I said, "and already they're getting divorced."

"They're just a la mode, dearie," he answered, lunching with me in the Atrium Club, an unlit cigarette between his teeth to keep him from smoking. "Chic. If they hadn't slept together at all, they might not be splitting."

"You're too sophisticated," I said. "And they're not English. They're not the Harold Nicolsons. Or Leonard and Virginia Woolf. And they're both heterosexual. At least I think they are."

Jerry was disdainful. "You're such an old-fashioned girl," he said. "I'm not talking heterosexual. I'm talking celibacy. I've been celibate two years now."

It surprised me to hear that. "What about Karen?" I asked. "Don't you live with her?"

"Live, yes. Sleep, no. I've no desire. I've told her, 'Have a fling if you like. Just don't tell me about it.'"

"And how does Karen feel about that?" I asked.

He ignored my question. "Really, Lila, you'd be better off like me. Celibacy's 'in.' You should try it."

"I'll think about it," I said, but I was dubious. Jerry put out his unlit cigarette and reached for the check.

"If you're celibate, what do you do about love?" I asked.

"Love," he said, "what does anyone do about love?"

One night when Max and I were working late, he asked, "You want to hear something really sick?"

"Depends how sick," I said, knowing he'd tell me anyway.

"Pretty sick."

"Oh, go ahead, tell me."

"Well, we were at this gay bar and the waiter told us that every once in a while, when he needed money, he'd hustle, it was so easy. So we asked him what was the worst thing ever happened to him, and he said it hadn't happened to him, but the worst thing he's ever heard about was some guy getting off on paying a guy to kill a bird."

"You're right. That's really sick," I said.

Alice is very upset about the sex-abuse scandals, kids in day care centers, two-, three-, four-year olds, babies. First in California, now in New York. Even the Minneapolis theater where she once worked. It's true, it's all over the place.

Alice wants to know why it's happening now.

I tell her it's always happened. Not that it's any comfort. It's just today, nothing sacred is sacred. Nothing profane is private. Look at Virginia Woolf. Her uncle abused her as a child and maybe it made her crazy. And everyone knows about it.

Look at Lucy. Lucy's uncle forced her to have sex with him for twelve years, from the time she was four. Her mother's brother. When her parents found out, they were furious with Lucy. It makes me sick. It made Lucy sick.

The Mayflower Madame is the newest, juiciest media scandal. "Mayflower Madame" is what the *Post* named her. They published her family tree which goes back to William Bradford. I wonder what Bradford would say about her.

The Mayflower Madame is demure, wears tailored black suits and plain black pumps, has one of those little Dutch girl haircuts. Of course, it was a cover, no pun intended. The Mayflower Madame ran a one thousand dollars a night call-girl operation. She has an MBA. Everyone says she's a great manager. Kept records on her girls' weight, menstrual periods. Put her girls on report when they gained a pound. When she hired them, the *Post* says, she told them deportment and conversational tact were very important. They never need stay with anyone they didn't like.

Could I have read somewhere that Mrs. Samuel Clemens deleted the "begats" from editions of Twain's novels. That doesn't sound right. I think she deleted all references to sex from his novels and took the "begats" out of his Bible.

Last week the Mayflower Madame was arrested. Her old boyfriend sold some seven-year old nude pictures of her to the newspapers. She looked terrific. He said she left him because he was Jewish. He said she was very classy. And well organized. Everyone agrees she was well organized.

Maddie says all her husbands took nude pictures of her. None of my husbands took nude pictures of me. I wonder, is that very common?

I once saw Maddie half dressed. She has big, round breasts. I tried to figure out how much more of them she shows when she's half dressed. That's the way she usually looks, she wears such low necklines. Max says everybody's tried to tell her she shouldn't go to see clients that way. It's so unprofessional.

Maddie always tells me I should dress snappier. When she says "snappier," she snaps her fingers and shimmies with her shoulders.

I'm perfectly satisfied with the way I dress.

Lucy says when they split, Jim took an apartment half a block away from his best friend Patrick. "Do you think that's significant?" she asked me.

"It's significant. We just don't know how."

I told Max I was going to put an ad in the Personal columns. He said it's dangerous going out with people you don't know. His cousin once picked up a guy and had sex with him and then they went to his sister's house to get something to eat. When they walked into the kitchen, the guy went crazy. Chopped Max's cousin up with a cleaver. He nearly died.

According to Max, his cousin was conscious all the time. He kept himself alive. He wanted to live. He's a mess now, Max says. One ear, crushed ribs. Lost a couple fingers. He figured there was no point telling the police. They'd have said he asked for it.

When my father asked me why I was divorcing Ben, I said I couldn't talk to him or sleep with him anymore.

"Well, sleep in another room," my father said.

"What do you think I'm going to get Pat for our anniversary?" Maddie asked me, after she told me he was sick in bed.

"A pornographic TV movie," I answered.

"How did you know?" She seemed surprised and disappointed I had guessed.

"I'm a writer. That's how I'd write it."

When I told Max, he laughed. "One day they hired me and Craig to clean their apartment and we decided to turn the mattress. We found three porno books, you wouldn't believe it. All of women's boobs."

"I hate that word."

"Which word?"

"You know which word. And you must have been expecting to find something like that if you turned over the mattress."

"We were."

Celia got Dan a gift for their fifteenth anniversary, a new bed with mirrors on the ceiling. I told her it sounded like their marriage was improving. She said it was. The only other person I ever knew with mirrors over her bed was Caryl Dee, the nightclub singer. I always wondered if that was narcissistic or pornographic. Celia says it's love.

Ted always used to quote Plato on love. He said Plato described two people in love like two halves of an egg, each needing the other half for completion. I think I must have told him that once and then he started quoting me quoting Plato.

. . .

I told Max that Alixandre is strange. Well, not strange, really, but sometimes I think she's coming on to me. When she comes over to tell me something she doesn't like about Maddie, she kind of rubs her chest up against me. I don't want to hurt her feelings because I like Alixandre. But I'm not interested in women as lovers. So I just ignore it.

Lucy called me up the other night, hysterical. She said, "We've only been separated three days and already Jim's sleeping with some other woman."

I said, "But Lucy, you asked him to leave. You said your marriage was impossible."

"But I always thought he'd come to his senses and beg me to come back."

"But you don't want him back."

"Yes, I do," she said. "I want him back."

I feel sorry for Pushkin, my cat. I named him that because he's half black like the poet, and beautiful. Living in the city, I had to have him altered. I also had to have his front feet declawed. I wonder what it feels like, to be altered. I know I had to do it, but it doesn't seem fair.

Max told me he knew a male belly dancer once. He said, "I was just walking down Avenue A and we passed each other in the street and he just stopped and looked at me. We both stopped. You know the way your eyes meet. I said to myself, 'It's now or never, Max.' So I went up and introduced myself and we went to his room. He showed me some belly dancing and we had some real hot sex."

"I thought you told me it was dangerous to go to bed with people you don't know."

"I did."

Two weeks ago I went out with a man I liked and we had a wonderful time. He wrote me a note telling me what a wonderful time he had. I asked Dan what I should do about it.

"Don't sit by the phone," he suggested.

.   .   .

Ted used to count the number of times we'd slept together. He'd say, "I figure we've slept together 370 times" or "470 times," or when we'd been married twelve years he said that was 4,380 days and if we averaged every three nights we'd be up to 1,460 times.

I loved him but I couldn't stand the counting.

He said, "You knew when you married me I was a number cruncher."

After he died, nights I would get in bed with a glass of gin and my notebook and count the number of days he'd been dead. I can't remember when I stopped counting.

Alice is the understudy in a Broadway play. She's making so much money she went out and bought herself a mink coat. Her husband Sammy was very upset. She can't make him understand she didn't marry him to buy her mink coats. She did it because it's something her mother would never do for herself. That doesn't make any sense to Sammy.

It makes sense to me because after Ted died and I was feeling very sorry for myself, I went out to buy a pair of gloves and bought a mink coat instead. I did it for the same reason Alice did. Because when I was a child, my mother was always bragging how she was the only woman she knew who didn't have a fur coat and my father told her, "So what's so smart about that."

The thing is, she wanted one. She really always wanted a mink coat. It seems like a silly thing to want, a mink coat, but there you are, that's what she wanted.

As for me, I never thought I wanted one. Like my mother at first, it was not wanting one made me feel rich. And afterwards, I was so embarrassed to own it, I didn't wear it for over a year. Even now, it makes me feel conspicuous. When I bought it, I tried on everything else that was simpler, but I have to say the mink looked best. I guess Alice and her mother and my mother and me, we're all imprisoned by symbols. I'd like to put a sign on my coat that says, "I'm wearing this because my mother wanted it. I'm not rich."

"There wasn't much going on in Mobile," Max said, "but there was this really attractive guy and we used to fool around a lot. Everybody fooled around a lot, whether they were gay or not. He used to do some trapping. Sometimes I'd go with him, just to go for a walk in the woods. It sure wasn't because of the trapping. And we had some pretty hot sex, but he just used to shoot off like a pistol. He couldn't wait.

"Well, he got married after I moved away and a couple of years ago I heard his wife killed him. Either shot him or stabbed him in the back. I always wondered if it was because he came so fast."

I arrived at the Center at nine a.m. today to interview Beverly for a story about the program she runs for homeless kids, but as soon as I heard her walking down the hall, I knew she was having a bad day. Beverly is seven months pregnant with her second child. She is pretty large in her red print dress, but as usual, she has on her pearls and her eyelashes and looks as elegant as anyone seven months pregnant can look.

"I can't do it," she said. "The weekend was awful. We had to kick one of the kids out when we caught him selling grass. I was so worried about what was going to happen to him, I was frantic. And then I asked myself what I was doing here on Sunday when I have a husband at home and a kid."

"What were you doing here?"

"Maybe I'm just hooked, but they don't have anyone else here. How are you?" Beverly asked.

"I'm okay. Actually I'm fine. Well, I wish I were in love."

"You really think that would do it? Having a man? Being in love? I mean, look at me, I'm married. I have a man. I even love him. And he loves me. And everything's a mess."

"At least it's a mess with love," I told her.

"You're such a romantic. You have kids. You've been married, haven't you?"

"Twice," I told her.

"You see," she said.

Max and I never talk about sex. I mean, I listen to his stories about all his affairs – "affairettes," he calls them – but we never talk about what they mean. I want to ask him, Is it just sex? Don't you really want friendship? Don't you really want love? Why are we so afraid to talk about love?

Instead I ask, "With two men, which of them goes to sleep first?"

Max says, "They both do."

Could that be love?

Ted was an ever-ready battery and a terrific lover besides. Except when he was drunk. Which was often. Then he got belligerent. And mean. "C'mon," he'd say. "Let's fuck."

"That sounds like the punch line of a lousy joke," I'd tell him. But he didn't laugh. He'd threaten to leave. Then he'd pass out. I'd end up sleeping on the couch.

It was just before the poetry reading, about two seconds after he said hello, that Jim told me why he left Lucy.

"I told her there was something fundamental missing. She just got up and left."

"What is it? What do you think is fundamental?"

"I don't know," Jim said. "That's part of the problem." He slapped at his leg with his squash racket.

"What's part of the problem?"

"That we don't know. That we all go around ad-libbing our lives. I'll tell you one thing, though. It's not sex. It's what comes before sex."

"Maybe it's chemistry," I said.

"Maybe." He paused. "You know how with some people there's just this attraction. You either have it or you don't."

"Maybe it's friendship."

"I don't know. Maybe it's love. Maybe that's what it is."

He didn't sound sure. But at least he was trying.

Alice was terribly upset today because her cat died. We met for dinner at my favorite Italian restaurant but she couldn't eat. She'd been rehearsing for a play and having one of her rare fights with Sammy and she hadn't realized the cat was really sick.

"I kept thinking I ought to take her to the vet, but I kept

putting it off. Then this morning, Mrs. Shaw found her dead in the litter box." Alice started to cry. She put her head down on the table. The waiter looked away discreetly.

I know how she feels. Three months after Ted died, my cat Kachina died. She had feline leukemia and she kept getting thinner and thinner. I was getting thinner and thinner, too, and I didn't notice that, so why should I have noticed that Kachina was getting thinner. And nothing I could have done would have saved her, the vet told me. Still, along with missing her terribly, I felt negligent. Rotten. I told that to Alice.

"I know," she said, "but I don't even have your excuse. And I keep thinking of her in the litter box."

"I keep thinking of Ted in the coffin."

"But you don't feel guilty about that."

"Yes, I do," I said.

I know it sounds flip, comparing those two boxes. How else could I deal with it? For years I thought life was over. Ted's death became my touchstone. I measured everything bad that happened – B.C. Before crash. A.D. After death – by how much worse that was. Worse than death. His death. My feelings afterward. It's apt, at least in this metaphor, that touchstones are black. Black crash.

The Mayflower Madame is on the cover of *New York* magazine this week, holding a rose. Some cover girl.

Andrea, a former employee of hers, is quoted as saying the Mayflower Madame always wanted the girls to be romantic, ladylike. They were never allowed to discuss money with a customer. And they weren't supposed to collect till the end. Andrea said she'd personally never heard of that before. "She had a lot of faith," Andrea said.

And the "clients," Andrea said they were lonely, regulars, successful businessmen, "habitual users," she said. It was maybe "distaste for entangling relationships," maybe the "simplicity" of the escort business that appealed to them. Andrea's a philosopher.

My daughter and I often discuss what we refer to as your "love life." We talk about sex, about love, about "relationships."

When we do, it seems our roles are reversed. She gives me advice. That's because at forty-seven, it's strange to be dating. Everyone I know who is forty-six or more and dating thinks so too. It's a sign of an unstable world. "God's not in his heaven," I tell Rebecca.

"Her heaven," she reminds me.

That's another sign. At her age, I didn't believe in God, but the God I didn't believe in was a man. At her age, we discussed kissing on the first date. Now everyone asks, What about sex on the first date. What about drugs on the first date?

"What about spontaneity?" a friend asked me.

"What about aesthetics," I said.

"Thank god, I thought you were going to say 'morality.' I thought you were going to say 'respect.'"

What about morality? What about respect?

Janice is sixty. She's still dating. She's been married and divorced twice. But she says she's through with men. She sounds like Jerry when he talks about being celibate. They both sound angry. And afraid. Like the Madame's customers who are afraid of entangling relationships. One pays. The other does without.

Janice rests her case on the grounds of male ineptness. "You know," she says, "men think they just have to stick it in and everything's fine. Or they just mess around a little bit with their left hand and everything's fine."

Janice says when she wants human contact she gets a massage.

"Every day?" I ask.

Evidently once a week is enough.

That's like my favorite line from *Annie Hall*, from the scene with the split screen. Woody Allen says to his shrink, "She never wants to have sex. Three times a week."

And Annie is saying to her shrink, "He wants to have sex all the time. Three times a week."

Why is everyone so confused about love? Even the *New York Times* tries to explain it. The *Times* quotes a Yale psychologist who says romance is not so important as sharing ideas and ideals. Sex is not so important either. What is important is how equal the love is.

One "eminent psychoanalyst," Dr. Otto Kernberg, opts for sexual passion, according to the *Times*. "An internal wildness" is what preserves a marriage, Kernberg says.

He describes a pathology of love, a continuum ranging from narcissism to mature romantic love. The latter is a very complex emotion. In achieving it, mystery is more important than orgasm. Mystery leads to transcendence, even though transcendence, he warns, has its perils.

That's where I stopped reading. I think Jim put it better when he said we're all ad-libbing.

When I met Lucy at the movies, she wore a new bright red coat. She looked absolutely beautiful with her long red hair and pink cheeks. She looks so all-American. It must be her midwestern background and her job with IBM. When I told her she looked great in the coat, she said, "I just bought it for two hundred dollars and it made me feel good for at least twenty minutes."

She has just been to see Jim's parents. I didn't have the heart to ask her why. "They were so mad at him," she said. "His father said, when he died, he didn't want Jim at the funeral."

Jim's parents are Orthodox Jews. They don't believe in divorce. When Jim married Lucy, they sat *shiva* because Lucy wasn't Jewish. Now it seems they're sitting *shiva* for Jim.

Jim's father has a wholesale dress business which he tried to get Jim to join. Lucy wanted him to take her in the business, and she would have been terrific. But Jim's father wouldn't hear of it. Women have no *kop* for business, he said, though I always thought the dress business was full of women. But he complained that she was a *shiksa*. That was the real reason he didn't want her in the business. Now, it seems, just by the act of wanting to stay married, Jim's family feels Lucy has become Jewish.

"I should have taken you in the business," Jim's father had told her. "Then Jim couldn't have left."

By now, Lucy has completely forgotten she asked Jim to leave.

.   .   .

I'm on an alphabet kick. What begins with L besides Love? Loss. Loneliness. When I told that to Rebecca, she said, "Lemons. Latkes."

"Nobody needs a daughter who's a smart-ass," I said. "You should feel sorry for me. I'm your mother."

"I do feel sorry for you, but you don't really need it. You feel sorry enough for yourself. One of us has to keep on going. How about L for Life. Levity."

Jerry told me a client of his is writing a book called *Love and Money. Money and Sex.* His client's thesis is that men buy sex with money and women buy money with sex. He thinks it's a revolutionary concept.

Alice explained to me that the next "in" thing is going to be part-time marriage. When I asked her how she knew, she said she read it in *Vogue* and all the kids in the theater are talking about it.

The baby-boomers are having babies now, it seems, and if they want to split, they find that divorce is a nightmare. Financially, that is. So it's better not to have babies. And real old-fashioned marriages with "togetherness" haven't been "in" since the fifties. People used to ask less of each other. Now so many women have careers they don't have time for either real marriages or babies. And so many men are afraid of intimacy, they can solve both the need and the fear with a part-time marriage.

"Alice," I asked her, "what is a part-time marriage?"

"I don't know what it is, I just know that it's 'in'."

It's odd what becomes fashionable. E.M. Forster is "in" now since they made a fashionable movie out of *Passage to India*, but what the book is really about isn't even in the movie. I think Forster is saying "only connect." Love, real connection was the important thing to him.

In his letters, speaking of his love for a poor, young Alexandrian tram conductor, he writes, "Upshot. In this as in everything, one is really after intimacy, however little one realizes it. Something more than physical hunger drives one."

. . .

Yesterday I met Peter for lunch at JJ's Ranch on Madison Avenue. Barbecued ribs are "in" now in Manhattan. Peter was looking fragile. Before getting down to business or even what we'd done with our respective children at Christmas and New Year, we had our usual conversation about the unavailability of suitable partners.

"I really want that old-fashioned thing, what's it called?" he told me right after ordering.

"You're right," I said, "it's old-fashioned. It might even be passé, like sleeping together."

"Oh, that's not passé," he said, "in fact that's the problem."

I didn't get it.

"I decided I'm really interested in intimacy, so I've changed my whole approach to women. I've started going out with older women instead of . . ."

"Chicklets," I said.

"Yes, instead of chicklets. And that doesn't work either. Like this painter I've been dating. Gorgeous. Smart. Obsessed with herself. Maybe I shouldn't date painters. How about something really greasy, like french fried onions and french fried potatoes."

"Maybe just skip artists," I told him. "And potatoes."

"On the third date," he said, "I felt I had to make excuses. I had to get up early Saturday, whatever, just because I didn't want to sleep with her till I knew her better. But I guess that's not acting like a man. She didn't go for it. She was furious."

"So you slept with her so you wouldn't be rude," I said.

"Sort of," he answered.

"It doesn't sound like love," I told him, "but it does sound familiar."

"Love? What can you do about love?" he asked.

Naomi Feigelson Chase

I think I survived my childhood thanks to my imagination. The year I was born, my father was elected to Congress and we moved from Pittsburgh to Washington. He was not around very much and my mother wasn't either. I was eight before my sister was born.

My mother was a very intelligent woman with a lot of ability, but she did very little with it outside of the immediate community. She was totally dependent on my father financially. Although she had gone to college and graduate school and had worked, she was terrified of poverty. She told me that when she first came to America, she lived in a boarding house in Baltimore and her mother would boil water on *Shabbos* (sabbath) so that the neighbors wouldn't know they had nothing to eat. Even though my father always made a comfortable living, she never forgot the empty pot. She did not go out and get a job, though I think she was very capable. She did not really look for ways of developing herself outside the community. When she died, I thought it was painfully sad that her life had passed without her doing something that meant anything to her. I decided early on, with the arrogance of youth, that I was not going to let that happen to me, that I was going to work, that I was going to be able to support myself. And I've bored my daughter ever since I can remember with the same advice.

Everybody in my mother's family had been some kind of a

writer but had never been successful. My mother's family was particularly verbal and literate and funny. They always made jokes, usually about each other. Whatever sense of humor I have is from my mother's family – peasant and rueful. Two of my maternal uncles were in public relations and wrote speeches for various government agencies. My mother told me she had written a lot when she was in college, though I was never aware of that when I was growing up. And many years later she told me she had written some stories and asked me if I would look at them. I didn't because I was afraid they might not be good and I didn't want to have to tell her that. It's difficult to say your mother was jealous of your success in writing, but I felt she was. For me there was a penalty about succeeding where everyone else in my family had failed. For a long time I was afraid to be successful. I think that I must have been aware of that without really articulating it as a child. I certainly became aware of it when my first book was published.

Besides her journals, which she kept on trips, my mother wrote voluminous letters, especially when I was in college. I must have gotten a letter or two a week. I used to say she wrote like Molly Bloom talked – a torrent of consciousness. It seems terrible to me now that I didn't save them. The other day I heard someone talking about her mother's letters to her, saying that her mother writes her all the time complaining. And she said, "I just skim the letters and then I throw them away." I think that's what I did. In fact I have a poem I call "My Mother Sent Me Gifts" in which I talk about the letters that I got from her all the time, a threnody of complaints. I've written about the sadness of her life in my poetry, and the lack of fulfillment in her life. And yet I credit her with my love of literature and music and art. Obviously my choice to write is in some way a fulfillment of her wishes for herself.

I started to write when I was very young. I can remember writing a story about a Scotty dog that belonged to our downstairs neighbors when I must have been six. It was a "lost and found" story: the dog gets lost, the dog gets found. I was the dog. As a child I thought about being a writer and knew that I wanted to write. I read a great deal; in fact I read all the time. It was my great escape. I was very interested in women who wrote, and bothered that so many of the women writers I was reading either were reclusive or went crazy: Emily Dickinson, Virginia Woolf, etc. I remember thinking that there was the possibility that if you got too involved in yourself, you might go crazy. Aside from my dog story, I didn't write.

In high school I had an English teacher, Elizabeth Evans, who was very encouraging. In fact I found a number of women like that who became substitute mothers. They were extremely important to me. I needed to feel a mother's support, so I guess I went out and found it where I could. When I was in sixth grade at Colfax School in Pittsburgh, the school principal, Hedwig Pregler, chose me to work in her office. That was considered to be a great mark of favoritism, a step above being teacher's pet. She once gave me something to read by William Allen White, a reporter who had written an elegaic essay about his daughter who was killed in a horse accident. I realized that she was telling me to be proud of myself and that she cared about me. She must have been more aware than I was of how uncertain I was about myself. Another important role model was my piano teacher, Emma Finkelpearl. She always told me how rebellious I was, but she was completely accepting and I loved her unreservedly. I have a poem about her called "Music Mother."

In high school Miss Evans encouraged me to write. I wrote a short story for a *Scholastic Magazine* contest and won. I thought that was incredible. I also published a poem in *Seventeen* when I was about seventeen. I wanted to frame my ten-dollar check but my father suggested I cash the check and frame a copy. I thought that took all the romance out of my gesture, so I just cashed it. The poem itself was an exuberant statement about immortality, about living forever. It surprises me now to think that I felt that way at seventeen. It's reassuring. I do remember keeping notebooks of what at the time I thought was poetry. The poems were probably terrible, but the fact that I was doing it was significant to me about my own identity. I was able secretly to think about myself as a writer. That probably was part of the romance of it. I certainly didn't take myself seriously.

One summer while I was in high school, I took a course in

fiction writing at the University of Pittsburgh with a well-known teacher, Ed Peterson. I remember how happy I was to be in that writing class. Peterson gave us a series of Hemingway-type exercises. Students could only write what they saw or heard. For example, describe what you see in a room, describe what you hear of a conversation, no judgments. Later when I taught a writing course at Harvard Extension, I used those exercises. They're very simple but they're effective for writers no matter how advanced they are.

When I was in college I worked one summer for a local newspaper, the *Oakland News*. I was allowed to write anything I wanted and I had my own column. I still have a scrapbook with all those columns in them; that was pretty heady, seeing my own picture and byline. Never mind that it was a throwaway paper. I thought I was Rosalind Russell in *The Front Page.*

I took writing courses when I went to college. They were all very influential, some positive and some negative. I went to Bryn Mawr for two years and then transferred to Radcliffe. I had wanted to go to Radcliffe mainly to take MacLeish's writing course. I didn't like Bryn Mawr very much but again I had one writing teacher, Bettina Lynn, who was very encouraging. I published poetry when I was at Bryn Mawr and started a novel about a time in my childhood when I lived with my grandparents. When I transferred to Radcliffe, the first writing class I had was with Albert Guerard. When I submitted that hunk of stuff I had written at Bryn Mawr, he told me my writing had a lot of energy. I didn't know what that meant but it sure sounded good to me. Energy! I was writing short stories in his class. He encouraged his students to try to publish our stories. One of mine won second prize in a *Harvard Advocate* contest in 1954. I had taken a trip with my parents to Europe and Israel – the story was about my relationship to my family and my relationship to Israel. The themes, personal and political history, are still themes that I write about. I sent that story to *Mademoiselle* as Guerard suggested. The editor, Cyrilly Abels, didn't accept it but later remembered me and became my first agent.

I wanted to take Archibald MacLeish's course at Radcliffe/Harvard, because he was supposed to be *the* great teacher. But I found that we were totally incompatible. He was very

New England, very Wasp, what I thought was very rigid. After I did my first assignment he told me I should write about things that I did not know about. That froze me. That was the first negative reaction to my writing. It was virtually impossible for me to write about things I didn't know about. I was too insecure or else just too naive to say to the great man, "You're crazy, what a ridiculous thing to say to someone who is writing." So I wrote poetry, because I couldn't write fiction for his class. And then I graduated from college and I stopped writing.

That was the beginning of a serious writing block. I'd been getting support and I'd been getting published. Except for MacLeish all the criticism up to then was very positive. It's too bad I didn't try to do something with that negative experience. It never occurred to me – I mean he had the word as far as I was concerned. I don't think I talked about it to anyone. It was a wound. The fact that it had such an effect shows how much it reinforced my insecurity.

I stopped writing anything creative for several years. I got a master's degree in English at Brandeis where I had a scholarship and then I got married and went to New York. There I got a job on a marketing magazine called *Tide*. That marriage did not last very long. Shortly after I was divorced I decided to go back to graduate school at Columbia. I was able to justify what I considered this self-indulgence because I got a tuition grant at Columbia and a job doing research for Hans Rosenhaupt who was then the dean of the graduate school. But Columbia refused to accept my Brandeis degree and also insisted I pass exams in French and Latin. I remember a winter of trying to read Latin on the subway until I concluded it was hopeless. I quit graduate school, got a job at a magazine, and met the man I subsequently married. Since he was going to the National Institutes of Health in Washington, I started to apply for jobs in Washington and decided to take a job teaching school in Anacostia.

I got pregnant while I was teaching and although many of my students had already had children, the rule was you were not allowed to teach if you were pregnant. I wanted to finish the first semester so I just lied about it. I was very attached to my students and when I left, my class gave me a shower. I felt that whatever I had done, I had some small impact. I think my daughter, Elizabeth, still has a blanket they gave me at that shower.

And then I got a call from the American Association of University Women, one of the places I had sent a resumé to before I decided to teach. They were looking for an editor for their quarterly magazine. They paid very little, but in those days a woman who was five months pregnant was not in a great bargaining position. I accepted. The editor there, Elizabeth Phinney, became another important person in my life because she was direct, supportive and encouraging. She told me to write something and there wasn't any way I could tell her I wasn't able to write, that I had a block. I wrote the back-of-the-book, called "News and Notes," which Phinney encouraged me to develop. I did a lot of editorial work. It was particularly important to me to succeed because of my relationship to her. I don't know whether "mentor" is the right word or not, but it is clear that it has been very important to me from the time I was a child to find people – and many were women – who would be helpful and encouraging. In my own work I can see the terrible impact that discouragement had. I hope I would not let that affect me today because I have a stronger sense of myself. Or maybe just more bravado. But it has taken me a lot of time to get there.

When my daughter Elizabeth was born, I continued to work at home and then went back to work part-time. I remember realizing, when Elizabeth was two months old, that I wasn't able to finish a thought, that I was totally unprepared for how tired I was going to feel and for the fact that I didn't know the first thing about taking care of babies. I had a maid/housekeeper at the time who was very good with Elizabeth – I used to worry that Elizabeth would think my maid was her mother. I wanted to have the time with her myself and yet I was so concerned with not being able to work. If I had known that I was going to be able to continue to work and in some way to make it, meaning to write successfully, to be a successful person, I would have been much less anxious as a young mother. It's too bad that there is no way of knowing that ahead of time. Working part-time was the solution for me, although I now regret every minute I missed with my children when they were little.

When Elizabeth was about two, we went back to New York from Bethesda. By that time I was pregnant with Jonathan. I had a job doing research on Alinsky, the Chicago radical, for Jay Schulman. It was the early sixties and New York City was involved in elementary school pairing. I was shocked at the way supposedly liberal upper-middle-class whites reacted to the thought of their six-year-olds going to school with black six-year-olds. I started pestering Jay to write something about it. Finally he said, "Why don't you do it yourself." So I did. I sat down and wrote an article about it and then I didn't know what to do with it. I called up Cyrilly Abels, the woman who had rejected my *Mademoiselle* story, with whom I had somehow kept contact. She suggested that I send it to *New York* which was then part of the *New York Herald Tribune.* They accepted it much to my surprise. That was really the beginning of thinking of myself as a professional writer. I did two more pieces for them, one of them about the decontrolling of luxury housing in New York. The writing was very important to me. Although I had started it because of the politics, I looked at it as fiction. I was caught by the people in the story and the feeling, the atmosphere. I must have rewritten that article thirty times. I wanted to get the feeling absolutely right.

And then after a prolonged strike, the *Trib* folded with my third piece about Lincoln Center in their drawer. One day soon after that, I bumped into Jules Feiffer, a neighbor, in the elevator of my apartment building. We were talking about writing and I told him I had done something for *New York* and he said, "If you can write for *New York,* you can write for the *Voice.* Why don't you call up Dan Wolf at the *Village Voice* and tell him I told you to call." I ran to the nearest pay phone. As a result, I started to write as a free-lancer for the *Voice.* The first piece I did, on a local congressional election, I rewrote at least as many times as my *New York* pieces. At that time the *Voice* paid twenty-five dollars an article, so you can imagine what I earned per word. But I was a writer! A journalist! It was the byline that counted. When that issue of the *Voice* came out, I went to the corner newsstand and blew most of twenty-five dollars on copies.

I wrote a number of articles for the *Voice* about local politics. And then I started to cover what later was known as the counterculture. I had also started to fool around in fiction. I was writing conversations, writing about what I observed or heard. I was also doing a lot of proofreading and editing to pay for an analysis. I was not aware that I was thinking about anything like a career. When my husband said to me at one time that our marriage could not sustain two careers, I thought he was exaggerating my work. "Careers," I said to myself, "what is he talking about?" And then I said, "Well, but that is what I want to do." But I said it very softly.

I got divorced after eight years of marriage, although I had worried for several years about how a divorce would affect my children. I had to go to work, psychologically and for the money. A neighbor who worked for NBC helped me get a job in what was then called the "News" department. It was actually public relations. Of course I thought I was totally inadequate as a writer, but I soon realized that I was at least as good at writing releases as the other people in my department. The idea of writing fiction and poetry was still buried somewhere.

In 1962 while I was at NBC, Cyrilly Abels called and asked me if I was interested in writing a book on the sixties for Funk and Wagnalls. When Cyrilly had suggested that I send my piece to *New York,* I sent her a check for 10 percent of what I was paid. And I continued to do that when I was writing for the *Voice* because I considered that she had helped me get a start. She got me my first book contract. I was ecstatic. I got a two-thousand-dollar advance for this book and, of course, thought it was incredible that anybody would let me write a book *and* pay me for it.

It was a very exciting time in America. It was clear that something unusual was happening but not many people were quite sure what it was. I just hung out in the East Village. The first person I met was Abby Hoffman and through him I met Jerry Rubin and Phil Ochs. Each person led me to another. It took me a little more than two and a half years to write *The Underground Revolution.* When I divorced I kept my married name because I wanted to have the same name as my children, so I published it as Naomi Feigelson. Because Funk and Wagnalls was going through problems at that time, they didn't send out enough review copies and they didn't do much to promote it, but it was a marvelous feeling to know that I had actually written a book.

I finished the galleys at Lindsay headquarters where I had gotten a job running the "negative research" office, and after Lindsay was re-elected, went to work as press secretary for Bess Myerson, who was then New York City Commissioner of Consumer Affairs. That summer I was at Cape Cod with Elizabeth and Jonathan when Cyrilly called me up and asked if I was interested in writing something about child abuse. Holt, Rinehart wanted a book on it. Although at first the idea of writing about child abuse was very disturbing, I was so provoked by the thought of finding out what it was – nobody appeared to know what child abuse was – that I decided to do it. The actual writing and research took somewhere between three and four years. I had an advance of six thousand dollars and the Ford Foundation gave me a grant, so I was able to quit my job and start researching the book which was published under the title, *A Child Is Being Beaten* in 1973.

.   .   .

For a long time I had wanted to write a novel. I even started an introduction – about a women's gym and the meaning of exercise. In 1974 when I sold the paperback rights to *A Child Is Being Beaten*, I misheard my agent, Joan Davis – to whom Cyrilly "bequeathed" me when she died – on the telephone when she told me I had gotten twenty-five hundred dollars for it. I thought she said twenty-five *thousand*. A friend of mine said, "Well, here's your big chance to write the novel you've always wanted to write." It was a very fortunate mistake.

I had remarried and my husband, my two children and I were living outside of Boston. I was working for the Massachusetts Arts Council. I quit my job and, in two months, wrote about half the novel. I had the most marvelous time doing it. Joan liked it very much and encouraged me to finish. I wrote the whole novel in six or seven months. I was forty-two years old.

That novel, *Life Exercises*, was very important to me. Look how many years it had taken me to do something I had secretly always wanted to do. I felt the time was really right, the theme was right. It was the beginning of the whole exercise craze. I was particularly interested in the way women dealt with each other in a locker-room situation which seemed to be very different from the way men did. With men there is a lot of braggadocio; with women there is much more complaining about what is wrong with their lives. Part of the book was about women living in New York in the violent seventies and trying to cope with their lives. There is a murder in the middle of the book which was meant to sum up the violence of urban life in the seventies. I loved it.

My novel was turned down by more publishers than I can count on my fingers. The rejections were very upsetting. I rewrote it and decided I would try to sell some of the individual chapters as short stories. I sent one called "The Stabber" around to a number of magazines. I started out by sending to the obvious commercial places, the *New Yorker, Atlantic, Harper's,* etc. It was turned down by almost as many people as turned down the novel. By that time I had started to write poetry and I sent the story along with some poems to the *Greenfield Review.* They accepted the poems but said they weren't publishing any fiction. Joseph Bruchac, the editor, recommended that I send it to *D'Arcy.* It was published there and Maxine Kumin read it and nominated it for a Pushcart Prize. That was wonderfully validating, a real antidote to rejection.

It does mean a great deal to be published, to see your name in print and to get some kind of feedback. You do really have to keep, not just working, though of course that is the important thing, but you have to be able to laugh through all that rejection. I think that really is difficult. I remember opening an envelope with a rejection slip when I was all dressed to go to a fancy dinner party. I headed straight for the kitchen and ate three bagels in a row. I did not eat at the party. I am not recommending eating as a coping mechanism – just illustrating how painful it can be. I ate the rejections.

· · ·

I had written poetry all my life, but I had never really taken it seriously. By that I mean I had never *rewritten* it. In the early

1970's, an acquaintance who knew I was interested in writing poetry asked me to come to the writing workshop she belonged to. It was a wonderful experience. The others in this workshop, all women, were in their twenties and I was forty-one. I had no fear about the fact that in terms of technique I was way behind them. I had studied poetry as an English major but my writing was much less formal than theirs. I felt I knew more about life. My big advantage was that I had lived longer. We met once a week or once every two weeks for about a year before the group broke up. And then the reviewer of *A Child Is Being Beaten,* whose friends in a poetry workshop were looking for another member, suggested to them that they call me. That workshop turned out to be one of the most important things in my life. It consisted of Miriam Goodman, Celia Gilbert, Suzanne Berger and later Carole Oles and, occasionally, Gail Mazur. Again I was way behind. Everybody had either already published a book or was in the process of having one published. I was the neophyte. But there was no embarrassment in bringing in something you thought was unfinished or needed a lot of help on or encouragement.

I don't think there is any experience that matches a good writing workshop in terms of instruction or support. That may be the most important thing, being with people whose very presence in that room says writing is worth doing. You learn how to weigh their comments and criticism and you realize that people may disagree violently about a word, a phrase or even a whole poem. And that throws you back to your own judgment. You have to sift out from what is said what you think is important and what works for you. Of all the learning and teaching I've done, that has been the most useful. And the support of the women was important because it counterbalanced the rejection we all experienced from time to time. It was a very nurturing atmosphere.

Several of the people in my workshop had been to Mac-Dowell or other artists' colonies, which I knew nothing about. They talked about them in very glowing terms and I decided I was going to apply to MacDowell. I was at MacDowell for six weeks. My husband was not crazy about the idea but there is no substitute for being in an environment where you don't have any work but your own. Whether or not you have a family or a spouse or live with somebody, there is always somebody else's presence, somebody else to take care of. If you have kids it's impossible not to think about whether they are going to have dinner – which you should be making – or whether they are going out at night. But when you are away from it, you are away. You only have to think about yourself. I found that really amazing. Being there makes you take yourself seriously. People respect each other's work and work time – it's regarded as next to holy. So *you* begin to think of it as that way too. Everybody I know who has been there or other places like it has found that very self-confirming, both people who are just starting or those a long way along the way. It was the most serious confirmation I had that I was really a writer.

In 1982, after my husband's death, I went back to New York. I was very worried about how I was going to keep up my poetry without a workshop so the first thing I did was to start a workshop with someone I'd met at MacDowell. And I took a poetry class with Grace Shulman whom I found very helpful and a fiction class with Peter Rand, both at the 92nd St. Y. It was in Rand's class that I started the story that's in this anthology. He was particularly helpful. "What Can You Do about Love" is an advance in my fiction, very different from what I've written before in style and, to some extent, in content. I started this story because I knew somebody like Max. His experience of love and the way he talked about it were new to me. There was something compelling in his stories and that was what I sat down with. And then the associations just came. It was like writing poetry in the sense that the associations and images led to each other. I didn't think about what I was going to do with the structure of the story until I had gone through the first draft of it. Rand suggested to me that I read Renata Adler as an example of how a writer distances herself from her narrator and I found that useful.

. . .

In sending my work out, I use *Coda* and the *Directory of Small Presses.* Some of my first poems were published in *Real Paper* and *Dark Horse,* both of which were Cambridge papers. One day, Tom Murray, the husband of a friend in another group of women writers I belonged to, said to me, "You really ought to have a book of poetry published." I just laughed. Tom suggested I send it to Bill Desmond who published the Archival Press. I got together a group of poems and sent them off to Archival. I said to myself, "Don't even think about it." I was going off for a three-month trip and when I came back and found out that Desmond had decided to publish my poetry, I was ecstatic. It was one of the most exciting things that ever happened to me. And when *Listening for Water* came out, although it came out at a very sad time for me, shortly after my husband's death, it was a milestone in my life. I am now getting together a second manuscript of poetry.

I have given a lot of readings. When I was living in Framingham, I thought there should be a poetry series there and decided to see if I could organize it. Part of the impulse was that my book was coming out and I wanted to be able to read. Eighteen people read in that series the first year. I got it funded by the Massachusetts Council on the Arts so that even after I left, it was something that kept on going. A number of us in the poetry group taught at colleges or had some other kind of entree and were very good about helping each other get readings. Miriam Goodman was teaching at Clark then. I read there. My daughter who was at Wesleyan organized a reading for me there every year and I would take somebody. About a year and a half ago, an actress I knew wanted to help organize some readings at La Mama, which is famous in New York for its experimental theater. They have an art gallery in which they were trying to get a series of readings started. I suggested it would be interesting to have a series on American women poets. Mary Tierney, an actress, asked if I would send her some poems, including mine, so I did. She then asked me if I would come and read my own. And then I was asked by Lawry Smith to help organize a series of women writers of fiction and poetry and I read in that series.

My husband and my children were very supportive of my writing. My children have always been very proud of my poetry and their pride has meant a lot to me. At times, it's been sustaining. The first poetry reading I ever gave was to my son's ninth-grade class. I was astonished that he invited me to give a reading at his grade school. Most thirteen-year-old boys don't even want anybody to know they *have* a mother. And now he gives my book to his friends when he knows they like poetry. At the last La Mama reading, Elizabeth came and threw flowers at me. My daughter has a very good critical sense and will often suggest changes to me. She liked the story that appears here and has read all the drafts and made some very helpful suggestions. I always consult her.

.   .   .

I think that artists really are the luckiest people in the world. There is nothing more satisfying than to write something; often just the writing is exhilarating, so much so that it's hard to judge what you've written. It is hard not to think of that as self-indulgent. But taking yourself seriously as a writer is the most important thing. If I had taken myself seriously as a writer when I graduated from college, it certainly would have helped. When I look at a publication list of mine, I realize that I have written an awful lot: I've published three books, I've written four and just put together a second book of poetry, I have a long list of magazine articles. Yet I don't feel as if I have done very much. Whether it's because I'm particularly conscious that there were long periods of time when I didn't do anything or whether I'm too hard on myself, I don't really know. I hesitate to say that that is a woman's problem, though I think women often have a greater problem justifying what they want to do. There is always the idea that somebody else is suffering for it, somebody is not going to have dinner, somebody is not going to have clean clothes, somebody is not going to have your full attention. Even now that my children are grown, though I don't spend an awful lot of time with them, I spend a lot of time thinking about them and attending to them one way or another. I must say they're as important to me as my work, if not more so.

I am sorry that I wasn't able to spend more time writing. I certainly think I am at a disadvantage in career terms. But the advantage of starting late is that one hopefully has a certain maturity. Being forced to deal with the world has given me a certain amount of confidence in myself. There's no substitute for that.

When my daughter Elizabeth read a draft of this interview, she said to me, "Mother, you've always been writing. You just couldn't identify yourself that way." She's right. Finally, I *have* identified myself that way. Perhaps, in order to do that, I had to give up the idea of being a victim. I recently told a woman who has an office across from mine that I was writing a novel and was having a wonderful time doing it. "You mean you're actually allowed to be happy with your work?" she said.

Yvonne Moore Hardenbrook

```
                  propping
     newly         up
     stacked         the old         stormfront
     firewood          shed          rising
```

Socks

Mama
cannot abide layabouts

Sitting last evening
on the loveseat
she matched socks
brought by the armload
warm from the dryer

Deftly
mating each pair
tops and toes together
she pulled them taut
tied a knot
gave it a lefthand flip
into the easy chair

The cat
pawed some air near her
ready to purr
or turn himself inside out
for a word or touch

Mama
through with the
matching and knotting
sat heavily
figuring
which chore to do next

Papa
danced a jig
on the cold morning floor
fumbling with his socks
hurrying
to get to work
on time

Night Vision

In the dusk of childhood summer
we stood in sober circle, counting
    ONE POTATO, TWO POTATO . . .
until one fist was left, and I was *it*.

Calling *RED LIGHT-1-2-3-4-5-6-7-8-9-10*
GREEN LIGHT, I heard you alternately dash
and freeze like statues without shadows.
Within the trammeled twilight
you dropped into secret pockets, crouched
there barely breathing, waiting
to be found – or run home shouting
    IN FREE! IN FREE!

I hunted the unlikely places – beyond
the yard, throughout the darkened
house – and found you
at my father's desk, swivel chair
creaking as you swung around
with his flashlight a ghostly glow
beneath your chin. You intoned
    ONLY THE SHADOW KNOWS . . .
and closed my startled scream
with such . . . a . . . kiss! It crossed my mind
we had outgrown these childish games.

I never knew your body warmth,
but that . . . one . . . kiss in darkness gave me
vision of the woman in the child.
Wartime took you from the mountains

the year we moved away.
Were you among the missing,
or did you come home free – to marry,
and find *your* children playing twilight games?

Today, the lost are found
with night vision systems of infrared
heat-seeking rays, undetectable
in war or love. Decades ago,
I sensed your heat print.
It lighted untried worlds where girls
turn into women, and are lost.

Pink Thread

My five-year-old says
>   *Mother . . . ?*
and I can tell he is serious.
>   *How did God make me?*
I am equally solemn as I reply
>   *What do YOU think?*
He looks thoughtful.
>   *God put a long thin thing*
>   *down from my throat*
>   *to my chest*
>   *and rolled it up*
>   *to make my heart.*
His fingers nimbly trace the lines.
>   *He put skin all over*
>   *and sewed me up with*
>   *pink thread. Then He planted*
>   *some seeds for hair . . .*
The grave voice trails off
as blue eyes suddenly widen.
>   *It took a LOT of pink thread,*
>   *Mother; where did God get all*
>   *that pink thread?*

He has me there, so I send him to play.
I cannot know that within a month
the pink thread will unravel
and I will lose my first-born.

I let him go, unanswered.

History Lesson

Talkin' about them killin's at Kent State
puts me in mind of Chicago's South Side in '37
when we was picketin' Republic Steel.
We marched peaceable for union rights,
not a Commie amongst us. Outa nowhere
come this solid wall of cops, charged us yellin'
    RED BASTARDS, YOU GOT NO RIGHTS!
They started in shootin' and we turned tail.
Point-blank, they volleyed – them
brave back-shootin' cops. The street run red.
We carried the wounded to Sam's Bar, and
seven men cashed in on the sawdust floor.
I seen the newsreel name it a massacre
but the *Trib* never even run a line.

We had to hustle in them days. I was a
forty-two-cent nobody when I joined the union.
I didn't wear no button – a button
was a sure way to get fired. Don't see
how a boy today startin' at three-thirty-five
with ever'thing laid out for him can understand
how it was when a man was nothin' but a cipher.
It was the Big Boys called the shots.

The strike was broke, but the
Wagner Act come along and saved the union.
We never made a buck till contracts for armaments
to Europe rolled in. *ARSENAL OF DEMOCRACY*
the Big Boys said we was, and the war in Europe
fed our families good. *SOLIDARITY FOREVER!*
PROSPERITY FOR ALL! Republic went closed shop,
the union made us strong, the Big Boys
made millions sellin' steel. The Government
chipped in . . . *they* called the shots.

Then it was *us* in World War II,
shippin' our sons overseas along with steel.
Prosperity, all right – ration stamps
for meat and sugar . . . shoes . . . gasoline . . . and
telegrams for *GOLD STAR MOTHERS!*
Thirty-three years later them kids at Kent State
was shot for marchin' peaceable, for
picketin' to protest our troops in Vietnam.
Didn't their folks never tell them
you can't win against the Big Boys?
It's WAR what sells the steel,
and the Big Boys what calls the goddam shots.

Scat Song

All music is about mortality.
　　　　　　　　　　　– William Matthews

In this moment, this square of our lives
between birth and dying, we sit at evening
listening as Art Tatum's hands cover, caress

black and white alike: eighty-eight keys
in harmonic fourths – strange intervals
of reconstituted jazz. You close your eyes,

say it's perfect how a blind man plays out
variations on the score, catches the changes,
improvises till he finds his voice. I take your hand,

trace the lifeline, say *Lover, you can do
anything if you come in and go out on the beat.*
When the words are lost we sing scat, playing

off each other with no paper music. We leave
the song in the understanding streets to pass
back and forth, like God changing his mind.

Pushing Off

from poolside straight ahead
in a deadman's float
till my lungs believe in death,
my weightless legs
create no wake.

Divorce is like that:
pushing off, face down, breathless,
heart pounding
in the skull – playing dead
long enough to get free.

I flip over to a frantic
backstroke, flailing, gulping air.
It is space I need
now, this space
in mid-pool with the others

who flexed their knees
and propelled headfirst
from slick concrete walls
to sink or swim
alone.

Breaking Away

Imagine her standing on the edge
of a girder, bruising her soles
on the I-beam's serif. Her resolve

quickens. She strides above air,
ascends to the face of the moon.
Imagine she reminds herself

that leaving one life is launching
another. She follows a valley
to the heights of steep craters, breathes

the must of a woman's dream.
She finds the moon cold, turns to see
earthlight, longs to summon the fire.

Unsure now, she pauses, hears her voice
whisper the words of a ballad.
Her eyes burn, sting with regret.

There is no way back. She steps
her raw footprints in dust on the moon.

Yvonne Moore Hardenbrook

There were a few artistic people in my family but only one or two made a successful living solely in the arts. One of my mother's brothers, Weston, whom I adored, was a professional musician. Her other brother, whom I didn't know, was a writer and when last heard from, a Boston newspaperman. My mother's mother was creative in her sewing, tatting and crocheting. My mother's father, who became a Baptist preacher, wrote poetry, short stories, newspaper articles and once submitted a scenario to a silent film studio.

My parents were also creative. My father, who was a Methodist minister in small towns of Virginia, Maryland and West Virginia, wrote poetry that was very traditional and simplistic and strictly for his own enjoyment. He loved poetry and hardly ever preached a sermon in which he didn't use lines from a poem to illustrate a point. I still have his copy of *Quotable Poems* and his small volumes of Shakespeare's plays. It was in his library that I first saw some of the classics.

Mother, who had been a school teacher, played piano and organ and had a beautiful contralto voice. Occasionally she would play the piano at home, but never as often as we wished. She was a workaholic, unable to "just sit." In fact, the first hymn I learned for piano was "Work, for the night is coming." Mother made many of our clothes. If we had to wear clothes from the missionary barrel, she remade them to fit us. And she designed her own hats from pictures – she would laughingly call them her Parisian creations. She always looked as if she had just stepped out of the bandbox. But Mother was very strict. Daddy left all the discipline up to her. If I broke a rule or displeased her, I had to go out and cut the switch myself for her to switch the back of my legs. This always took place in an empty room where I was left until I was through crying. My brothers got the same and sometimes she would just not speak to the miscreant for hours on end.

Both parents read to me and sang me lullabies at bedtime. We almost always had a live-in housekeeper, but it was Mother or Daddy who would rock me in the wicker rocking chair that creaked and squeaked as I fell asleep. I loved being read and sung to – songs, I realized later, that had been sung to them as children. I still have some of the first books they gave me, two of them poetry, yellow with age. I can picture the book of Bible stories Daddy read from every morning at breakfast. We had daily devotions but it was never forced, never a didactic teaching.

From the earliest I can remember, I sketched and colored. In the 1930's there were paper dolls in the Sunday comics, like Tillie the Toiler, and dresses you could fit on the doll. By the time I was nine, I was drawing my own. I wanted to take art lessons at the Catholic convent with some of my friends but Mother said I had to take piano, even though I didn't have any talent in piano. My ability in art came in handy making new friends, since we moved every three or four years. I would sketch a girl – like the paper dolls – and someone in the class would see it and say, "Draw *me* a girl."

I don't remember writing on my own, except letters – I left friends behind everywhere. I did write a poem in the fourth grade as a result of an assignment. I didn't want to admit it was a made-up story, so I wrote it as a dream. When I let Mother read it, she gave it back later with a word changed; I didn't write any more. But I really enjoyed drawing more than writing. I was like a camera – not very creative, but technically I was pretty good. And I got more reponse to my drawing and painting than to my writing.

I enjoyed school, I enjoyed reading. I loved listening to

people talk, hearing new words and trying them out myself. But I was often embarrassed using words I'd seen in print and hadn't learned to pronounce correctly. I once said "stiff-ling" instead of stifling, to everyone's great amusement. It was then that I started studying pronunciation guides.

When I was in the early grades, the granddaughter of a next-door neighbor was the best storyteller! Her characters had exotic names, like "Sylvia Winthrop." We were used to ethnic names, German, Italian, Greek, Lebanese, as well as Jones and Brown, but *Winthrop* – there were none of those. By the sixth grade we had moved from Maryland back to Virginia and I became the neighborhood storyteller. Mine were mysteries and my listeners loved to be scared by my tales.

Other than assigned themes, I didn't do any writing until my senior year in high school when, in journalism class, I was asked to do a series of feature stories for the high school paper. I called the feature "The Office Clock" because it was under the big wall clock that miscreants had to sit when they were sent to the office. I wrote this series of feature stories as if I were the clock and what I was seeing.

The idea that writing was glamorous occurred to me during the war. In my sophomore and junior years, when some of our teachers were drafted or left when their husbands were called to military or government service, we had a few makeshift teachers. One of them was an author, a pipe-smoking, tweed-wearing, slouching character who seemed at ease in any situation. I hung on his every word and often stayed after school just to talk with him. Another substitute teacher, who was called in to teach geometry but had no background in math, would read poetry to us an hour every day. I heard Poe's "Annabel Lee" and "The Bells" and "The Raven" read so dramatically that I still get "goose bumples" just thinking about it. When I wasn't staying after school to talk to teachers, I was stopping at homes of various friends to read magazine stories. We didn't get *Redbook* or *Ladies' Home Journal* at our house, just magazines such as the *Christian Advocate* and *American Legion*. At home, I felt stifled and spent as much time as possible writing letters, reading or sewing in my room.

And I fell in love. It was not really a romance. When I was

introduced to the freshman class my first day in the new school, he was the only one who reacted – and with a *whistle!* Since my mother had impressed on me how homely I was, I thought he was making fun of me. The rest of that year and the next, we did a sort of ritual courtship dance, keeping our distance but always aware of each other. He would show me his drawings and stories about the lost continent of Atlantis. But when I reached sixteen and was allowed to date, he didn't date at all. One morning that spring he gave me a beautiful rose that matched exactly the roses in the chintz skirt I'd finished making the evening before. The rose wilted as I carried it around all day and the skirt lost its "permanent" sheen forever when I washed it. Through the rest of our relationship, such brief beautiful incidents were always followed by a tragedy of greater or lesser magnitude. That sounds melodramatic, but it's true.

After high school I went to West Virginia Wesleyan, a Methodist college in central West Virginia. The student body numbered around two hundred, very Wasp. I did pre-med studies and had a minor in English. I took the one journalism course offered, but didn't like the deadlines; I wanted plenty of time to write and rewrite. The creative writing for English classes was fun and I usually got "A's". Although we had spoken of marriage, a misunderstanding ended the high school "romance" in my sophomore year. I was so stricken that I told myself I'd marry the first man who asked me; I didn't care what happened to me or my dreams. That was in 1946, when the influx of veterans dramatically changed campus life. I dated one of them about a year, he asked me to marry him and I did. I was twenty.

I enrolled in education courses to support us by teaching; he continued in pre-med. By the time I graduated in 1949, I was pregnant. In 1950, on a temporary certificate, I began teaching in a coal camp near my husband's hometown in southern West Virginia. I enjoyed teaching, especially art, music, creative writing and play production. Our son, Britt, was the light of my life but the marriage was rocky almost from the start. I had a second child, Michael, and just after his birth I became pregnant again. My husband, who had been fired from his job, became abusive. I left him just a week before Mark was born, lived with my family and returned to teaching. But six months later when he promised to get straightened out, I said I would try again.

Soon after we moved to Columbus, in 1955, making a new start, with three small children and me still with no permanent teaching certificate or any way to make a career, our oldest son died very suddenly. Doctors said it was like crib death, but he was six so that just meant that they didn't know. The doctor had treated his "intestinal flu" with seconal; he went into a coma and never woke up. Britt had been such a marvelous person. Even at six he had a distinctive personality. Everyone, when they expressed their grief, said he was dear, he was precious. We'd had some amazing conversations, he and I, one of which is in my poem "Pink Thread." I thought, This kid, in just six years, made such an impact on everyone he knew. I've lived twenty-seven and if I died nobody would miss me. I have to *do* something with my life.

After some serious talks with the Lord, I decided teaching was where I belonged. There was no chance of my going to graduate school, medical school or any other school. I would be the best teacher I could be. Teaching in Columbus, I was eligible to pursue postgraduate work in education tuition-free at Ohio State. (I completed my teaching certification requirements in 1959, but did not earn another degree.) One of my courses was Children's Literature. Even though we were studying the Newbury and Caldicott award books, I thought, I can write as well as this. What came was not children's stories, but poetry inspired by my own children. And I wrote several poems that year during and after my hospitalization for major surgery. The first was "To the Nurses on Two-Town," the name of the hospital wing. It was well-received and posted at the nurses' station for all to read. That experience encouraged me to write more in the next few years. My serious pieces in free verse used very "poetic" language, such as "soft wind thrusts its way through the tall grass." I became more introspective, even dredging up memories I had previously felt unable to verbalize. Like my dad, I was entranced with rhyme and meter but generally reserved that style for humorous poems.

I began reading more poetry, teaching it in my English

classes, getting the kids to write more poetry. When the other teachers found out I was doing this, they asked me to write a verse to introduce each teacher at our first PTA meeting of the year. Several Christmases, I wrote a humorous poem to each teacher for our faculty party. One year I composed verses and designed valentines for each of my students, which I really loved doing. Usually I wrote poetry for specific occasions and it was fun, not serious at all. It gave me pleasure but I didn't see that it would lead anywhere.

My latent ability in journalism was tapped in 1965 when Columbus Education Association asked me to edit a monthly newsletter and sent me to Syracuse University for a week's crash course in educational journalism. Within a few months, with long-distance help from my Edpress "coach," I had built a journal out of the newsletter. I was still teaching but spending every extra minute on writing, interviewing, editing, proofing, layout and meetings. I applied for graduate school in journalism at Ohio State in the winter of 1966 and started with one evening course, feature writing, in which I got an "A." But I never finished.

My career and my life were interrupted by a series of accidents. In 1962, while driving through downtown Columbus, I had been hit by a delivery truck, injuring my spine. My treatment was periodic traction and physical therapy but the pain continued, so in 1963 the doctors turned to surgery to remove the ruptured discs. I had elected stainless steel clamps rather than a body cast, and as the fusion healed I returned to teaching. I applied for a junior high position to get away from the playground duty required of elementary teachers and had been teaching there for several years when, in June of 1966, the kids were in a rioting mood. I had as many kids in the classroom as could fit and was holding the door against the ruckus in the halls. But they pulled open the door and slung me, hanging onto the doorknob, out into the hall. The steel clamps were torn loose and had to be removed surgically a few days later. Although another fusion was attempted the next year, it proved unstable. The doctors experimented with one medication after another for the excruciating pain in my back and legs. I gave up the *CEA Bulletin* and in 1968 took a disability retirement from teaching.

At forty I had no career, no future, not much of a marriage. I became quite dependent on, rather, addicted to the pain medication and was hospitalized for withdrawal many times with very little success. I couldn't deal with any part of my life so the doctors tried electric shock therapy. I couldn't make decisions, my memory was gone, I was a cipher, a nothing. The acquaintances I'd thought were friends, the bridge playing, dancing, drinking friends, gradually dropped me. They were confused and frightened by my need for psychiatric care. They were going ahead with their lives but I had given up. My parents, brothers and sister, and of course my sons were equally confused; apparently my husband gave them no details of my emotional illness or my treatment, including the shock treatments. But a neighborhood prayer group I had been part of, and some friends in my church and a few others still kept in touch.

My husband was away from home for long periods without explanation. Most of the time our only income was my pension and disability benefits. For these and other reasons, we separated, sold our home and divorced in 1972. I was living with our sons in a townhouse complex when, two days after the divorce hearing, I asked where they were going in their Sunday best. "To Dad's wedding." I was absolutely floored. I had been blaming myself for everything, but had no idea he'd been living with someone else or was planning another marriage so soon. I attempted suicide several times. Then one day in 1974, when I was hospitalized and in traction for a fall from a horse, I realized this was the picture for the rest of my life if I depended on myself. I had a very deep religious experience in which I gave the whole thing to God. That was the beginning of the long climb back to normalcy. Later, I was told by my friends in the prayer group that they had been praying for me that very night, that they, too, had had a religious experience.

.   .   .

That same summer, my son Michael wanted to bring a friend home so I could see his poetry. Mike had warned me, "Mom, I know he's spaced out on drugs, but he wants you to read his poems and tell him what you think." Mike remembered that I had once written poetry! This poor kid *was* spaced out but he had some lovely lyrical lines. I started thinking about writing again and did a long narrative poem about one of our singles group parties. It was published in our newsletter along with the bowling scores and everyone got a kick out of it.

But I still wasn't emotionally stable and my behavior was not consistent with promises I'd made to God and myself. I'm just now realizing it was probably the shock "therapy" that made me so irresponsible, even with my new direction and renewed faith in God. My life really fragmented when, in 1975 I met, married and was deserted by an itinerant charmer who had shown up at one of the singles-club dances. Soon after that I met and married another charmer – this time a local one. He said he wanted me to write and gave me all the time and space I needed. But he was so abusive that nothing would come. In a few months he found his sixth wife and I found a really fine psychiatrist who didn't hospitalize his patients or prescribe shock treatments. He saw me once a week, then every two weeks for eight years; he helped me figure myself out, deal with my returning memory and regain my sense of self-worth.

By 1978 I was over three terrible marriages and enjoying a sane-and-sober single existence. I resumed church and community activities, rejoined my choral group, even wrote a drama to be performed by the women's society at church. The poem I was asked to write celebrating the seventy-fifth birthday of Columbus Branch, AAUW was a hit, and the research that project required provided the direction and impetus to write more. A neighbor in my apartment building kept stopping by after work to chat because his folks had moved to Florida and he was lonely. I loaned him books to read that I had enjoyed, including poetry. That was Carl, who is now my husband. When he found I wanted to write, he said in his youthful naivete, "Well then, why don't you?" And I thought, Why don't I indeed? I am doing all these other things as if to avoid what I really want to do. That was in 1979; I was 51.

The *Citizen-Journal*, a now-defunct Columbus daily, had a poetry column in its Saturday edition and I began reading and clipping the poetry. Eventually I submitted the first two poems

I had written at Ohio State in the 1950's and they were accepted and published. I was hooked. Then, in the *Columbus Dispatch* Sunday magazine, I saw a notice of the "World of Poetry" competition. Carl encouraged me to enter so I began work on a poem that was very tightly rhymed and metered, like most of the humorous pieces I'd done. But this was a serious subject I'd long wanted to write about: my first ride on a carousel that featured a brass ring. I got the brass ring, all right.

I was so new to poetry competition that I made the mistake of entering an updated version of the same "Merry-go-round" a few months later in an Ohio Poetry Day contest for beginning poets. (The annual observance was organized by the Ohio Poetry Day Association and featured a selected Ohio poet-of-the-year, a workshop and an awards luncheon). I was notified of the OPD second prize and the World of Poetry fourth prize at about the same time. I preferred the Ohio award, especially since that entry was the better poem, but since the other had been earlier, I withdrew the Ohio entry. I was very straightforward in my explanation, but I have avoided simultaneous submissions ever since.

The Ohio poet who had sponsored and judged the Beginner's Luck contest was Amy Jo Zook, who became my mentor and very close friend. She invited me to join a state-wide poetry group of which she was then president: Verse Writers' Guild of Ohio, a fifty-year-old group that met monthly for a poetry presentation, critique session and social time. My activities in Verse Writers Guild led to my being elected vice president, then president. During my tenure we instituted an annual competition and day-long workshop called Poetryfest, which we opened to the whole central Ohio poetry community.

I also took on the OPDA publicity job for two years and won for Ohio a third-place award for my 1981 Poetry Day publicity. But I felt I was wasting time doing the nitty-gritty things an administrator has to do, when all I wanted was to study and write poetry. So I resigned, first the VWG position, then the OPDA job. In a flurry of writing, I went on to win five cash prizes in the 1983 OPDA competition! I was also studying the haiku form which I had first seen in the *Citizen-Journal*. I wanted to become an "expert" in haiku, keeping in mind, however, a favorite quotation of my mother: "An 'expert' is just a little spurt a long way from home."

I had served my time and paid my dues, so to speak, but I soon missed the activity and decided to reach beyond the traditional aspects of these two organizations. I liked being a poetry pusher! Women's Poetry Workshop, a group of writers formed from an Ohio State writing workshop, was convening the Community of Poets Awards and invited all the poetry organizations in central Ohio to be represented on its committee. Six or seven poetry groups were cooperating, one gay, one avant-garde, some large, some small; I offered to serve for Verse Writers Guild. Our aim was to offer opportunity, support and exposure to the poets of Ohio. Ohio Arts Council gave us financial support. The editors of a widely circulated newsletter, *Writers Grapevine,* helped fund us and worked on the committee. We built up a mailing list of fifteen hundred poets in Ohio, and sponsored state-wide poetry competitions with recognized and respected Ohio poets as judges. We offered substantial cash awards and publication in a series of chapbooks. The winners and judges were featured in a series of poetry readings, one in 1985 at the Governor's residence with Governor and Mrs. Celeste actively participating in the event.

As the COPA publicist, I met many other poets from around the state and enjoyed the benefit of much exchange of ideas as well as hearing and reading some fine work. One of my poems was selected for *Centered on Columbus,* our chapbook of poems honoring the city in its 150th year. Two summers later, an excerpt from that poem was published on one hundred Central Ohio Transit Authority bus posters. My poetry was appearing in several small press publications, and I won honorable mentions in contests in other states and nationally. My haiku and related forms appeared often in a number of publications. A high point in my haiku development was during my membership in the Yuki Teikei Haiku Society when the distinguished Japanese haikuist Teruo Yamagata selected *four* of my haiku among the twenty best that season. One of my greatest thrills was when a student usher at an Ohio State concert recognized me, saying she had heard me read and liked my poetry. Twice, members of my audience told me after a reading that they had driven a hundred miles to hear me!

Margaret Honton, with whom I worked on the COPA Committee, invited me to visit a critique/support group called Montage, that she belonged to. I was invited to join the group and Margaret offered to publish my first chapbook through her small press, Sophia Books. *Whalebone and Royal Blood* was published in the spring of 1985. I sold more than one hundred copies to bookstores, gift shops, libraries and individuals. From the review copies I sent out, I received some very fine reviews and at fifty-seven, I was, at last, beginning to believe in myself. In 1986 I was granted full membership in the National League of American Pen Women. The *Pen Woman* magazine published much of my work, as well as a good review of my chapbook.

My last big poetry-pushing effort before we moved to the Pittsburgh area was for Poetry in the Park, an annual summer series of the Columbus Recreation and Parks Department "Music in the Air" program. The Thursday evening readings featured selected Ohio poets, June through August, at the Whetstone Park of Roses gazebo in a natural amphitheater. Each reading featured three poets for about twenty minutes each, and once each summer a nationally known poet, such as Denise Levertov or Marge Piercy, brought out the crowds. I was among the poets who performed from 1984 through 1986.

But along with all this support and activity, I wanted to study with a famous poet. A few hours with Diane Wakoski at the Midwest Writers Conference hadn't been enough, and I found it hard to identify with her. Ohio State had resumed its writer-in-residence program and a limited number of non-students could apply for the two-week workshops. My applications were turned down for two years but finally, in the winter of 1986, I was one of the poets from the community accepted into William Matthews' workshop. About fifteen of us took turns reading our poems aloud for Matthews and the class to critique. The author was not allowed to say anything, which I liked. If you have to explain the poem, you haven't written it right. Line and stanza breaks – that was the main thing I learned from Bill Matthews. You should have good reasons for where you decide to begin or end a line or stanza. He said a poem is lopsided when all the important words are on the right, at the end of the line; you need some of those strong words at the beginning of the next line to balance the poem. Matthews called this the central technical question in writing free verse. His comment on line breaks for a breath pause? "Stupid." He taught us to keep the upper hand, not let the poem impose *its* will.

.   .   .

I have earned some money writing publicity, but very little writing poetry. The first poem I sold to a poetry journal was "Delirium" to *Pig Iron* in Youngstown, for two dollars. The most I earned was for my 1986 Poetry in the Park performance. I receive one dollar for each acceptance by *Modern Haiku;* the one about my son and grandson, I framed, dollar and all! But the biggest payoff is knowing someone else appreciates my writing, whether by audience applause or an editor's acceptance. When I became a regular in the *Citizen-Journal* poetry columns, people I didn't even know complimented me.

When I've been asked to do a reading, it's because someone heard me do a poem in an open reading, or when I've received a prize or won out in the selection process from general submissions. I have read my poems at public libraries, at a retirement community home, in classrooms, on the radio. Whatever my reason for being at the microphone, my knees knock and my hands are like ice. But when members of the audience compliment me later, someone always admires my "composure." People often come up afterwards and tell me what they liked the most. For Poetry in the Park readings, a favorite was "Pink Thread." At a Poetry Forum reading I was invited to do at Larry's Bar in Columbus, I got an amazing response to "History Lesson." Men came over to me from the bar, where I hadn't any idea they were even listening, and said, "You got it! That's the way it is." They didn't even question how I knew. It was Studs Terkel's book, *Hard Times,* that started me writing about the Great Depression, which led to more research. I heard the vernacular in his taped interviews for that book and his later *Working,* but it wasn't strange to me, since I had heard it in the coal camps. I had a steel worker on strike read it recently and he also said, "You got it!" But he added,

"We don't call them 'big boys,' we call them 'fat cats.'"

Through all this activity, my best critic and most loyal fan has always been my husband, Carl. He is very well read, extremely intelligent and creative, and has an amazing vocabulary. He knows me so well, he can spot a bad line, a lazy short-cut, any wordiness. If I protest, he's been known to say, "If you like that line so much, use it in another poem!" He has been a part of almost every poetry activity I've participated in, providing the sound system, taping, operating the video camera. He has washed dishes after banquets and helped me entertain visiting poets.

.   .   .

I write something every day even if it is just a line. I've learned to write down thoughts as they come, no matter where I am. I keep note pads all over the house. Periodically I gather up all the pieces of paper, copy off the lines and drop the typed pages in my "idea" file folder. Every trip, every Sunday afternoon drive, we take our cameras and I take my notebook to record special things. Sometimes I can look at a snapshot from an outing and recall what I was thinking at the time. Many poems have come like that. Inspiration can come from anywhere. For example, "Night Vision" was inspired by an ad in *Smithsonian* about the night vision systems that are used to find lost seamen. "Scat Song" grew out of research I was doing to prepare publicity for Allan Ginsberg's Poetry in the Park appearance. At the precise moment I was reading his description of Whitman's influence, a jazz pianist on the radio was explaining how Art Tatum's technique had affected his own. I wrote down some lines and when I had read more about Tatum and Whitman, "Scat Song" began to develop. Because Matthews is also a jazz lover and has written about it, this was one of the poems I submitted at his workshop. The first thing he said was, "What is Ginsberg doing in there?" He let me know my preoccupation with Ginsberg was detracting from what I was trying to say, which is, as he put it, that all music is about mortality. Ginsberg was taken out. I realized from this experience that what you start with doesn't have to be what you end up with. Months later I asked Bill Matthews' permission to use his remark as an epigraph for the revised poem. "Scat Song," by the way, just received second prize in a Pittsburgh area contest sponsored by the Westmoreland Arts and Heritage Festival.

.   .   .

I see writing poetry as revise, revise, revise – which in itself should be a learning process. I get the feel of the poem in typing it, almost like listening to the words on tape. Some poems come more easily than others but everything I've written has been a learning process. The poetry I was raised on had rhyme and a regular meter, so when I first experimented with writing poems I started with the forms I was familiar with. I don't know at what point I realized that the tail was wagging the dog; I was sacrificing content and intent for rhyme and meter. In 1979 my son Mark asked me to write a Thanksgiving poem for the small town weekly he was editing, but he didn't like the first effort which was "R&M." He said it seemed trite and oversimplified. And the editor of *Pudding* kept rejecting my R&M poems, equating the form with triteness, and almost forced me into contemporary forms. So my transition was partly supply meeting demand. But I had already begun to see that poetry was not clever rhyme or intricate meter. Earlier I was doing humorous stuff, using rhyme in a clever, even cute way. I went for the cheap laugh! In recent years I have discarded that. I have to say, though, that my early appreciation of R&M was an education in the music of our language and intensified my regard for the spoken word. I used to be too wordy, loved those adjectives, but needed stronger nouns and verbs. Doing haiku helped me be more concise and insightful in my other poetry. I learned to listen to myself on tape to pick out wrong words and phrases. Probably because of my age, my change is happening more dramatically. I feel I don't have as much time to horse around.

.   .   .

One obstacle in starting to write so late is the apparent failure of my immediate memory; I can't absorb as readily when I study, my attention span is shorter. Another, which was always true, is my preoccupation with keeping a neat, clean house. Then, when I finally get around to writing, I don't want to stop.

Carl is diabetic, but we both need to get on a more regular schedule. We've had trouble getting organized since our recent move to the Pittsburgh area. I'm "going like sixty" since I started writing seven years ago, but I'm going *on* sixty and I feel that time is slipping away. I don't have time to waste being dishonest or pussyfooting around, unsure of myself.

I constantly regret the years I have missed. But they weren't really a waste, because all those experiences, even the worst, I have learned from. As Soren Kierkegaard once said, "Life must be lived forward, but it can only be understood backward." Now that I understand the past better, I have a rich background to work with and write about. I'll never be a "promising *young* poet," but it's never too late to be promising. My best poem is my *next* poem.

Jeannette S. Guildford

. . .

Excerpts from *Twelve Months at Arethusa*

Preface

My great-grandparents, Charles and Lucinda Webster, bought Arethusa Farm in Litchfield, Connecticut in 1868. It is named for the small, wild, pink orchid that grew in a swamp on the land. Charles was a storyteller and happily he was followed by two other superb storytellers. Through the one hundred and thirteen years Arethusa Farm remained in the Webster family, there have been listeners by the dozens.

I am one of them. I never had to go out to the cattle barn on a January morning, electricity off and temperature ten below zero, to milk cows, feed chickens, pigs and horses. I never had to mow hay when the fields simmered, the sun blazing down relentlessly, as waves of heat shimmered like desert mirages from the windrows of mown hay. I never slaughtered cattle nor worried about feed bills. Never did I roll beneath a tractor tumbling down a steep bank, and I certainly never had to try to catch a bull running loose in the barnyard. So when the day came for Arethusa Farm to leave the family, I had the luxury of being unabashedly sentimental about it and its place in our lives.

Hadn't it been my mother's childhood home? She had been married from there and her first son was born there. When her father died, and many years later, my father, we had gathered within the hospitable walls of the farmhouse to grieve together. Eleven years after her husband's death, we met again to weep for dear Tollie, my mother, "who was called home by her Heavenly Father." Six years went by and once more the family, grown from its original sixteen to include thirty-two great-grandchildren, said our goodbyes to our grandmother who was ninety-seven.

Months crept by as the house was emptied and prepared for new owners. I wanted to save it for the family forever and wandered through that final day before it left Websters, seeking an aura, something tangible that would remain to say our family had been born there, lived and died there. In three poems, I tried to catch an essence. They weren't enough. And slowly the idea of writing down the tales, told over and over in that farm house, grew in my mind. I would write one for each month.

Are the stories true? Yes, and again, no. The scribe did not live one hundred years ago. The one-hundred-year-old story-teller to whom she goes to check her facts changes little details. Sometimes the racing horse with mane flying and tail blowing is Frank, the buckskin, and sometimes flighty Pony-horse. The self-appointed scribe takes some liberties too. But the names are real and the incidents are real.

The *imprimatur* was given to the scribe when she read to her one-hundred-year-old uncle the dearly loved tale of his older brother's pranks. He laughed, nodded his head and said: "That's just about the way I remember it."

.   .   .

October 12, 1892

> *Today we honor Isabella Regina,*
> *Columbus, her captain, and crew.*
> *The Pinta, the Nina, the Santa Maria,*
> *And 1492!*

>   Arthur Guiterman

The shiny round kettle sat on the stove, rocking ever so slightly as puffs of steam rose above the black stove, wood inside crackling merrily.

But to Tollie, rocking beside the window in the great big rocking chair, holding Fanny close to her, the song of the kettle seemed anything but cheerful. She whispered to Fanny, "It keeps singing, 'Today's the day. Today's the day.' And I don't want Papa and Mama and Bennie and Ern to go away. I don't want to go over to Grandma's and Grandpa's. I want to sleep in my own little bed, Fanny."

Fanny was only a doll and she couldn't answer. But Tollie seemed comforted by looking into Fanny's eyes which looked back at her sympathetically, Tollie thought. Two tiny round tears began to slide down Tollie's cheeks. She lowered her chin – Papa and Mama didn't like tears – and she tried to hide them.

Almost before she heard footsteps, she found herself in Papa's lap and he was rocking her and holding both her and Fanny. His brown eyes twinkled, but his face was tender as he asked, "Do I really see tears, Tollie? Can this be my little girl who often teases to sleep at Grandpa's and Grandma's where Jack and Zip come up and sleep on the bed with you and Fanny? And where Grandpa takes you out to the barn to see the calves?"

"Oh, Papa." Now Tollie wailed. "But then you and Mama are right here in the cottage. And if I need you, Grandma can ask you to come right over. Or Grandpa will carry me home in Bennie's wagon. Now you'll all be in a place I've never seen, and what will I do if I'm lonesome?"

Papa answered gravely, "Tollie, you will be Mama's and my brave little girl. Grandma and Grandpa are so happy to know you can stay with them overnight. You must do your best not to let them think you are lonely. They would feel very badly if they think you are not having a happy time." Papa sighed a little bit, for he knew exactly how Tollie felt. He, too, liked best of all sleeping in his own bed, in his own house, with Poodlekins curled up at the foot of the bed.

Then he began to smile, thinking of a visit from the Chestnut Hill cousins when he had told them Poodlekins could talk, and he asked Tollie if she remembered. She nodded slowly. She never did understand why it was so funny to Papa and Mama and Ern and Bennie. Catherine had asked, "Can he really talk, Cousin Wilbur?" And Papa nodded, "Of course." Turning to the placid tabby sound asleep on his blue cushion beneath the stove, Papa would say, very seriously, "Poodlekins, what would you like for supper?" And Poodlekins would say, "Nothing." Tollie had turned four only two weeks ago. She knew that was why she didn't quite understand: she was too little. She smiled politely as Papa chuckled.

"Tollie," Papa asked, "would you like to get my shaving soap and brush? It's time for me to shave. Jennie and the boys and I have to begin to get ready to leave. We'll only be away for today and tomorrow. Grandma asked me to tell you she has a surprise for you, and Grandpa says he'd like to have you walk down to the Red Barns with him. And then you can stop here and feed Poodlekins. He'll be lonely, too."

Tollie's face brightened. She had two things to think about: helping Papa and wondering what Grandma's surprise was. She opened the cupboard by the sink, taking out Papa's shaving brush and soap. Papa stropped his razor slowly on the long leather strap which hung on a hook beside the sink. Slowly Papa lathered his face. She giggled when, in the mirror, he made a funny face at her and dabbed a little bit of soap on her face. It smelled good.

While she and Papa smiled at each other, Bennie ran in calling, "Oh, Tollie, I've never been so excited in my whole life. It's my very first time riding on the cars. How I wish you could come too."

"But Mama says I'm much too little and I would get too tired," Tollie said sadly. "And I'm going to stay with Grandpa and Grandma. And Grandma has a surprise for me. And Grandpa and I will go to the Red Barns and feed the chickens and Poodlekins . . ."

"Ho, what kind of fun is that," added another voice. "Going to New York City on the cars. Now that is really fun," Ernest chimed in. "Maybe when you are a big girl, you can do it too, Tollie," he added magnanimously, neither of them dreaming a day would come when Tollie would take the cars all by herself to go to New Haven for music lessons.

"Well," Tollie said, "I think I'd be scared to go to the

White's house in New York City. I think their Big House here that Papa takes care of is scary. And Miss Eliza and Miss Caroline are so tall. I guess I'd rather stay home, but I do wish I could sleep in my own bed."

Bennie squeezed her hand, grinning at her. Like Papa and Tollie, he liked his own home best, but at seven, he was old enough to look forward to a new adventure.

Mama hurried into the kitchen, giving Papa a quick hug and kiss, admiring how soft his face was after shaving. A hug and kiss for Tollie. A suggestion to Ern, "Ern, won't you look out the north window and see if the trap is coming yet from the livery stable. And Wilbur," she said, turning to Papa, "you'd better hurry and change and I'll help carry our bags downstairs."

"I can carry Bennie's and mine," Ernest offered enthusiastically. "I don't see the trap, but here comes Grandpa and Grandma. They're in front of Benton's already."

Before he had quite finished speaking, all three children ran out in time to see Grandpa help Grandma down from the buggy. Bennie helped tie Jessie-Mare to the hitching post beneath the tall maple, its leaves crimson and gold in October sunshine. Grandma held Tollie's hand and they swung arms together, strolling to the south porch.

Cheerily, Grandma asked, "Is Fanny's little trunk packed and ready to come with us? And do you have your nightie and a dress for tomorrow?"

"Fanny and I are all ready, Grandma, but . . ."

"Don't worry, Tollie." Grandma gave her a big hug. "Of course you'll miss Papa and Mama and the boys, but Grandpa and I think it's a fine treat to have you visit us, and we'll take good care of you. After dinner would you like to go up the Plains and visit Grandpa and Grandma Wooster? I know they'd love to have us call. And the two Grandpas do love watching the funny cat. Smart, isn't he, to wait until the fire dies down before jumping up on the warm stove."

Tollie nodded rather solemnly. She loved hearing Grandma Wooster play the pretty rosewood melodion. She always sat beneath, watching Grandma's feet pumping the pedals which made the bellows work. Much more fun than a cat, Tollie thought.

Grandpa picked her up and tickled her face with his beard, a game they always played together.

"Well, Puss," he whispered, "you and Fanny ready?" When she nodded, he picked up her little carpet bag and Fanny's trunk and carried them to the buggy. Then he went back to the porch for the bags and picnic basket and stowed them in the livery trap which had drawn up in the driveway.

The boys scuffled in the leaves on the lawn, until Mama finally came out with Papa. After goodbye hugs and kisses all around, all four Websters, waving back to Grandpa and Grandma and Tollie, drove off with Julius Treadway.

Julius Treadway and the livery trap trotted smartly up the Plains past Grandpa and Grandma Woosters, up the Old South Road and down the hill towards the train station.

Mr. Landon, the station agent, greeted them. "Well, well! Where are all these Websters going so early in the day?"

"To New York," Papa answered rather shortly.

"Ever been there before? What takes you there today?"

"Yes, I've been there," Papa replied. "Mrs. Webster and I have been to the Whites several times. And well I remember my first trip when Father Webster and I returned from driving those cattle from Echo Farm down to Flushing, Long Island."

Mr. Landon chuckled. "Seems to me I do remember about that trip, Mr. Webster. What's going on today?"

Ernest spoke up importantly. "Mr. White invited us to see the big parade tomorrow."

"Parade?" Mr. Landon echoed. "I haven't heard about a parade."

"Well, there is one to celebrate Christopher Columbus who discovered America four hundred years ago this year."

"Well, now," said Mr. Landon slowly, "that's an experience you'll be bound to remember all your life. I'll look forward to having you tell me all about it, Ernest, when you come back."

Ernest grinned, a little shy now after speaking so openly.

The family climbed onto the cars, settled themselves comfortably on two seats facing each other, the boys choosing to ride backwards, thinking that would be much more fun. Mr. Landon called, "All aboard!"

Two or three more people hurried to get on, greeting the

Websters as they, too, found seats. And slowly, with many puff-puff-puffs, the engine drew away from the station and away the train went. First of all, the boys recognized West Cemetery where all the South Plains neighbors had bought lots and where Papa's own mother, Lucinda Baldwin Webster, was buried. The train poked through pine trees as it made its way to Bantam, slowing down to a crawl and stopping alongside the station where Mr. Crossman took charge of loading dozens of milk cans in the baggage car behind the coal car.

Mr. Crossman shouted exactly as Mr. Landon had done. And this time Ern and Bennie echoed, "All aboard!" Perhaps when they grew up, they could be station agents and wear an important uniform and peaked blue hat.

The whistle blew. The train crept so slowly Papa laughed and told the boys what the local people frequently exclaimed, "We could walk to Hawleyville faster than this train runs."

Now the Bantam River rippled and sparkled below the track. There was a stop in West Morris and in Washington Depot. By now the baggage car brimmed with hundreds of milk cans. The boys looked startled as the sun disappeared and the car grew dark as it rumbled through the dark tunnel below the gorge at Steep Rock. They were at Roxbury Falls when the train emerged from the tunnel. The next stop was Hawleyville and the station agent shouted vigorously, "All out! All out! Change here for Bridgeport, New Haven and New York. All out!"

The two little boys were wiggly and restless. Papa and Mama helped them jump down from the high train step to the platform. "There, boys," Mama encouraged them, "this is a fine time for you to run around. Do be careful not to get in the way. All those milk cans have to be taken off and loaded on the next car, so you have time for a good run."

Prancing and dancing quickly, the boys played Jim-Horse, Grandpa Wooster's horse, and Jessie-Mare. They snorted and stamped and shook their heads, almost forgetting they were on a day's outing.

When the next "All aboard" resounded and the boys got back on the train, Mama opened the picnic basket and the tall thermos filled with warm cocoa she had made before breakfast. Brown-bread sandwiches filled with ham slices from Arethusa pigs were demolished by the hungry horses. Fat gingersnaps and fall apples from the orchard completed their hearty lunch.

The boys yawned unexpectedly. "Jeannette," Papa smiled, "I'll sit over there with Ern, and Ben can stay here with you." Mama nodded and quietly began humming, "Listen to the Mocking Bird," which seemed almost like a lullaby as the boys' heads drooped, eyes closed, and tired children napped. Even Papa and Mama dozed off. When the family awakened, the boys could see water shimmering in a vast sheet which stretched as far as their eyes could see. Awed, they looked at Papa.

"Where are we, Pa?" Ern whispered.

Papa explained, "We've just left Bridgeport and that water is Long Island Sound. Yes, Bennie, the very same Long Island Sound Grandpa and I crossed on the Port Jefferson Ferry when we took those cattle to Flushing."

The boys could see a boat which had a rounded front and back moving steadily across the Sound.

"That's very much like the ferry we rode on, sons," he added. "It will be another long while before we reach New York. Shall we play Colors or Letters?"

"Colors are easier for me, Papa," Ben answered.

Mama took a turn first. "What's in this car that's *blue?*"

.   .   .

The wheels clickety-clacked, squealed now and then on the tracks, and the miles and miles rolled by. Papa and Mama and the boys played games, told stories, sang songs, until Papa suggested they look out at the bridge they were crossing.

"This," Pa said, "is where we begin to come into the city. I know you will want to look."

The boys' eyes were round as they looked at the huge city. Nervously, Bennie inquired, "How will we ever find the White's house?"

"We'll take a hack from the station, Ben. Their house is right on Fifth Avenue, not far at all from the station."

"Six-o-nine," whispered Ern, who had learned the number by heart, fearing he might become lost in the train station and could at least tell someone where he was supposed to be.

The huffing and puffing of the train grew slower and slower. The train drew in beside a platform which stretched farther than Ernest and Bennie's eyes could see. Awed, silent, overwhelmed by throngs of people, they clung to Papa and Mama as they walked along the platform towards tall gates far ahead. As they neared them, the boys suddenly began dancing in delight.

"There's Thornton! There's Thornton!" they shouted together. People smiled at the two little boys so pleased to see a face they knew so well. Thornton slept at Grandpa's when he came to the Big House in the summer.

"Mr. Webster. Mrs. Webster." Thornton's grin was as contagious as the boys. "Ben! Ern!" He hugged each boy, then reached for their bags. "Miss Eliza thought it might make it easier for you folks if I came and met you in the victoria she's hired for your stay. Suggested that after you rest a bit and change, I can take you for a ride and show you the sights. She is sure the boys would like that."

"How thoughtful of her," Mama replied quietly. "I know we will all enjoy that and I'm pleased the boys will see something of the city."

Out the west door of the station, they followed Thornton to the victoria. He loaded the bags, helped them in. "Ern, want to sit with me?" Thornton asked. "Ben, you can have a turn next."

"This is Forty-Second Street," Thornton told them. "It divides Uptown and Downtown." And as he turned the cob smartly into Fifth Avenue, "This street divides the West side from the East side. Not far to go now." Very quickly, he turned into a circular driveway at 609 Fifth Avenue.

"No wonder Miss White always wants balconies at the Big House," Mama remarked dryly. They all looked up at a balcony which looked over the drive and onto the avenue.

Thornton chuckled. "I've already been instructed about carrying out extra chairs for all the guests tomorrow, so you can watch the great parade from the balcony. Even Lena and the maids and I are going to be able to watch it, so we've been told."

At the handsome front door with its large silver knocker, Thornton rapped lightly. When the door opened, there was another familiar face, Lena Braen, the housekeeper. "Oh Mr. Webster, Mrs. Webster, Ernest, Bennie! What a treat to see you here in New York."

Shyly the boys shook hands, following their parents and Lena into the grand front hall with its marble floor designed in diamond patterns. Up the broad stairs Lena led them and then into a large drawing room filled with flowering plants and bowls of cut flowers. A country feeling despite being in the city.

The Whites greeted them somewhat formally as was their usual manner, Miss Eliza directing Lena to take them to their rooms. Through many large, elaborately-furnished rooms, Lena led them, the boys looking with amazement at the paintings, books, thick rugs beneath their feet, and everywhere, plants and flowers. The rooms they were to use were the servants' rooms behind the butler's pantry, the flower room and the kitchen. Lena caught Mama's eyes and grinned at her mischievously.

Mama all but sniffed. Papa said, "Now, Jeannette . . ."

Lena went on, as though completing an already begun sentence. "I quite agree, Mrs. Webster, but at least you are here and you will be fed and warm."

Mama smiled back. She and Lena understood each other very well. And at least in these bare, sparsely furnished, unattractive tiny rooms, there was no worry about what two lively boys might get into.

Quickly the Webster family refreshed themselves, then followed Lena once more into the morning room.

"Did Thornton inquire whether you would enjoy having him take you around the city," Miss Eliza asked. "Perhaps you are too tired after your journey."

"We are all looking forward to the drive very much, Miss White," Papa answered. "We think it's very thoughtful of you to suggest it." Lena left the room to call Thornton and soon, down the grand stairs they went, out the front door and into the victoria, four pairs of eyes turning from right to left as Thornton proudly pointed out all the exciting features of this vast and growing metropolis, so different in every way from quiet Litchfield.

Bennie wasn't so interested in the city. He and Thornton

talked steadily about the farm, the cats, how many calves there were, did Grandpa have any new horses. Thornton assured Bennie that if the ladies went to the Big House next summer, he would continue to need Bennie to bring milk for his barn cats. Bennie was content.

Making their way through horse-cars, drays, carts, carriages of every size and description, they found themselves at a huge wharf. Thornton explained that this was the North River.

"This is where the huge ocean liners dock," he informed them. "And this is where the milk from Echo Farm and ice from Bantam Lake are loaded to go across the ocean."

The boys were surprised when Papa told them this was the great Hudson River they'd heard him read about to them. For some reason, in New York, it had a different name.

Ferry boats were coming in, loading and unloading carriages and people. There was a constant bustle, shouts, whistles. Thornton said regretfully, "Too bad we have to get back for supper, or we could have a ride over to Hoboken and back. Perhaps you'll be down again and we can plan to do it then. It's quite an interesting thing to do. Sometimes there are people who play accordions and sing, people telling fortunes. A very entertaining ride."

Reluctantly Thornton turned the cob, and back they wove their way to that house with the magic number, 609 Fifth Avenue.

When she learned the family were to eat in the servants' dining room and not with the family, Mama sniffed again. But she and Lena quickly began visiting about Litchfield neighbors on South Plains. Thornton told funny stories about his adventures hiring out and driving for all sorts of people. Papa listened quietly, not saying much. They all felt, if not at home, comfortable. Soon the yawning sleepy boys were tucked into bed, while Mama and Papa sat with Lena in the servants' sitting room.

In her dignified manner, Lena said she didn't think much of having guests eat with the servants. "But there, Mrs. Webster, you know as well as I do how they think about people who work for them."

To Mama's amazement, when breakfast was served, there

were exactly five eggs for four people. And exactly four pieces of toast. Mama had had enough. Her peppery tongue could not be contained any longer. "Never, never can I imagine anyone treating guests like this," she exclaimed. "I'll not let them think we are hungry."

Each person ate one egg and the inadequate, lonely fifth egg was sent back to the kitchen. Some cookies and apples were still in the picnic basket. Mama flounced over, took them out, put them on the table, and Papa and the boys and Mama too each nibbled until they had enough to eat. Papa shook his head at Mama, but he too was glad of the extra food.

They waited expectantly for Lena to come and take them to the balcony. At last she arrived and they went through all the grand rooms again into the drawing room. Tall windows were open out to the balcony. Many other guests were there, but quickly room was made for the two little boys to kneel at the railing's edge to look at the splendor below. Never had they imagined such music and bands, such gaily decorated horses.

"Oh Ern, how Tollie and Grandpa would love the music and horses," Ben whispered to his brother.

There were banners and marchers dressed in brilliant costumes. There were floats with Queen Isabella and King Ferdinand, the three ships with Spanish flags flying high in autumn breezes: the Santa Maria, the Pinta and last the Nina. There were sailors in funny old-fashioned hats and uniforms waving and shouting to the crowds. There were streamers and confetti.

The boys' eyes were round in amazement as they watched the vast, never-ending spectacle parading beneath them. Firecrackers popped, balloons burst as though they couldn't contain their excitement at the grand parade honoring Columbus. At last came the most splendid float of all. On it stood Columbus himself raising the flag of Spain, and kneeling at his feet were half a dozen Indians.

The last band disappeared down Fifth Avenue. The boys craned to see the drummers as they slowly marched out of sight. Miss White rose, sighing a bit, as though she too were sorry to see the end of the parade. She led the way back to the enormous dining room where on a huge table a vast picnic lunch was ready for everyone. Once more, the eyes of the boys were saucers as they saw lobster salad, fruits they didn't even know, platters of sliced ham, turkey, roast beef, deviled eggs, cheeses. After the hours spent in brisk October air, the grown-ups were as hungry as the children. This time there was food for all.

All too soon that astonishing morning was over. Mama and Papa took their little sons into their rooms to gather their bags and wait for Thornton to take them to the station. The late afternoon train would take them to Bridgeport and Haw-leyville, then on to the Shepaug Railroad and back home to Litchfield.

Lena came for them. They said their formal goodbyes and thank-yous. Down the stairs they went into the marble hall, out the grand door with its silver knocker to the circular drive where Thornton was waiting, smiling again as he helped Mama and Papa into the carriage, then lifted the boys in.

"It has been a real treat having you here," he said as the cob trotted smartly down Fifth Avenue, around the corner into Forty-Second Street, swinging into the entrance to the station. He helped them board the train and shook hands warmly with each of the four Websters.

"We hope we'll see you next summer," Ern called after him as the last good-bye had been said and the conductor was shouting, "All aboard!" Thornton heard and waved once more.

The train jerked a little, the wheels began turning and out the station it crept, slowly at first, bell ringing merrily, then gathering speed. As the wheels seemed to sing on the tracks, Ben's eyes closed, then Ern's. Once more, Mama held one, Papa the other and everyone napped as they sped toward Litchfield and the farm. Half in his sleep, Bennie murmured, "I wonder what Tollie's surprise was."

Jeannette S. Guildford

My mother was a very fine pianist. Her idols were Louise Homer, one of the great opera singers in the early 1900s, and Sidney Homer who accompanied her. My mother heard them when she was a child and that became her ideal, to be an accompanist. And she certainly did accompany and teach music all her life. My father was a minister, an excellent public speaker. His father spoke the most perfect precise English of anyone I've ever known, never used slang of any kind. He was very fond of Poe and would recite a lot of Poe's poetry by heart, so my grandmother told me.

There was lots of singing around the piano when we grew up, lots of duet playing and, when we were able to have two pianos, two-piano compositions. I didn't play well and it was always very disappointing to me, because my mother, brother and grandmother were excellent pianists. I adored dancing and always wanted to be a professional dancer. A girl in my grade at school was a dancer and it was exciting to see her in costume dancing on the stage, toe-dancing they called it in those days. I was consumed with envy, but my parents didn't think it was proper for me to have dancing lessons.

My father's church was very small. There were only, at the very most, four people in the congregation who were on salaries; all of the rest were production workers in Waterbury industry. When times were hard, which they were most of the years I was growing up, there was a difficult cash flow problem, as we would say today. But I wasn't aware of it when I was a girl. No matter how poor we were – we may not have been able to pay the light bills – my parents always had season tickets to the concerts in Waterbury, Connecticut where I grew up. As soon as I was old enough, I was allowed to go with them. In those days the rich dressed in evening clothes at these concerts, so it was very romantic for a child. I heard Grace Moore, Tibbet, Melchior, Paderewski.

I was sick a lot until I had my tonsils out when I was about eight. The doctor's prescription was always, "Send her to grandmother in Litchfield. The Litchfield air will help her." It was the nearest to heaven I reached as a child. I suspect it was easy for me to run a temperature when the treatment would be "going to Grandma's" and Arethusa Farm. I remember trying to hide in tiny closets within closets when my parents came to take me home – I wanted to stay at Grandma's forever. Grandma sang and recited – she often recited poems as I snuggled in bed with her early in the morning. She told stories about Mother and her brothers when they were growing up, about Grandma herself being a tomboy and always preferring to be with her cousin David than with her sister Nell, who was proper and loved to sew and embroider. Her stories entered my memory intact.

I had three brothers, no sisters. I didn't find very much in common with the girls in my neighborhood who were not encouraged to read and didn't have to have piano lessons and practice every day. They played with dolls – I never did. I played with the neighborhood boys, very active kinds of games. The area was still not built up, so there were lots of fields where we could play and rocks to hide behind. We had a ball team. I couldn't run very fast, but I could almost always get a hit.

We read aloud almost every evening after supper. And before everyone was on different school schedules, we had prayer every morning after breakfast. I don't know that we did anything more than each taking a turn reading a psalm or a chapter of the Bible, but I'm sure that the rhythm of that wonderful language was a very important part of what my ears became accustomed to. I remember the first word I ever read. I was in first grade and the teacher wrote "candle" on the board.

I was the first one in the room to get it, probably my only triumph in elementary school. I started reading then and my favorite presents for birthdays and Christmas were always books. I remember I was convalescing from some illness when I was about eight and mother started reading *Little Women* to me. When she would go to do other things, I would sneak out of bed, get the book and read it under the covers. She couldn't stand it, because I kept getting so far ahead of her.

I was the storyteller in my family. My brother and I had an arrangement: whoever cleared the table, washed the dishes and whoever scraped the dishes, dried them. While we worked, I would tell my continuing stories. My brother was enthralled, my mother enjoyed it too, but the water would get cold, the soapsuds would disappear, he'd be wiping the same plate over and over, and my mother would say: "You children get through!" One of the tales was a marvellous yarn about a land called "B.B." which stood for Before Birth. It was modeled on any number of fairy tales, with lots of rich jewels, struggles for power, battles between good and evil. In all the stories, money was never lacking, as it was constantly in our home. My brothers and I and our summer friends at Bantam Lake were always making up plays and pageants and dressing up. Most of the make-believe was based on *The Boy Allies at Jutland* or *With the Submarine D-32* or *Dick Prescott at West Point*. And of course Robin Hood and the like. I remember we had an illustrated guessing game based on silently acting out nursery rhymes or Bible stories. Perhaps those creative games were such fun that the energy needed to put words on paper didn't seem necessary.

But I always wanted to write. At nine or ten, I started writing a book. My best friend was the daughter of my family doctor; on his desk there was an hour-by-hour appointment pad that came as an advertisement from a pharmaceutical company. I was given that and on it I started writing my first novel – I can remember my awful handwriting, the pencil smudges. Again, lots of money, and this time, fantasies about decorating the rooms of the two heroines. That was when I decided my living room, when I grew up, would be green and gold.

At college I had a double major in English and sociology.

Of course I always wrote excellent themes. I've thought about that, that I had at least two outstanding English teachers in college and neither one of them encouraged me to do more with writing, although they were so impressed with the work that I did in their classes. Perhaps, in order to get that kind of encouragement, I would have had to do things like writing for the college newspaper or going out for the yearbook, but that never interested me. I made one other early attempt to write. In my early twenties I wrote a tiny book – seventeen pages, 4 by 6 1/2 inches – and had it printed. In it were the stories I'd heard from my grandmother and my mother, the same ones that are now in the Arethusa collection. For that little book, called *Connecticut Yankees All,* I used oral history, a notebook that said "Wooster Genealogy" on the cover but contained a lot more than lists of names, and Grandma's Bible in which she collected newspaper clippings related to family doings. Reading the little book now, it seems strange that after years of school and college writing, I didn't know words had to be put together with connectors – the sentences were short and unadorned. I didn't know anything about how to flesh out an anecdote or make up dialogue or embellish a story, so it was very sparse.

I gave them for Christmas gifts that year and was practically disowned from the family because I had revealed a family secret in that book: that my grandfather's brother had been married and divorced. I had heard that from my grandmother who said that Uncle Fred had married a "loose woman" and she cheated on him. The word came down that my uncle was furious. I was heartbroken because I enjoyed him enormously and thought he would be very pleased at my effort to keep the stories. He was not amused. I threw them all out. I thought, I can't do this.

·   ·   ·

When I was in college, I felt called by the Lord to become a social worker. When I graduated in 1936, right in the midst of the depression, I had a job that began the next day in an agency called Lincoln House Association. Our clients, sent to us primarily by the City Welfare Department and Visiting Nurse Association, were people out of work because of the Great Depression whose problems needed more individual attention than was possible at the Welfare Department. I started at something like eight dollars a week; my parents supported me. In retrospect, the worst decision I made was to go back home after college. There was only one of my whole group who was brave enough to go off and make her way. Leaving home was not the cultural thing to do in those days – I lived at home until my father's death five years later when I was twenty-six.

I found that I was extraordinarily gifted in what I did. I got my master's degree in social work in 1945 and worked for several years in Elmira, New York. I learned I could create my own life without being my parents' daughter, but I was homesick for the mix of nationalities and ethnic groups of Connecticut, as well as our cottage at Bantam Lake and all the relatives. I took a job at Fairfield Family Services where the clients were even more diverse than I had worked with elsewhere, and in 1953, a year after my mother died, I applied and was hired as director of the Litchfield County office of Children's Services of Connecticut. I was the first MSW in what was then a very rural area. I worked with the Community Chest, the Child Welfare Association and other local and county organizations, provided direction for volunteers and did monumental fund-raising to support the agency. There was a constant need for finding foster homes for infants and babies and specialized foster care for children with special needs. My other charge was to begin a family-counseling program.

In 1966 I retired as director but continued to work there part-time. By then, women's issues were increasingly visible and I became involved with the politicizing of women and the clarifying of issues they had to deal with. I think that was really a flowering of my own knowledge. And then, after I retired from the agency, I had the unexpected bonus of several years of a very rewarding private practice. I have been fully retired since 1983.

Obviously there was not much time for writing in those years. I guess I kept a diary for perhaps seven or eight years. When my son, John, was in fourth or fifth grade, I wrote a wonderful story about our cat, Mrs. Cat and one about John's first dog. The next time I really tried to write was when my son asked me to, many years later when he was married and a father. I think he knew that his child would hear the songs and stories he had been regaled on and he felt the same sense of mortality as I had with Grandma, so it seemed time for me to write. I wrote because I had a goal – John asked me. But it didn't become just those stories, it became a collection of significant happenings I had experienced either personally or as part of our neighborhood. Every morning before I went to work, I would type a minimum of two to three pages double-space. I have a thick folder of that stuff, about three hundred pages, of which seventy-five pages are the original family material. But when I showed some of the things to John, he corrected them like a high school English teacher, which he was. He has told me since how much he regretted that and I realize now that it's quite all right, that someone has to make corrections, but I didn't know that at the time. I was heartbroken. I didn't put fingers to the keys again for a long, long time.

I have to remind myself, though, that I was writing all the time. I was doing thousands of words of case records, reports, papers to present at workshops. The secretaries in any agency where I worked used to love to transcribe my tapes; it was the quality of aliveness which I think is in my writing in general. And I am an obsessive letter writer. So there was never a time when I have not been writing, though there is a great difference between that kind of writing and other forms. What I have found, with retirement, is that the creative energy I used as a therapist suddenly became available for other sorts of creation. And my skills have developed – to some extent *because* of John's comments. His schoolteacher corrections were "embellish here" or "elaborate there" or "expand here." That was an important concept for me to grasp, that it couldn't be the journalistic thing you do when you are doing a workshop with very specific material. You have to make it come alive and the way to do it is to feel freer with how you use your words.

Since retirement, I've written in a variety of categories: poetry, autobiography, journals, children's stories, historical pieces about Great-grandfather and his Yankee peddling days and about two houses I've lived in, a group of stories I call Litchfield County Frivolities and, especially important to me, the twelve Arethusa stories. I really felt a tremendous sense of accomplishment about those, because that was a specific goal I'd set for myself. But still, the greatest amount of writing is my incessant letter-writing: I've used almost two hundred stamps since Christmas three months ago!

Each kind of writing is a different voice: the dark side in the serious autobiography, my constant sense of the ridiculous in the Litchfield County Frivolities, which get their name from the fact that residents of Litchfield are apt to take themselves and the village so seriously. I see the poems as creating colors and pictures I'd like to draw but can't. And the historical pieces are a commitment to save experiences of the past to share with others.

Somehow, everything appears to me as a story. Once I mastered some of the technique of creating dialogue, the Arethusa project was an important next step. I hated knowing that Arethusa Farm was leaving the family after one hundred years and yearned to save it for the children of my grandmother's grandchildren. Not one of them, as it turns out, is the least bit interested. I realized then that I was writing them for me. But written words take on a life not necessarily planned by the writer – I didn't dream they would become the basis for "show-and-tell" programs for clubs, classrooms, women's groups. At my most recent presentation to the Women's Forum in Litchfield, I was stunned to realize that the demographic changes in the five years since I started the project have been so enormous that almost no dairy farms remain. So the tales have gained significantly in historic importance.

I've done a lot of autobiography. I suppose I've always been introspective. I am much more with the real world than I was for many, many years of my life, but I think it was those years of introspection that have made it possible for me now to go back to that time and recapture some of my own struggles in growing up and becoming an adult. What I want to share is the struggle we all have, if we are willing to be honest with ourselves, in just growing up and taking responsibility for our lives and not blaming other people or circumstances for the course our lives take. And I feel a sense of responsibility about getting down this information about what it was like to grow up in my particular period of time doing the kind of work I was doing.

I've done a number of fragments but have not been able to discipline myself to work steadily at them and make them become a cohesive whole.

.   .   .

Without knowing it was going to happen, I've found many chances to read my work. In 1986, for example, I had seven or eight speaking and reading engagements. They come about in a number of ways. One of the women I swim with at the Y, who has always been thrilled at the thought of my writing and frequently asked for progress reports, invited me to read to the group of retired people she belongs to. I read one Arethusa story and one Litchfield County Frivolity to fifty or sixty people, many of them retired farmers who knew the "characters" in the Arethusa story. A women's church group called up and said they heard I did programs. I read them my story about the bare-breasted woman at a Christmas cocktail party. The only man in the audience, the minister, very young and brand-new at the church, was trying enormously hard to be serious and dignified. He had his chin down and his chest and shoulders were shaking and the women were wiping their eyes from laughing so hard.

I give programs for children as well as adults. Three or four years ago, the children's librarian asked me to do a program for her "Bookaneers." She told me to bring my writing "tools," so I brought a dictionary, an encyclopedia, a thesaurus and pens. She loaned me a typewriter. We covered them all on a small table and had the children guess what my tools were before we took the cover off. It was a shock to *me* to discover that two of the children, no bigger than a minute, were already published writers in state-wide magazines that provide contests for children to submit their works. The Morris Historical Society, which I belong to, sponsors programs in the elementary school illustrating facets of life at a different period of time. I read stories of the adventures of my Yankee pedlar great-grandfather and showed an exhibit of things which might have been carried in a Yankee pedlar's wagon. I always let children handle everything, sometimes holding my breath, but that's what gives them the real flavor of things and gives them a chance to say,

"My grammy has something like this in her house," or "What do they use this for?" I make the point that there is always someone who *listens* to someone who *tells* stories. Once, three children came up to me and told me that they knew their grandmothers' maiden names – they had an enormous amount of interest in their grandparents' attics.

I used the autobiographical material in two lectures I presented at a nearby college. To share the realities of my life as experiences which are probably universal, is a serious and necessary task for someone like me, who is in love with words. And I don't see any point in writing anything about the years before unless I am really open about it. A young woman at one of the lectures, "Transitions in Women's Lives: Women Helping Women," said I had articulated feelings about her life which she had not been able to define.

Most recently I presented "The Arethusa Program of Show-and-Tell" at the Litchfield Women's Forum. I took posters I've made of pictures of the farm in early days, clothing like my grandfather's baby clothes and a great-grandmother's hat, all carefully labeled in proper Historical Society display fashion. There were between fifty and sixty people present, including a number of men. There was a gasp when I appeared in costume and the men roared with laughter as I read about my two uncles trying to teach the Banty chickens to fly, the mischievous Ernest switching horses and cows to startle his father and grandfather. One young woman spoke to me in tears after the reading, saying her father is still alive and no one has taken time to listen and record his history for the family.

. . .

I understand now that I've been a "closet" writer. I don't think it has been important for me to think of an audience – I've done it for my own delight. It was such a shock to me when I read Edna St.Vincent Millay's letters a couple of summers ago to realize that an enormous amount of her time was spent, not in writing her poetry, but in selling her poetry and planning to have it published advantageously. I'm not entrepreneurial-minded. I think that is the reason why I never really moved beyond where I am in terms of finding an audience for my writing other than the Arethusa stories. It never occurred to me that I should do anything about them. I never think of publishing the autobiographical material, it seems too intimate; yet I know that isn't correct. But I wanted to have the Arethusa stories in print. A year ago I talked with an agent in Amherst who gave me a number of excellent ideas. She felt I had not sufficiently explored the resources here, that the library or historical societies might have funds to help publish the stories. And she said that the more reading aloud I did and the more presentations I made, the more that would give credibility for my body of work to be published. And that is how it's come about. Someone who heard me at the Women's Forum thought my stories might fit the format of a new local paper, *Foothills News*. My very first story, "Mrs. Cat," was chosen. And now the same paper is bringing out an interview of me and, month by month, each of the Arethusa stories.

.   .   .

In regard to my writing routine, I like to sleep till seven-thirty, have breakfast, read the paper, do whatever household chores need doing – I generally go through the house with a dry mop and shake it out the back door – and then sit at my desk and try to stay there until twelve. I can't write when I have lots of pressures coming in on me, or lots of things that I have to do or be responsible for. I really have to be very quiet within myself and within my house to write. I have scrap after scrap with ideas on them, a constant stream of ideas about things that I would like to do. But I interrupt myself constantly instead of really narrowing down and sticking with it, so that is the other side of the coin. In the afternoon I do the other household things and then have time to read, another very important part of my life.

Various things support my writing. In recent years I have turned for nourishment to the enormous body of work written by women: journals, diaries, letters, biographies, autobiographies which provide constant encouragement and permission to be open and honest. The Arethusa stories are written at one level, but my other things are written at a very different level where I need the permission to reveal and not be afraid that I am going to expose secrets. I have been a May Sarton reader for many years – I began in the McCarthy era with the novel *Faithful Are the Wounds.* When she began in her journals to reveal her constant struggles with depression, which has been my lifelong struggle too – not as dramatic as hers but certainly painful enough to me – it was very opening for me. And women have begun to be open in talking about sexuality. In my life I have only had one friendship – Iva died many years ago – in which we were equally able to be open about our sexual life and experiences. I put that in the autobiographical writing. I used to think that was a secret that had to remain within me, and I don't feel that way anymore.

As far as obstacles are concerned, I blame everything on the problems of women! Last night I started getting supper at four o'clock, ate at six and I still had to go back into the kitchen to do another hour's work to clean up. Our life is not complex by any means, but still *someone* has to do the housework. And I find that that does stop me many times from settling down and working at my desk. I have commitments to things outside my household. I am on the vestry at church and do once-a-month volunteer work there. I am the family social secretary. To be available to friends and family for chatting, visiting, having lunch together or social kinds of things – I need all of these pieces of my life. The Morris Historical Society can make a variety of demands on me at various times of the year. That doesn't sound like very much, but sometimes I feel I have as many commitments as when I was working. I don't think there is any question that I use them as a way of avoiding getting into the autobiographical stuff which is so painful. When I am working at it, I become so preoccupied that it is very hard to come back into the world and to make connections.

Some of the things that are obstacles to writing are simply part of the pattern of my life. A very important one has been swimming, something I was determined to do for myself when I retired, to keep up my health. In order to do that, I have to plan my morning's work around when the Y pool is available. And I make other excuses to myself: for forty years, from 1936 to 1977, my time was totally controlled by demands from the outside to earn a living, and so I find it very easy to say I am going to do something that gives me personal pleasure. Writing is very hard work; I find it hard to justify doing that.

I didn't have any idea when I retired what I was going to do with my time. I was not one of those who was always waiting until I retired to hook a rug or whatever – I just knew it was time to stop working. But a friend of mine, who became a sculptor after retirement, said to me my first summer after retirement something I've quoted over and over to friends as they have retired: "Don't worry about retirement, Jeannette, you take yourself into retirement." And what I realized immediately is that if you have always been a busy person, you will always be a busy person. It's just a question for me of learning how to give myself permission to use the energy for writing.

One of the advantages of writing at this age is the feeling that you have nothing to lose by being as open as you choose to be. As an older person, I have already created an identity for myself. I am not dependent as an eighteen-year-old starting out on her first novel, who is having to create an identity along with whatever work is going to be produced. I already have had a rich life and rich history and an identity. I don't have anything to lose, I only have something to gain in creating an identity in another form.